AF505693

VIOLENCE IN RURAL
SOUTH AFRICA, 1880–1963

Africa and the Diaspora:
History, Politics, Culture

Edited by Tejumola Olaniyan,
Neil Kodesh, and James H. Sweet

Violence in Rural South Africa, 1880–1963

Sean Redding

THE UNIVERSITY OF WISCONSIN PRESS

The research for this book was supported by grants from the
Amherst College Faculty Research Award Program, funded by the
H. Axel Schupf, '57 Fund for Intellectual Life.

The University of Wisconsin Press
728 State Street, Suite 443
Madison, Wisconsin 53706
uwpress.wisc.edu

Gray's Inn House, 127 Clerkenwell Road
London ECIR 5DB, United Kingdom
eurospanbookstore.com

Printed in the United States of America
This book may be available in a digital edition.

Library of Congress Cataloging-in-Publication Data
Names: Redding, Sean, author.
Title: Violence in rural South Africa, 1880–1963 / Sean Redding.
Other titles: Africa and the diaspora.
Description: Madison, Wisconsin : The University of Wisconsin Press, [2023] |
Series: Africa and the diaspora: history, politics, culture |
Includes bibliographical references and index.
Identifiers: LCCN 2022018270 | ISBN 9780299341206 (hardcover)
Subjects: LCSH: Violence—South Africa—History. | South Africa—Social
conditions—19th century. | South Africa—Social conditions—20th century.
Classification: LCC HN801.Z9 V5684 2023 | DDC
303.60968/09034—dc23/eng/20220707
LC record available at https://lccn.loc.gov/2022018270

For
PETER *and* DAN

CONTENTS

ILLUSTRATIONS

PREFACE

My interest in analyzing violence in rural South Africa emerged from my research on an earlier project that looked at the connections between the South African state's imposition of colonial rule and Africans' beliefs in the supernatural. What initially motivated that study was how few open revolts against the South African state had occurred in the eastern region of the Cape after the initial conquest.

As I worked on that project, I concluded that explaining the long quiet periods between revolts against the state left much of the violence within African rural communities unexplored. While it is possible to discuss this more local and intimate violence as a kind of displaced political resistance, that interpretation seemed superficial. It gave too much agency to the state and did not engage with Africans' ideas of what they were trying to accomplish through their actions. I went back to my sources to better understand what drove some of the violence Africans committed in the countryside as they navigated the constraints the white state had imposed on them.

Many of my sources are criminal and civil court cases, and my engagement with historical violence is partly an artifact of relying on them. Court cases rarely document society at its most functional and pleasant. But there is a more profound reason to investigate the violence that goes beyond the availability of sources: state policies often relegated Africans living in the rural areas to the margins. As long as Africans were not actively rebelling, their lives were rarely central to the planning of white policy makers. Officials frequently discounted the local violence that occurred, viewing it as evidence that Africans needed more restrictive laws with more robust enforcement. Yet in reading the court transcripts, one sees that Africans were using violence, sometimes strategically, sometimes opportunistically, to achieve specific goals, including securing a more stable family life. In many cases, these goals were aligned with what people deemed to be "traditional" life: people invoked traditional practices in their court testimony as the rationale for their actions. The combination of tradition and violence was potent, and the question of which traditions were legitimate and legal spurred ongoing conversations and alterations in what the magistrates' courts accepted as traditional. The shifting category of tradition thus became an integral part of my study of violence. But people's invocation of tradition, particularly in the context of a legal proceeding, cannot always be taken at face value. Trials and official commissions were high-stakes negotiations over the exercise of legal and social power. Discussing the links between violence and tradition is complicated and often disturbing, and I have tried to engage this topic sensitively. I do not mean to suggest that all traditions are violent or that Africans are traditionally violent. Instead, I hope to show that violence became inscribed in various traditions as people interacted with state officials and the legal system.

My own experiences of South Africa provided another reason for investigating the roots of violence within rural areas. These are personal memories, and, while I don't claim that they give me any special insights, they do provide the personal background for why I, as a white American woman, undertook the project. I have traveled to South Africa, including the rural eastern Cape, since 1979, initially to teach in a secondary school in Engcobo. At that time, some students had been sent by their parents to relatives in the rural areas and away from Soweto and other cities to avoid politics or the police or both. From the mid-1980s onward, my trips have focused on historical research, and I have spent time in the various provincial capitals working in archives as well as in rural areas doing limited oral historical research. This forty-year period of South African history has seen a lot of violence. While I have never personally witnessed brutal acts of physical violence, I have seen many of the longer term impacts of it and also the mundane, structural violence instituted by the South African state and its policies. These episodes of more mundane violence included, in the 1980s, watching policemen stop Africans on the street to check their passbooks. They also included passing through police roadblocks in the 1980s and 1990s, with police snipers at the side of the road aiming directly at each car as police searched it. In the course of doing some historical interviews, I watched an older African man pull decades worth of tax receipts and official documents from a beaten-up metal trunk in his hut, records he kept to ward off harassment from the local headman and police. I interviewed another older man who asserted that working in the mines for several years had made him "a little bit crazy." Several African women recounted their illnesses, body aches, disturbing dreams, and loss of family members. They often attributed their troubles to spiritual failings or attacks by supernatural actors, blaming themselves for the harm caused by poverty and racism. Everyday violence shaped their lives and their personal stories.

The impact of the structural violence imposed by white colonization has a long history in South Africa and perhaps also a long future. Structural violence was the backdrop against which Africans lived their lives. It colonized people's traditions and created enforcement systems that encouraged or allowed Africans to use violence as part of these reconstructed traditions. State policies embedded violence in everyday routines and relationships that persist to the present.

Let me provide a couple of notes on the location of archives and orthography. The Cape Colony took over the region that is the heart of the book, the Transkei, in the 1878–94 period. The twenty-seven administrative districts of the Transkei were a "Native Reserve" under Cape colonial control until 1910. After the creation of the Union of South Africa in 1910, the Transkei was administered by the Native Affairs Department, later renamed the Bantu Affairs Department in the 1950s, based in Pretoria. However, at the local, district level, the administrative structure was the same before and after 1910. The Transkei's administrative archives, including magistrates' reports and court records from the 1880s through the mid-1960s, are deposited in what was the Cape Provincial Archives and is now the Western Cape Archives in Cape Town. Trial transcripts and court records for the period after 1902 are incomplete because they were culled by retired magistrates before they were deposited with the archives. For some districts, the culling was extensive, for others a larger number of the trial records remain. It is unclear what the criteria for culling were or indeed if there were any standardized criteria. Documents relating to national issues, such as government commissions and topics of interest to the central Native Affairs Department, are in the National Archives in Pretoria. In 1976 the Transkei became an "independent" homeland under the grand apartheid scheme; many of the documents from the 1970s onward have not survived, although some are available in the Mthatha (formerly Umtata) Archives. In addition to the archives in Cape Town, Pretoria, and Mthatha, I have also used the provincial archives of KwaZulu-Natal in Pietermaritzburg. The spellings of numerous places, like Mthatha, have changed since 1994. I have retained the spellings as they appear in my sources. Some provincial boundaries have also shifted. The district of Umzimkulu, for example, was part of the Transkei through most of the twentieth century. After 1994 the provincial boundaries moved so that it is now in KwaZulu-Natal, while most of its archives remain part of the Transkei's archives. The bibliography contains a full list of the archives consulted.

Like all authors, I have multiple debts. The research was supported by grants from the Amherst College Faculty Research Award Program, funded by the H. Axel Schupf, '57 Fund for Intellectual Life. In terms of primary sources, my most significant debt for this book is to the archives of South Africa, especially in Cape Town and Pretoria, where the archivists were consistently helpful and knowledgeable. As I began to write, I presented partial chapters as papers at several conferences, including various African Studies Association annual meetings; a 2011 conference, "Permanent Persuaders," at the University of Fort Hare; the Berkshire Women's History Conference; and the New England Workshop on Southern African Studies. Part of chapter 3, "Deaths in the Family," was published in the *Journal of Southern African Studies*. I thank the journal's editors and anonymous reviewers for their comments, and I am using the material taken from that article with the publisher's permission.

Colleagues on the Five College African Studies Council provided suggestions and feedback, particularly in the early stages of the project. For several years, my friends and colleagues Eliot Fratkin and the late Mitzi Goheen were coeditors with me of the *African Studies Review*. I learned a great deal about the multiple faces of colonialism from working with them and absorbing their insights. Catherine Higgs, a friend and scholar of South Africa, also provided valuable comments on two chapters. My research trips to Cape Town were more fun because Julia Teale generously allowed me to stay with her on several occasions and go for walks with her and her dogs. Three trips over the 2011–15 period to Engcobo and the surrounding districts allowed me to have multiple casual conversations with people about their lives and how they have and haven't changed since the end of apartheid. I enjoyed the generosity of many South Africans who offered me both tea and advice.

The book manuscript benefited from the criticisms and comments made by the two reviewers for the University of Wisconsin Press, Jacob Dlamini and Hlonipha Mokoena. There are undoubtedly still errors and inconsistencies in the book, despite their best efforts to set me right. My thanks go to Derek Gottlieb for his excellent work indexing the book. I'd also like to thank the editor in chief at the University of Wisconsin Press, Nathan MacBrien, and the series editors, Neil Kodesh and Jim Sweet, for their support.

Finally, my deepest debt is owed to my family, including my husband, Peter Siegelman, and my son, Dan. Both were incredibly understanding and supportive even when my research and writing took me away from them. Both read early drafts of chapters and offered tactful criticisms. My love goes out to them.

Violence in Rural South Africa, 1880–1963

Introduction

A History of Violence,
a Question of Tradition

In 1936 a young African man was on trial in the magistrate's court in rural Ngqeleni, a district in the Transkei, in the eastern part of the Cape Province. The court had charged him with accusing his father and his father's second wife of witchcraft and of physically assaulting them. What emerged at the trial was a complicated story of disputes within the family, compounded by concerns over who had the right to farm the land allocated to his father by state policies. These disputes had ultimately escalated into a physical attack. The young man's father complained that his son had tried to run him down on horseback and then drove him and his wife away from their home: "He came at me with his horse which ran over me but did not trample me. He chased me with the horse. He said that they must chase the witch away." The wife testified that the son had accused her and her husband of killing the younger man's child by using supernatural substances "to press down the top of the head. He told us we should go away. He assaulted us with a stick. He accused me of being a witch."[1] Other witnesses spoke of a long history of family disputes that ranged from individual jealousies to arguments over household goods, and the local headman revealed that the son had never gotten along with his father's second wife. In his defense, the son denied making the witchcraft accusation. Instead, he accused his father of misappropriating the bridewealth paid for his two sisters and neglecting them. And he also asserted he had the right to till the farm on which his father lived because it was the land that his deceased mother had farmed: "I have claimed my father's kraal [homestead and farmland] as I am his son. It is mine now."[2]

The confrontation, although filled with acrimony and threatening behavior, resulted in little physical harm to any of the people involved. Yet the potential for harm was there, stemming from grievances over the death of a child, the welfare of the defendant's sisters, and arguments over land. The son hoped to stake a claim to the land and control his sisters' bridewealth. He claimed that his father was using the sisters' bridewealth for the second wife's upkeep, a situation that, if true, would be "contrary to custom," according to the headman's testimony. Unfortunately for the young man, under the South African state's version of "customary law," he had no legal claim to either the land or the bridewealth. The magistrate presiding over the case rejected the son's criticisms of his father's conduct, ignored his assertion of a right to the land, and convicted him of imputing witchcraft to his father and the father's wife. The magistrate's sentence revealed how seriously he took the imputation of witchcraft: he sentenced the young man to three "cuts with a heavy cane" and three months in jail.[3]

Such disputes and violent threats were evidence of a complex reality in which government policies inflamed local tensions among and within rural families. Government laws regulating land availability to African farmers and the system of patriarchal control formed the backdrop against which this episode took place. While unique in its details, this case was broadly representative of how people in rural African communities engaged with the economic and legal realities constructed by the white-controlled state. They attempted to navigate their situations by invoking the idea of "custom," or using the state's court system, or alleging or hinting at the use of witchcraft, or by violent threats and acts. Sometimes they tried to use all these strategies at once, hoping to find one that worked.

The intricacies of the stories behind many acts of violence stand in contrast with the views commonly held by white officials at the time. Magistrates and native commissioners were the frontline officials of the South African state in the rural areas. Their attitudes and prejudices toward Africans inflected the decisions they made and the policies they enforced. In 1931, for example, a native commissioner in Bulwer, Natal, replied in a questionnaire from the Native Economic Commission that "the natives are well behaved and there is little crime among them." But, he continued, "crimes of violence such as faction fights and assaults on each other are fairly prevalent and are more in evidence when the natives have reaped a good harvest and kafir beer [home-brewed beer] is plentiful. After a poor season there is a considerable amount of petty pilfering of foodstuffs and the European farmers' crops and flocks of sheep suffer. They are also somewhat given to stealing each others' sheep and goats in native areas."[4] This official's report was echoed by comments from another magistrate (from Idutywa in the Transkei) to the commission: "Witchcraft is sometimes a contributory factor to such crimes as murder, serious assaults, etc. Assaults, however, chiefly arise out of beer-drinking."[5] These comments represented widely held opinions among white officials: that rural Africans were inherently "given to stealing," especially from each other, and that physical assaults typically resulted from drinking and witchcraft allegations. Their reports oversimplified and distorted the causes of rural Africans' social and economic problems and implicitly denied that disruptions caused by decades of white rule may have played a role. Yet these reports—and others like them—informed many state policies in the rural areas and shaped the way magistrates enforced the laws: they saw violence as an inherent feature of African life that was largely unrelated to problems of poverty or the effects of state policies.

The different understandings of the sources of rural violence are at the heart of this book. The book's central argument is that violence among Africans in rural South Africa was evidence of Africans attempting to navigate the complex and hazardous reality that had emerged under white rule in South Africa. Africans' actions were a form of "social navigation" similar to that discussed by Henrik Vigh in his study of young African men in Guinea. "Social navigation" was his translation of a local term, *dubriagem*. Vigh explained *dubriagem* as people shadowboxing with reality—bobbing and weaving to "the push and pull of social forces—not as static constraints or positions of power in a social field but as social effects that engage social beings and bodies within the social environment."[6] Other scholars have used the term social navigation to discuss immigrants, unemployed youth, refugees, and ex-combatants surviving in environments that are hostile to them.[7] While the people in this study of rural South Africa were neither refugees nor ex-combatants, they did have to operate in a social environment that was in flux. As Julie Archambault's study of youth in Inhambane, Mozambique in the 2010s, has noted, "the concept of 'social navigation' offers a heuristic analytical framework for those interested in everyday lived experiences and life trajectories and therefore deserves to be extended to also capture everyday life in less volatile environments."[8] Social navigation provides a way of capturing the purposeful actions of individuals in a world that they cannot fully control.

This study looks at violence in the rural eastern districts of the Cape (the Transkei) and adjacent districts of KwaZulu-Natal to find connections between intimate and community violence on the one hand and political and structural violence on the other. It is impossible to draw a clear line between political violence and nonpolitical violence in most cases. An episode in which political activists attacked a chief for his progovernment views might fall easily into the political violence category. But it is also worth considering whether the case of the young man who attacked his parents after accusing them of witchcraft was also resisting political constraints as well as responding to familial jealousies. Masculinity or a sense of patriarchal rights was frequently bound up with acts of violence, directed either at the state or at family members. However, there was often more at stake than masculine identities, and it was not just men who committed or instigated violence.

Among Africans living in the countryside, white rule and various state policies shifted the social environment and the contours of what was legal and what was traditional. The concept that transformed some uses of violence from illegal to legal was that of "tradition," as understood by state officials and as approved by state policies. But as we saw in the opening court case, some traditions—such as patriarchal control of the family—were acceptable to white officials, while others—such as beliefs in witchcraft—were not. Tradition became the idiom through which Africans and whites contested morality and agency; Africans' strategic use of violence often became the realization of that agency. Using the concept of social navigation as a lens through which to analyze Africans' movements through the changing environment highlights both their agency and the limits of that agency.[9]

Rural life became routinely violent for many Africans under white rule during the first half of the twentieth century. Those people who landed in court because of their use of violence often characterized and tried to justify the violence as a legitimate element of traditional practices. White officials, for their part, frequently suggested that violence committed by Africans was traditional, a suggestion that allowed them to believe that the violence was neither new nor an expression of resistance to state policies. Throughout the book, however, I will show that violence within families and communities in the rural areas sprang from the same roots as political violence directed against the state and addressed many of the same problems.

For historians, the framing of violence among rural communities as traditional and often insular has meant that most scholarly studies have not investigated it to the same degree as violence in towns and cities. While organized political violence and gang violence in the urban areas have received the bulk of the scholarly attention, violence in the rural areas has a history of its own. People's use of violence often addressed rural problems that emerged sometimes from local troubles and rivalries, sometimes from the results of state policies, and sometimes from both.

Much of southeastern South Africa—what is now the Transkeian region of the Eastern Cape Province—came under white control from the 1880s onward. Before the 1880s, Africans in this region had contacts with white settlers through trade, armed conflicts, and missionary activities. However, most still lived under the rule of African chiefs and continued to practice a vibrant culture. The onset of white rule in the 1880s provoked a reordering of rural African life more extensive than the "invention of tradition" literature has documented.[10] Whites partly justified the expansion of colonial rule into the Transkei based on their beliefs that warfare and violence among Africans was customary. Officials' decisions to use some of the local customs (as whites understood them) as the basis for control created a hybrid system that served white interests well, although it was not consistently legible to African subjects.

Historians have demonstrated that colonial powers actively invented traditions as part of their project of establishing political control over indigenous populations. The literature on invented traditions has explored the enshrinement of "customary law" in colonial Africa, but it has not explored how the colonial state and some Africans came to accept violence as part of the customary.[11] Scholars have largely ignored the ways that colonial rule allowed and even, in some cases, promoted acts of violence committed by Africans as elements of tradition.

White rule colonized African traditions. "Tradition" and "custom" remain contested terms: cultures are dynamic, and in a living culture, traditions often change in response to changing circumstances. Historically, attempts to ossify various cultural practices under the rubric of the customary have been, effectively, attempts to hold onto power.[12]

Since the end of apartheid in 1994, scholars have charted how current African leaders have used the idea of adherence to tradition to add to their authority and justify their use of violence, often for political purposes or to enhance certain legal claims, particularly to land.[13] But much of the more recent literature has focused on Zulu culture and ideas about tradition in postapartheid society. This book's focus is on the Transkei region of the Cape Province and some of the adjacent districts of Zululand in Natal. The time frame encompasses the first eighty years of white rule in the region, including the ascendance of segregation and apartheid policies through the early 1960s. This region and period provide greater depth to the discussion of the historical roots of violence, particularly violence that existed in a supposedly traditional space. New themes emerge from investigating how both Africans and whites defined tradition and custom in the shifting context of government policies, court cases, and the documented responses of Africans to various social and economic pressures. The violence that became embedded in traditions and customs was fundamentally a historical construction of colonial polices and African attempts to navigate these policies and retain some agency.

The next section explores scholarly analyses of violence among Africans. While many of these analyses are present oriented, they often look for historical roots of violence. Deeply historical studies have focused on violence stemming from increasing poverty and shifts in attitudes in African society about masculinity. While both greater poverty and changes to gender identities were significant factors, they are often too broad to serve as explanations for violence within African rural society; they do not capture the intentional use of violence in Africans' responses to the challenges they faced. This introductory chapter will briefly sketch how violence became incorporated into colonized traditions. The chapter will end with a brief synopsis of the rest of the book.

HISTORIES OF VIOLENCE

Recent accounts of violence in South Africa have often focused on current problems. Massive and increasing levels of economic inequality have been singled out as a primary cause of tension, as the transition away from the apartheid state and its policies did little to mitigate wealth differentials between rich and poor.[14] The decades following the end of apartheid, with their neoliberal economic policies and anemic reforms, have hardened political corruption and heightened social and economic stratification, even as new generations of South Africans, born after the end of apartheid, have become the majority.[15] Violence has persisted in structures of governance and industrial production, and it surfaces in discourses surrounding race, gender, sexuality, and identity.[16] Black protesters have organized political campaigns against policies of the African National Congress–governed state, and the state has sometimes responded with sharp police crackdowns reminiscent of apartheid-era police actions. Meanwhile, in the rural areas, the state expects traditional leaders and family patriarchs to maintain public order even though many of the structural tensions created during the period of white rule—including widespread poverty, land shortages, and inadequate social services—persist.[17]

In the post-1994 period, interpersonal and intercommunal violence has competed with political and economic violence for news headlines and scholarly analysis. Xenophobic clashes with immigrants from elsewhere on the continent have stemmed from cultural differences and rumors as well as from economic competition.[18] Violent acts committed against intimate partners, family members, and members of the LGBTQ community have also come more prominently into the literature as documented assaults have increased since 1994.[19] The persistence of social and economic problems in the postapartheid era, compounded by a political leadership that has lacked either the will, the skill, or the resources to address these problems, suggests that violence will continue to be a significant feature of South African life and a focus of future scholarship.

For the most part, these recent studies have investigated violence in the informal settlements, mining compounds, and walled and razor-wired gardens of the urban, suburban, and peri-urban areas.[20] Although studies of violence between intimate partners in the rural areas has been an exception to this generalization, violence in rural settings has not received the attention that dramatic scenes in urban spaces have. Partly this emphasis on the urban reflects the current demographic realities: the vast majority of South Africa's population now lives in cities or peri-urban regions.

The current demographic distribution, though, is different from that of the first half of the twentieth century. Well into the 1960s the majority of Africans either lived (at least part-time) in the rural areas or had extensive family connections there. Coercive government policies had hampered population movements from rural "black" areas to urban "white" ones for decades. The rural basis of many Africans' lives was not less real for being partly coerced; many Africans had much of their savings and personal and familial identity invested in the countryside. The habits and happenings of rural life were central to the lives of people as individuals and as members of communities and families; the violence that occurred in these rural spaces thus carried considerable significance. One enduring feature of rural life that marked the expressions of violence was that migrant labor was strongly skewed for much of the twentieth century toward male migration. As a result, women's roles in rural households and the complex relations between sexuality, gender, land rights, and wage earning frequently stoked domestic violence and violence within communities.[21]

The history of all South Africa during the colonial and apartheid periods is a history of forced dispossession of African land and lives and of the construction of a society that white rulers intended to be unequal. Historical studies of violence under colonial and apartheid rule note that the state routinely used violence against Africans. Consequently, violence committed by Africans against the state has been relatively straightforward for historians to portray as politically driven resistance. However, violence also erupted *within* African communities. William Beinart stated, in his survey of the histories of violence in southern Africa, that "explaining and understanding African political violence as a response to conquest, dispossession, and the authoritarian nature of colonial rule or apartheid has not been particularly problematic. . . . More difficult has been the related issue which [Frantz] Fanon raises: that of violence within or between African communities."[22] Beinart asks a big question about how to explain violence within African communities and whether there was a connection between violence within communities and political violence against the state.

In the context of looking for connections between different episodes of violence, we must discuss the meaning of the word "violence." Any study of violence in the colonial and apartheid periods in South Africa runs immediately into definitional issues. David Chidester notes in his study of "wild religion" in South Africa that "violence, by definition, is force gone wrong, the wild force that blows up bridges, breaks laws, and disrupts order."[23] Donald Donham defines violence as a "force that directly threatens bodies and the bare life of bodies." He notes that "however the culture, the political, and the economic come together, we might say that violence is red,"[24] a comment both on the spilling of blood and the grip of emotions that frequently drive people to violence. In the case of South Africa's rural areas from the 1880s onward, much violence was indeed red and often threatened individuals' lives. But violence also had a more cold and calculated aspect as it emerged from white control over the state and the economy, along with the long-running social disruptions caused by migrant labor and land dispossession. These circumstances were particularly stark in the Transkeian region of the eastern Cape Colony (later the Cape Province and, post-1994, the Eastern Cape Province) and in Natal (post-1994, KwaZulu-Natal). Occasional outbreaks of violence directed against the state coexisted and overlapped with interpersonal and domestic violence. But it can be difficult to distinguish between political and personal motivations among those who committed some acts of violence.

In South Africa, the meaning of the word "violence" reflected the disposition of political power. If violence is force gone wrong, as Chidester alleges, it was usually those who had governing power who decided the difference between rightful and wrongful force. Government documents in the archives did not use the word "violence" to describe, for example, the canings meted out by white magistrates as punishment to many youthful African offenders, including the young man in the court case cited at the beginning of the chapter. However, they did use it to describe stick fights and faction fights between groups of boys and men. State records did not use the word "violence" to describe government policies that restricted African ownership of land while granting expropriated land to whites. However, they did use it to describe the fights that periodically erupted among rural African families over access to land and other resources once white rule was imposed. When a government official described an act as violent, he almost always conveyed the notion that the act was illegitimate and possibly immoral, just as when a political dissident described the state's use of force as violent, he or she implicitly called the state's legitimacy into question. Similarly, acts of violence against the South African state have often been dubbed "resistance" by historians—thus recognizing the acts' political weight and conveying a sense of legitimacy—while state officials labeled such violence as "criminality" or as "unrest" incited by "outside agitators"— thus implying the state's right to suppress those acts. The use of the word "violence" often carries with it a political judgment.[25]

The administrative and legal context imposed by an oppressive regime is often called structural violence. Enmeshed in a comprehensive system of rule, people exposed to the violence of the colonial and apartheid systems did not always respond by committing violent acts. Nevertheless, people's reactions to the state's violence, whether those reactions were themselves violent or not, arose out of their understandings of their social roles and opportunities. Donham writes that "there is no doubt that the notion of structural violence has its uses. It reminds us of all the silent and unremarked-upon factors that, just as surely as the blow of a machete, snuff out life. And it is clear that factors such as exploitation can contribute to patterns of physical violence, though it is also clear that they do not always do so."[26] Donham continues by suggesting that, if we accept that violent reactions are not inevitable, we have to explain why people do respond with violence in some situations and not in others; we have to look at each act of violence as being a purposeful choice rather than a reflex. This insight makes a break with how colonial officials frequently saw Africans' commission of violent acts as reflexive expressions of an inherent propensity for fighting. Instead, Africans chose how to respond to state violence and policies. Frequently, when they used violence, they did so strategically as a way of navigating the colonial landscape. And they made those choices with the knowledge of how the colonial environment limited them. Historians should look for the meanings in violent acts and the social constructions that brought them about rather than focusing solely on the physical, social, and political outcomes. Throughout the book, I will use "violence" to mean using force that caused or threatened to cause physical harm. Although that definition is expansive, it allows a deeper investigation into how certain types of physical force became socially and legally accepted.

Violence and Masculinity

As scholars have discarded efforts to explain Africans' use of violence by invoking racially based concepts of hardwired tendencies toward brutality, they have made numerous attempts to fill the analytical space with more recent social-scientific studies on the causes of violence.[27] One set of explanations has explored violence, particularly urban gang violence, as resulting from competitions among men over honor and status. Gary Kynoch's work, for example, concludes that the high level of violence perpetrated by male gang members against both women and other men resulted from the extreme violence of South African society generally and from personal attempts to establish dominance and status. Harsh working conditions in the mines and other workplaces, brutal policing, and shared experiences of violent crime socialized men to resort to violence to survive and to preserve their identities.[28]

Analyses of violence in South Africa almost immediately merge with discussions of gender. In his study of violence in South Africa's labor hostels, Glen Elder wrote, "Violence is always gendered."[29] South African scholarship is not alone in seeing the performance of masculine identities as strongly implicated in questions of violence. Still, as many who have written about masculinity note, the fact that men are the most common perpetrators of violence should not simply be attributed to naturalized biological identities but, instead, needs in-depth, social explanations. Cultures create distinct definitions of masculinity, and although an association between men and violence may be shared across cultures, different cultures may assign positive or negative values to specific acts of violence as well as having divergent ideas of what acts fall into the category of "violent." Violent acts committed by young men may, in certain circumstances, have positive associations, and at least for members of their own peer group, those actions would not be "force gone wrong." For example, men, as well as some women, who fight in wars may do so to preserve their societies and may not be primarily concerned with a demonstration of personal "masculinity."[30] The idea that certain types of violence may preserve or construct group identities is present in many analyses of gangs, but it is also present in the discussion of the use of violence to establish ethnic or national identities.[31] While people might use force to claim a gendered identity, they can also use force to preserve or defend larger groups and cultural norms.

Beyond competing notions of masculinity, broader changes in gender roles often sparked conflict. The historian Anne Mager has looked at rural African culture in the mid-twentieth century for the precursors of violent masculine identities in South African towns. Mager argues that from the 1940s onward, African society in the Ciskei region of the Cape was regendered, with men's and women's social roles and expectations scrambled by the effects of white rule, industrialization, and competing cultural norms. The social and economic changes "destabilized masculinities" and made violence more likely to be a component of how men asserted their masculinity.[32] Mager's analysis of gangs in East London argues that the violence of *tsotsis* (urban gang members) was more than an alternative way of acquiring adult male status; the violence emerged "in the context of the new culture of the urban slums and, above all, in the turmoil of changing gender relations."[33] Moreover, women participated in urban violence. She notes that, in East London, gang members included women—*amatsotsikazi*—and the gangs used violence to subvert old gender identities—both male and female—as well as to perform power and acquire money.

Despite Mager's finding that some women engaged in gang violence, much of the literature continues to draw a strong connection between men and violence. The dual association of violence with men and with the colonized condition has contributed to a reevaluation of men's violence: the violence of the male subaltern often acquires a heroic cast in nationalist and resistance narratives.[34] Those who commit violence in a domestic context may claim that it is a legitimate exercise of their roles as patriarchs and that patriarchy is a form of mastery that negates the colonial condition of subordination.[35] However, in glossing violence in this way, scholars may end up rendering those who have been harmed by violence, including both African men and women, as collateral damage in the struggle between colonizer and colonized, with women in particular relegated, in Daniel Magaziner's words, to the roles of "mourners-and-mothers."[36] The construction of African violence as both heroic and masculine thus may preclude a deeper discussion of the meanings of violence committed by both men and women and narrow the discussion to overtly political acts of defiance by men against state actors.[37]

Too narrow a focus on anti-state violence also obscures the degree to which state policies fostered certain types of violence within African families and communities. Colonial and apartheid laws appropriated aspects of African culture in ways that made intrafamilial violence more likely. The altering of particular aspects of African culture to suit the needs of the regime is an issue taken up in Mark Hunter's exploration of the meaning of manhood among Zulu informants in the first decade of the twenty-first century. He notes that "racial stereotypes of violent black men are omnipresent worldwide and negate the violence of racism itself. At the same time, it is not possible to simply blame intimate violence on 'apartheid,' 'poverty,' or 'emasculation.'" Hunter argues that "apartheid's form of racial rule . . . did not simply emasculate men but worked through the patriarchal home and created patterns of respectability amid plural ideas of manhood."[38] As he details the meanings of Zulu masculinity and sexuality, Hunter thus embroiders on Belinda Bozzoli's analysis of colonial society being made up of a "patchwork quilt of patriarchies," in which both men and women wrapped their ideas of community, family, and self.[39]

Multiple patriarchies, however, created conflicting notions of tradition, and these different notions fueled violence. A major theme of this book is the ways in which some acts of violence that might superficially have appeared to be nonpolitical were actually connected to the political and historical context in which they took place. This was particularly true in the colonial context, where certain cultural traditions were legal while others were criminal.

Mark Hunter's analysis of the connections between patriarchy, traditions, and white rule demonstrates the alterations that occurred in these ideas during the twentieth century. Traditions were not just a collection of abstract ideas about cultural practices, they were concepts employed by both Africans and white officials in the construction of policies and the legal system that governed Africans. While laws constructed categories of legal and criminal behaviors, they also regulated African family life, including inheritance, marriages and divorces, women's status as legal minors, and control over land. These were all vital concerns for African households. Africans often had to defend themselves against the state, but as we saw in the court case discussed at the beginning of the introduction, they also had to defend themselves against other family members with contending claims of power and authority.

While state policies dubbed African life traditional and implied that it was unchanging, they changed Africans' lives and set the stage for Africans to compete with one another for restricted resources.[40] In the rural areas, the most limited resource was land, as the creation of the Native Reserves along with the passage of the 1913 Native Lands Act and later laws sharply limited the amount of land available to the African population. In 1913 only 7 percent of the land in South Africa was available for Africans to reside on and farm independently; that percentage only increased to 13 percent in the 1950s under apartheid policies. While the 1913 act itself was never implemented in the Cape Province, other measures that limited African land ownership and tenure had a similar effect. For a rural population that remained economically dependent on farming, the land shortage was an economic crisis. But the shortage of land also evoked broader social crises involving family life and the cultural meaning of adulthood.[41]

The land shortage for African farmers was a creation of state policies that were fundamentally coercive and violent. Clifton Crais, in his study of poverty in South Africa's rural areas, links poverty directly to the conflicts that arose from land shortages. He asks, "How might the story of rural poverty in South Africa 'look' if we bring the problem of violence toward the center of its analysis? To what extent was violence both destructive and formative, or constitutive of new and durable social and economic patterns?"[42] Crais argues that colonial violence in the countryside created a series of crises within African communities that fundamentally changed them, making them both more impoverished and more likely to use violence themselves.[43] He likens the condition of living through colonial conquest and rule to a condition of trauma—at both the individual and social level.[44] Crais is correct to point out that the experience of white settler conquest and rule directly injured African societies and families, even as it institutionalized systems of oppression. But the following chapters will argue that even within the oppressive system of white rule, Africans exercised some choices as they tried to navigate toward goals they desired. Violence became integrated into rural society and normalized as part of a newly reimagined set of traditions from which Africans derived identities and meanings.

The Myth of Traditional Violence

In the early to mid-nineteenth century, multiple wars between white settlers and Africans as well as the wars that surrounded the creation of the Zulu state fostered the construction by whites of a myth of Africans as inherently prone to conflict and rough justice.[45] Whites' interpretations of these events then informed the construction of the legal system that they imposed on Africans as the Cape Colony expanded eastward in the latter half of the nineteenth century and as whites established colonial rule over Zulu speakers in Natal. Colonial magistrates claimed that they used African "customary law" or "native law" to decide criminal and civil cases brought to their courts, and they claimed that these precepts derived from discussions with African elders and their own knowledge of what they termed the "native mind."[46] Still, magistrates and policy makers refracted their interpretations of custom through their own religious and cultural codes as well as through their (mis)understandings of African life. When specific violent acts ended up in courts as criminal or civil cases, the ways that magistrates adjudicated these cases over the years in turn helped to mold Africans' ideas about what violence was legal and acceptable and what was not. Additionally, insofar as magistrates believed some acts of violence to be part of traditional culture, they made choices about whether to criminalize them, depending on whether they saw themselves as upholding the preexisting African social order, reforming it, or scrapping it. A. H. B. Stanford, the magistrate of Umtata in 1881, claimed that he administered "Kafir [*sic*] law as far as it is not repugnant to humanity and justice," with the implied message that white magistrates were the appropriate arbiters of "humanity and justice."[47]

Beyond the colonial court system, other institutions strongly influenced African culture as practiced in the rural areas and helped condition many people's ideas of what constituted traditions and customs. State policies governing marriage, inheritance, and land rights reconstructed a version (or perhaps a better word is "mirage") of traditional African life. Many whites and some Africans glossed particular acts of violence as traditional features of African society over which the state could exercise only marginal control in the short term even if it wished to reform them over the longer term. As we will see in upcoming chapters, these acts included large-scale fights among young men and marriages forced on young women. Officials accepted and reinforced many other customs as part of their attempt to control Africans at a relatively low cost to the state.[48] Allowing patriarchs as well as chiefs and headmen to use certain types of violence in the exercise of their traditional authority was thus pragmatic, and officials were wary of interventions that might generate unrest and undermine their authority or the authority of elders on whom they relied for the maintenance of social order. Africans navigated a complicated and shifting social reality by using those reconfigured traditions to make claims, protect their autonomy, and achieve their desired goals.

One of the few types of traditional violence that state officials actively tried to eradicate from the onset of white rule was violence resulting from allegations of witchcraft. Whites saw witchcraft beliefs as superstitions and often failed to comprehend the social, economic, political, religious, and health-related foundations of many witchcraft allegations. The defendant in the court case discussed at the beginning of this chapter found that when his complicated history of family strife and economic constraints appeared in court, the magistrate reduced it to a question of whether he had accused his parents of witchcraft. Despite the physical threats he made and the allegations of abuse of patriarchal authority that he leveled at his father, he was ultimately convicted of the crime of making a witchcraft accusation and not of committing an assault. His father's possible abuses were not investigated, and the magistrate was also not interested in the broader social critique that emerged from the case's details. Paradoxically, the fact that the state criminalized witchcraft accusations may have bolstered beliefs in the existence of malevolent supernatural powers and increased anxiety over their use.[49] The state punished Africans who named and took actions against witches, but it could not prevent people from fearing witches or legislate an element of African culture out of existence.

Violence, the State, and Tradition

As many scholars have noted, violence was an essential attribute of the colonial state. Violent acts committed by the state were physical manifestations of power and dominance; they were also performances meant to forestall challenges to authority from the colonized population. The colonial state had few limits on its use of the power to coerce and kill. And violence often extended beyond episodic confrontations between the colonial state and the colonial subject and became institutionalized as part of mundane interactions between people and state policies.

This mundane violence marked many of the experiences of Africans in rural South Africa as the segregationist and apartheid states advanced their control. In the last two decades of the nineteenth century, white officials articulated the idea that the state had to rely on preexisting structures of African rule to slow the pace of change and prevent extensive unrest. Theophilus Shepstone in Natal was the master of this system, adopting the title of "Supreme Chief" of the Zulu and attempting to impose his own ideas of civilization gradually by ruling through and over Zulu chiefs.[50] Expanding his influence, Shepstone gave lengthy testimony to the 1883 Native Laws and Customs Commission convened by the Cape colonial government in which he strongly recommended that his system of ruling through chiefs and headmen be adopted by the Cape.[51] Walter Stanford, perhaps the most influential administrator in the Transkeian region of the eastern Cape in the 1880s, made similar comments about the need for the colonial administration to draw on local norms of governance to facilitate white rule.[52] Cape administrators meant to harness the authority of the chiefs for the purposes of white rule.[53]

While Shepstone and Stanford saw white rule as a benevolent force of civilization, by 1903 at least a few white magistrates understood that colonial rule was coercive and authoritarian. One longtime Transkeian magistrate, J. C. Garner, testified to the South African Native Affairs Commission of 1903–5 that "up to the present we have governed them [Africans] from the effects of their own tyrannical treatment, which caused the Natives to look upon those in authority with fear and trembling who could not be disobeyed. We unconsciously governed on this unknown reason, considering it to be their thankful confidence and love toward our laws and customs."[54] As Garner came close to acknowledging, rather than accepting the colonial state as benign, Africans were instead cognizant of its ability to deploy force at any time to maintain control. In Garner's view, the use of tyranny by the state to govern was traditional. However, the reconfigured roles played by chiefs and headmen within the colonial administrative structure was a novelty masquerading as tradition.

In the early stages of colonial rule in the Cape Province (particularly in the Transkei) and Natal, from 1880 through the 1920s, the white-controlled state framed policies and defined what constituted crime among its African subjects.

However, the enforcement of laws was often haphazard and depended on individual Africans reporting crimes and enforcing policies. Outside of periods of active rebellion (particularly in 1880–1 and 1955–63), state control was rarely a matter of brute force continuously exercised over the population.[55] Throughout the whole period from 1880 through 1954, Transkeian districts with populations as high as forty thousand to fifty thousand people often had minimal police forces, sometimes numbering three or four African constables and one white officer. Similar population-to-police ratios existed in rural Natal districts. Chiefs and headmen supplemented the police forces and were deputized by magistrates (also called native commissioners and, beginning in the 1950s, Bantu Affairs commissioners) to enforce the laws. Chiefs and headmen were more than state employees and deputies—they were also typically the most trusted informants on the topics of Africans' precolonial laws and customs for magistrates and government commissions. In the early decades of colonial rule in the region from 1880 until the mid-1920s, chiefs and headmen could shape and mitigate the laws enforced by the state by defending various practices as elements of tradition. They were also often in a position to make decisions about whether to enforce various laws or not at the local level.[56] The system particularly favored older African men: relying on what they understood as Africans' traditional deference to elders, white officials accorded older men autonomy within the family as patriarchs, just as they accorded headmen and chiefs some autonomy as traditional rulers. This personalized and localized system of control and enforcement left Africans some openings to use local networks to their advantage.[57]

Rural governance became more bureaucratized and rigid in the 1920s with the passage of the Native Administration Act of 1927.[58] Simultaneously, violent acts among rural South Africans became more frequent. Some of the increase may have resulted from differences in how people defined and reported crime, but some of it was undoubtedly a real rise. This escalating violence emerged as people living in the rural areas felt harsher social and economic pressures. The strains of intensified engagement with the South African economy combined with laws restricting African land ownership and the flow of Africans from the rural to the urban areas to push state officials to impose new measures to manage and contain the rural African population. The structural violence of the systems of governance and migrant labor were persistent forces in most Africans' lives around which they had to navigate.[59]

More active policing of the rural population emerged in the mid-1920s as part of the effort to streamline and systematize segregationist laws to entrench white control. This process then accelerated from 1948 into the 1950s as the newly empowered apartheid state imposed ever more unpopular and intrusive policies on the African population. In 1951 with the passage of the Bantu Authorities Act, the apartheid state developed policies to create "independent," self-governing homelands for Africans that placed additional administrative powers into the hands of chiefs and headmen, who in most cases were chosen by and worked under the supervision of white officials.[60] The Bantu Affairs Department had already been actively promoting various agricultural "betterment" plans, including livestock culling and fencing. These plans were unpopular among Africans, but chiefs and headmen were expected to impose them on their local populations. They quickly found themselves in an awkward position: as state employees, either they could enforce the new policies and suffer the effects of popular distrust and anger or they could criticize the policies and lose their jobs and their status. Either way, the policies, their enforcement, and individual officials often encountered resistance. Some of this resistance turned violent, and by the mid-1950s and early 1960s, rebels were openly targeting the regime with violence. At the same time, many people who had little direct connection to the state also were on the receiving end of violent attacks by members of their own communities who accused them of collaborating with the regime. Rebels were, in many cases, accusing "collaborators" of immorality and witchcraft.

During this long period of social and economic turmoil, Africans attempted to hold onto the autonomy of their family lives. They often took up the colonially reconstructed images of African traditions, modified them, and defended them to "move toward positions they perceive[d] as being better than their current location and the possibilities within them."[61] The imposition of white rule did not wholly remake African society. Africans retained some of their older beliefs and social norms, while preexisting ideas of appropriate and inappropriate uses of physical force merged in idiosyncratic ways with the superimposed violence of the settler state.[62] Africans attempted to work through, around, or against state violence while still maintaining an African identity distinct from the one that government officials mapped out for them.

Not all the violence committed by Africans during the period of white rule was overtly political or politically transformative. The violence within African communities demands more discussion and analysis. This was violence that was not aimed directly at the state or its officials but was internal to the family, or occurred between neighbors, or initiated abduction marriages, or erupted between groups of mostly young men. This intracommunal and intrafamilial violence was partly a reaction to and outgrowth of repressive policies and therefore was political in its structural causation even if the individuals involved had no personal political motivations. But the specific patterns of violence that emerged were also informed by preexisting cultural practices. Violence became one of the methods of navigating the limitations and structures of the changing rural social environment.

Structure of the Book and Sources

In researching this study of rural violence, I have relied principally on archival evidence. My research includes court records and magistrates' reports for eighteen (out of twenty-seven) districts of the rural Transkeian region and documents from the Transkeian chief magistrate's office (in the Cape Town and Mthatha archive repositories) and three adjacent KwaZulu-Natal districts (in the KwaZulu-Natal archives). The court records include transcribed testimony and evidence from civil and criminal trials across the entire period (1880–1963).[63] In the National Archives in Pretoria I have also examined the archives for the Ministry of Native Affairs/Bantu Affairs Department and the collected records of two major commissions: the South African Native Affairs Commission of 1903–5 and the Native Economic Commission of 1930–32. In addition, the published evidence and reports of other commissions, especially the Cape Colony's Native Laws and Customs Commission of 1883–84, have also been important sources.

Archival materials such as these have several strengths, including describing economic and social issues over an extended period. Official reports give a broader picture of life while revealing the prejudices and miscalculations of magistrates, police, and other officials. While colonial government archives are notably biased, they provide considerable detail about Africans' daily lives from testimonies in court cases and at commissions. The range of transcripts from local trials, both civil and criminal, that I use has received little attention from most historians analyzing life in the rural areas. The trial testimonies provide a wealth of information, not just about criminal activities or searing social problems. They open a window onto the interactions between the colonial and indigenous social orders, the workings of the legal system at the most intimate and immediate levels, and the lives of ordinary people and what they thought was important. These testimonies show Africans actively navigating the policies and laws of the South African state as they participated in court cases, framed their testimonies, and tried to control the outcomes. My research also includes contemporaneous newspaper articles and missionaries' publications to supplement these government sources. Church officials and journalists had blind spots as well, particularly given the cultural, linguistic, and political dynamics of writing for predominantly white audiences about the lives of the African population. Still, their articles provide details and perspectives that official sources lack.

The people who crafted these documents and curated the archives had disparate interests, some of which are clearer than others. Historical archives, as Ann Stoler observes, have "itineraries of their own."[64] However, Africans were not passively victimized by the state's creation of records. They initiated many civil lawsuits relating to marriages, property, family relations, and the stresses imposed by labor migration and state policies. They used the information they gleaned from court decisions to shape their interactions with state officials and institutions. They actively tried to mold policies through responses to government commissioners' questions. As Poppy Fry has noted as part of her discussion of women's roles in the Fingo Emancipation of 1835: "The colonial archive must be read not as the definitive account but rather as a jumble of information in which a range of patterns, stories, and perspectives may be discerned."[65] Imperfect though they are, the documents provide vital evidence about African rural life and the violence that sometimes marked it.

Synopses of Individual Chapters

The idea of Africans using violence as part of their attempts to navigate colonial laws and social norms emerges in several different contexts. Rural families were not constantly in conflict with each other, and well into the 1950s and later, many households were socially stable even if quite a few were poor. But there were stress lines in African families and in rural society generally. Along these stress lines violence became more common.

One such fracture was the fighting among adolescents and men known as "faction fights." Chapter 1 discusses the violence at the center of these fights and how the fights became more lethal during the twentieth century. Ben Carton and Rob Morrell have argued that twenty-first-century headlines have too strongly influenced scholars who have investigated the history of rural fighting. The historical reality, they suggest, was that Zulu boys, when they learned to stick fight, also learned "honorable restraint."[66] Boys were not training to be killers but were learning discipline and how to command respect within a particular social system. At the same time, the enthusiastic support and encouragement given by older girls and young women to the fighters legitimized and socialized the fighting.[67] My evidence suggests that fighting among older boys and young men in the Transkeian region became common and more lethal in the rural areas by the late 1920s and was seen by many observers (both white and African) as disturbing and harmful. These observations provoke questions and a need for more analysis. Did these more lethal fights continue to fulfill socially prescribed tasks? Was their increasing lethality a symptom of broader problems in rural society resulting from the violence inherent in white rule? Did the state's acceptance of stick fighting as a supposedly traditional blood sport facilitate the increased incidence of more lethal forms of fighting? What connections existed between fighting and violent political unrest directed against state officials in the 1950s and early 1960s? The chapter will engage with these questions and discuss the disparate motivations that fed into these fights.

Rural expressions of violence frequently stemmed from conflicts over gender roles and family troubles. Chapters 2 and 3 investigate how the white-controlled state and some Africans condoned and presented certain violent acts committed within families as traditional. In chapter 2, the physical force that frequently accompanied abduction marriages (*ukuthwala*) by the 1920s and later was not traditional violence, at least in the sense of being well grounded in historical practice. Even though abduction marriages had occurred in the precolonial period and were called by the same name—*ukuthwala*—the levels of violence used to complete the abduction and the frequency with which abduction marriages took place increased during the period of colonial and then apartheid state control.[68] As we will see in this chapter, officials' gradual acceptance of abduction marriages as legal and legitimate coincided with a shift toward labeling such coercion as traditional. Some women also came to accept coercion in the creation of these marriages, which many believed was evidence of their adherence to traditional culture and identities. Women's acceptance of such violence as traditional provides a clear instance of social navigation: women had to make choices about what they would accept on the basis of their reading of the shifting cultural and social situation.

Chapter 3 explores the topic of violence within families and communities, particularly violence involving allegations of witchcraft against wives, widows, and unmarried women. It engages the literature on men's violence toward women, and it also analyzes women's violence within the family. The chapter uses multiple court cases as evidence. In some cases, women were accused of committing acts of physical violence within their families; in others, family members committed violence against women who were named as witches. Within rural African culture in the first several decades of the twentieth century, people presumed that women's violence was immoral and associated with witchcraft familiars and harmful medicines. I argue that these assumptions about women's power to do evil were a way of framing common anxieties about the long-term absence of adult men as migrant laborers and the declining economic health of rural families. Allegations of witchcraft were closely intertwined with the imposition of white rule and the expansion of male labor recruiting. But witchcraft allegations and beliefs in supernatural beings were also ways of diagnosing and attempting to redress personal and familial problems.[69] Africans tried to navigate an often harsh economic and social reality by enlisting the assistance of diviners and ancestors. How women came to be blamed as the source of multiple social problems, and how they became strongly associated with supernatural powers is the focus of the analysis. At the end of the chapter, we will look briefly at the ways in which witchcraft accusations often appeared in the political violence that developed in the rural areas in the 1950s, much of which was also rooted in local conditions and grievances stemming from government policies.

Chapter 4 builds on the previous discussion of witchcraft and violence in family and community settings to investigate political violence targeting apartheid-era homelands policies and leaders in the early 1960s. The apartheid state's creation of "homelands" for Africans was the regime's attempt to define Africans as perpetual foreigners in "white" South Africa. The Transkei was the first of these designated homelands to achieve "self-rule" (in 1963) and "independence" (in 1976). The chapter analyzes the rise in regional violence against state policies in the 1950s and early 1960s. These acts of violence emerged from local, rural grievances and incorporated the methods of the local and regional violence discussed in previous chapters. I then look for the links between this local violence and two particularly dramatic acts in late 1962 and early 1963 in the Transkei: an attempted assassination of Chief Kaiser Matanzima, the African official who was collaborating with whites in the creation of the Transkei as a homeland, and the murder of a white family at a roadside camp in the Transkei. Both acts were committed by male members of Poqo, the armed wing of the relatively new nationalist organization, the Pan-Africanist Congress.[70] Although they took few lives, the attacks garnered sensationalist news stories throughout South Africa, stories that conveyed the official government narrative of Africans, and particularly African men, as inherently violent and culturally alien. While this narrative worked to legitimate among whites the idea of the homelands as a permanent way of segregating South African society (and keeping white political and social privileges safe), it fundamentally misread the causes of African political violence. Among Africans the attacks were an expression of legitimate grievances, but they were also symptomatic of divisions within African society. Ultimately, the resort to direct armed attacks against state officials demonstrated that rural life had become unstable and difficult to navigate for most Africans. The erosion of the old system of social navigation led to increased use of violence by both Africans and the state.

A brief concluding chapter discusses the themes explored in the book, particularly the historical construction of violence as traditional in the segregationist and apartheid context and Africans' use of violence as one way to navigate the world. This book is not a comprehensive history of violence in South Africa but instead looks at the use of violence in the rural Transkeian region of the Cape Province and in adjacent rural areas of Natal. The violence that occurred was often intimate or communal, but even so, it frequently emerged from the restraints imposed by the white state. Segregation and apartheid as systems of white rule promoted policies for rural Africans that did not control every aspect of their lives but that significantly altered their lives nonetheless. Equally important, exploring this relationship also helps us develop a stronger historical sense of the changing roles that violence has played in rural South Africa.

I

Neighbors and Rivals

Faction Fighting and Traditional Violence in the Rural Transkei

In his autobiography, Nelson Mandela incorporated his memories of learning to stick fight as part of his rural boyhood in the Transkei region of the Cape Province. "From an early age," he wrote, "I spent most of my free time in the veld playing and fighting with the other boys of the village. A boy who remained at home tied to his mother's apron strings was regarded as a sissy. . . . I learned to stick-fight—essential knowledge to any rural African boy—and became adept at its various techniques, parrying blows, feinting in one direction and striking in another, breaking away from an opponent with quick footwork. From these days I date my love of the veld, of open spaces, the simple beauties of nature, the clean line of the horizon."[1]

Mandela's memoir presented stick fighting as part of an almost idyllic childhood. He glossed over the potential for inflicting real physical harm, even when the sparring turned into more dangerous battles: "As we grew older, we organized matches against boys from neighboring villages, and those who distinguished themselves in these fraternal battles were greatly admired, as generals who achieve great victories in war are justly celebrated."[2] His memories depicted not just a love of physical contests—Mandela became an avid amateur boxer as an adult—they also expressed a quiet approval for the kinds of values that such martial games instilled. The comradeship with peers and the exhilaration of skillful fighting made these contests, in his view, an essential part of young men's socialization.

Stick fighting was historically a rural game for boys who jabbed and swung at each other with long sticks and staves. Despite Mandela's idyllic depiction, these fights occasionally resulted in injuries or even deaths. Still, Mandela was not alone in describing stick fighting as a character-building outlet for youth. It has become part of an accepted story about the pastime, exemplified in a

2011 article from the *Guardian* about a revival of stick fighting as a martial art in some South African cities. The reporter cites Mandela's description approvingly as a prelude to reporting about the emergence of new stick-fighting clubs: "The ancient art of intonga (stick fighting), practised for centuries among rural herders, is making a comeback in the bleak landscape of Cape Town's townships. In the past six months, a dozen clubs have sprung up. Contests with prize money of up to 1,000 rand (£90) are held most weekends."[3] According to one club's founder, the clubs kept children away from crime and allowed for the creation of healthy relationships among peers: "For years, township youngsters saw stick fighting as a backward pursuit. They preferred guns. Now that is changing. They can see that stick fighting teaches them to endure pain, and they want to reconnect with that." He acknowledged that minor wounds resulted from these bouts but hoped that learning to stick fight would teach discipline as well as how to endure pain.[4]

Historically, while most sources agreed that stick fighting was recreational, they also agreed that such fights could take a lethal turn. These more lethal fights were often called faction fighting, and they typically involved combat between well-armed groups of older "boys," often in their teenage years or twenties.[5] They featured all kinds of weapons, including knobkerries (a category that included stout, knobbed wooden cudgels often studded with nails or iron spikes), battle axes, pickaxes, knives, pangas, and occasionally guns. Participants sometimes set fire to the huts and crops of their opponents and stole and killed livestock. Severe injuries and deaths were common. Participants in faction fights could face prosecution under laws prohibiting affrays or public fighting as well as for assault or homicide. While recreational stick fights could escalate into faction fights, the different types of weapons used and the different levels of harm inflicted made them two distinct—if related—kinds of encounters.

Under white rule in the Cape Province, stick fights were not illegal while faction fights were. In practice, however, distinguishing between the two types of fights was not always easy. One observer of rural culture in the 1920s and 1930s, the Methodist minister J. H. Soga, captured how closely related the two types of fighting were in his description of the "Boys' Battle" or "Um-Ngeni." He wrote: "These fights are often very serious affairs, and it is quite a common occurrence for one or more boys to be killed in the course of them, or to die later of wounds."[6] He noted that these fights were frequently among "boys in the prime of health and strength of body, who are nearing the stage of circumcision," and concluded that "their battles are often terrible affairs, and frequently end by involving the men of the respective locations [wards or sub-districts]."[7] Faction fights thus went beyond the sparring between peers that characterized stick fights and in some cases became real armed conflict.

By the early 1930s, Soga and other observers of African life thought that such fights were increasing in number and becoming more dangerous. They condemned these fights as threats to public order and morals, criticisms that were echoed in official reports. Many white magistrates, for example, saw such fighting as evidence of young men's insubordination to their elders or of the breakdown of African society's moral order. A 1944 comment from the Flagstaff magistrate exemplified this view: after describing several faction fights that resulted in deaths, he stated: "The Natives in this district are far too addicted to violence."[8]

The frequency of lethal fighting posed questions for contemporary observers and later scholars. Contemporaneously, white officials often wrote about faction fights as traditional and suggested that fighting was an expression of African culture's inherent violence and "tribalism." Fights, from this perspective, were about one tribe attacking another because of long-standing animosities dating back to the precolonial period. Officials recognized other causes of faction fights, including, for example, drunkenness, delinquency by older adolescents, and personal quarrels, but the designation of "faction fight" carried with it an implicit trivialization of African political and economic grievances. As historian Jabulani Sithole points out, in his analysis of faction fighting in Zululand in the 1930s, magistrates had biases that came into play as they documented fighting. Sithole notes that they were writing "primarily for metropolitan audiences, aiming to justify their violent actions against the recently colonised and subjugated peoples." They presented Africans as "intrinsically violent and barbarous" while depicting themselves as "peacemakers and civilizers."[9] By the late 1920s and early 1930s, as the numbers of these fights rose, officials began to see them as having a potential for social disruption that could undermine the foundations of continued white rule.

Some scholars have seen deep political and economic motivations behind the increase in fighting. State restrictions on access to, and ownership of, land fostered competition among Africans, and that competition sometimes fueled armed combat. At the same time, fighting became an element in the ongoing reconstruction of ethnic and tribal identities by both the white-controlled state and Africans living within its constraints. In this analysis, faction fighting directly emerged from land shortages created by government policies in the Transkei, Zululand, and other native reserves. Competition over land initiated a vicious cycle of violence, killing, and revenge.[10]

Other scholars have focused more on social aspects of such fighting, particularly in urban settings. In an extensive study of life in residential compounds attached to South African gold mines in the 1980s, Dunbar Moodie looked at the large-scale, often lethal faction fights that took place. Moodie observed that such fighting "in its immediacy and perturbation and bonding may even be enjoyable" for many participants.[11] Fighting promoted cohesion within social groups in the compounds even though not all men participated.

The idea that fighting promoted peer group cohesion resonates with many analyses of urban gang violence. Fighting another gang could be part of an effort to construct strong, in-group social networks in anomic contexts like urban neighborhoods or workers' compounds. In the South African context, many urban gangs and mine compound factions organized around ethnic identities that both state policies and mine labor practices reinforced.[12] Several scholarly studies suggest that faction fighting—both in rural and urban areas—was part of a violent performance of masculinity in a country where adult African men had little political voice and diminishing economic power.[13]

However, the motivations for fighting in towns and compounds may have differed from the motivations behind rural fights. Labor migrants living in single-sex compounds and young men growing up in town lacked the social structures and deep family influences that persisted in the countryside through the mid-twentieth century. Men did move routinely between rural and urban settings as they chased wage-earning opportunities, but the challenges they faced in those two settings were vastly different. As they returned to rural families, they often brought with them experiences of urban brutality and weapons, such as battle axes and knives, which undoubtedly altered how they engaged in fighting in the rural areas. But rural fights were fundamentally about rural issues, and such fighting has not received the same depth of scholarly analysis that urban fighting among gangs and factions has.

The concept of social navigation, as developed by sociologist Henrik Vigh, provides a different perspective for viewing rural fighting. Vigh noticed that his Guinean informants often physically moved their bodies as they described how they used their few resources to survive the uncertain circumstances of their lives. His informants seemed to be shadowboxing as they dodged the (metaphorical) blows thrown at them by powerful people and social currents. Vigh gradually understood that their physical movement "was an embodiment of the concept [of social navigation] itself. What my informants were moving and shifting their torsos in relation to, I realized, was the push and pull of social forces—not as static constraints or positions of power in a social field but as social effects that engage social beings and bodies within the social environment in question."[14] Social navigation, as practiced by Vigh's informants, was a process of constantly adjusting to a social environment that was stable in some ways but unpredictable in others. His informants were not simply reacting in the moment; instead, their adjustments had roots in history and personal experiences and were directed toward specific future goals. Life in Bissau in the 1990s (when Vigh conducted his research) and in the rural Transkei in the first half of the twentieth century were very different settings. But social navigation provides a more general framework for understanding individuals' and groups' attempts to impose order and agency on a social context they cannot fully control or predict. Viewing rural South African faction fighters through this lens may let us see how these men drew on rural traditions, responded to local grievances and opportunities, and tried to achieve long-term goals. It also may allow us to see broader trends in rural life as the practices of faction fighting changed.

This chapter will first discuss the historical basis for fighting among older boys and young men, dating back to the region's political and military circumstances in the early to mid-nineteenth century. These circumstances are the traceable historical roots of both stick fighting and faction fighting. Next, the chapter will look at accounts of several specific fights taken from trial transcripts and official reports to unpack some of the motivations and causes of the fighting. The chapter will explore why these fights became more frequent and brutal from the late 1920s onward. And finally, the chapter will discuss how young men with experiences of faction fighting became available for participating in regional political battles that emerged in the 1950s.

This chapter will argue that fighting had multiple short-term motivations. Some fights were attempts by young men and older adolescents to burnish their adult identities and to acquire honor or respect, and others were the equivalent of barroom brawls. These multiple motivations led historian Sithole to adopt the label *izimpi zemibango*, or "wars as a result of disputes," in his analysis of faction fights.[15] This term has been used by many rural people and commentators themselves to discuss these fights, and it captures the ad hoc character of many fights.[16] However, it implicitly denies that the motivations behind the fights had much in common or that they can be meaningfully analyzed as a group. My research suggests that these fights became emblematic of what magistrates and other white officials saw as a kind of traditional violence. When magistrates discussed fighting as traditional, they were consciously understating its political significance. African participants, on the other hand, often positioned fighting as traditional to protect it from official oversight and to preserve it as an avenue for expanding local control over land and people without necessarily engaging in outright confrontation with the state. Some "faction fighting" was thus an embodiment of Vigh's "shadowboxing." The consequences of any specific fight could extend beyond combatants' personal motivations, however. And as we will see below, by the mid-1950s, faction fights did more commonly confront state officials and policies directly.

Fighting: A Short History of Combat in Transkei and Zululand

Violence historically had a place in rural society. Africans had used violence prior to the colonial takeover of the region to protect their homes, their extended families, and their chiefs. Herd boys had to know how to fight with sticks to defend livestock from theft, and young men had to be able to fight to defend their societies. But even sparring with fighting sticks could result in serious wounds that led in some cases to death.[17]

Yet occasional stick fighting and training for battle was not evidence of high levels of lethal violence in the early nineteenth century. Ludwig Alberti, who traveled through the Cape Colony and its eastern frontier in the first decade of the nineteenth century, noted that the Xhosa-speaking people he met "cannot really be called a war-like people; a predominant inclination to pursue a quiet cattle-raising life is much more evident among them." He went on to note that they were "nevertheless ready to strike, when it comes to defending or validating certain real or imaginary rights, and which is then done with courage and resolution."[18] Alberti's narrative only briefly mentioned recreational fighting between boys or youths, and then only as part of the celebration concluding circumcision rituals. After a large feast marking the youths' new re-integration into society, they received from their elder male relatives "javelins and knobkirries [*sic*, knobkerries or knobbed fighting sticks]," and were told that they were to "regard themselves henceforth as men, [and] that weapons have been placed in their hands for the protection of their chief."[19] The timing of Alberti's observations is important: although there had already been conflicts with encroaching white settlers in the 1779–1803 period, most Africans living east of the Cape Colony's borders retained control of their land and their political independence.[20] Consequently, there was little need for youths to be as thoroughly prepared for war as later generations had to be.

The succeeding decades of the nineteenth century witnessed significantly more armed conflict throughout southern Africa. From the early 1810s onward, there were political and military disruptions in both the eastern Cape and in what is now KwaZulu-Natal. The warfare and population movements that accompanied the creation of first the Mthethwa Confederacy and then the

Zulu state meant that fighting was not just a pastime, it was a necessary skill.[21] With the consolidation of the Zulu kingdom, Zulu forces attacked the (Xhosa-speaking) Mpondo in the 1820s, refugees and raiders moved across the countryside, and white adventurers carved out their own small chiefdoms from which they too conducted raids for cattle and people.[22] Other frontier populations such as the Griqua grabbed territory, people, and cattle, and some African societies did the same.[23] Multiple groups of refugees entered the eastern Cape, some as supplicants but others as raiders themselves.[24] These unsettled conditions lasted well into the 1840s, only to be followed by increased tensions and conflict with white settlers and the colonial states of the Cape and Natal. Additionally, the cattle killing of the 1850s among some Xhosa-speaking populations in the eastern Cape created its own set of social disruptions and launched another generation of refugees. The aftermath of the cattle killing saw a new expansion of white settlement that gave rise to a series of new frontier wars. These wars battered African political structures and eroded their economic independence. By the early 1880s most of the eastern Cape was under colonial rule and most of Zululand was under British control.[25] This long history of conflict in the region through the 1800s made fighting a requirement of survival even if it did not ultimately prevent colonial conquest.[26]

Beyond the impact of a century of conflict, there were also social and economic factors that may have caused fighting to become common in the rural areas by the late 1800s. Some of these causes, such as beer drinking and peer rivalries, are significant because they trace deeper social roots of fighting. It was these roots that made it possible for people to later portray faction fighting as traditional.

Beer drinking at dances and feasts appears in several reports as an explanation for outbreaks of faction fights. White officials assumed that beer drinking and fighting were regrettable but traditional pastimes for young men, even though older Africans often condemned excessive drinking and the fighting that resulted. At the 1883 Native Laws and Customs Commission hearings, government officials and missionaries testified that both home-brewed beer and distilled liquor were connected to violent crime and fighting among Africans. Some of the African men testifying agreed. One African man stated that home-brewed beer was a common feature of marriage feasts, and "the drinking that ensues leads to fights without cause, simply through drunkenness. . . . The fighting which results is a very bad thing."[27] There was a common assumption that excessive drinking was particularly problematic among young men. Historian Michael Mahoney notes that there were waves of faction fights among Zulu in Natal in the late 1880 to 1910 period, most of which were deplored by elders—at least when they spoke to white officials about the fights—as evidence of youths' increasing insubordination. Mahoney concludes that some of the fighting erupted at parties attended by young men who, after drinking a great deal of beer, became keener to test their fighting skills and perhaps also quicker to feel insulted by peers.[28]

Fights that broke out at parties and feasts feature in trial transcripts from the Transkeian region as well. For example, in 1909 the Umtata magistrate noted that there was very little crime in his district, but, he added, "there have, however, been a number of cases in which faction fights, generally arising out of beer gatherings, have resulted in the loss of life. Prosecutions for culpable homicide invariably follow, but very often fail, as in the melee when each one hits the first head that comes within reach, and all are more or less under the influence of beer, it is sometimes very difficult to ascertain clearly who delivered the fatal blow."[29] In 1907 the African self-help organization known as the Native Vigilance Association (also known as Iliso Lomzi) of Umtata expressed similar concerns about parties, drinking, and fighting. The association sent a letter to the Umtata District Council (a local administrative body made up of chiefs and headmen) requesting that the council "emphatically force the Chiefs, Headmen, and Citizens of Locations [subdistricts or wards] to prevent the gathering of kaffir [*sic*] boys and girls at night," because such gatherings led to "rape and fight [*sic*]."[30]

Nearly half a century later, in 1951, a wedding party in the same district devolved into a faction fight. In this later episode, however, the impact of new weapons made themselves felt. At least forty-five people were involved in the conflict, with the majority of the participants being in their late twenties or early thirties. Most men had come to the party armed with knobkerries as well as assegais (stabbing spears) and battle axes. According to witnesses, the fight began after attendees had consumed a substantial amount of beer and traded insults. Three deaths and multiple injuries resulted.[31] The links between beer drinking and fighting were thus still present after decades of white rule, but the increasing use of axes and assegais made the fighting more serious.

By the 1940s and 1950s, magistrates assumed that fighting was a virtually inescapable outcome of large parties. Rather than looking at the particular circumstances behind the fights, they often attributed such fighting to traditional rivalries. For example, in his notes on the guilty verdicts he had rendered in a case in 1948, the Xhalanga magistrate commented: "Tribal fights and disorders usually begin by a series of beer drink fights and affrays such as the one under consideration." When that particular case went to the Supreme Court on appeal, the court remarked that "there was a great deal of beer and

"Xhosa people talking, Transkei, South Africa." Photograph by Constance Stuart Larrabee, 1947. EEPA 1998-061258. Used with permission of the Constance Stuart Larrabee Collection, Eliot Elisofon Photographic Archives, National Museum of African Art, Smithsonian Institution.

many gathered in the afternoon at this kraal [homestead]—and the inevitable fight occurred."[32] The statement that such fighting was an inevitable result of a party was revealing of white attitudes that saw Africans as inherently prone to both drunkenness and "tribal fights and disorders."

Beer drinking and fighting were linked in recorded incidents of fighting, but they were also connected to changes in rural African life. Economic patterns in the rural areas changed substantially from the 1850s onward, partly in response to the expansion of trade and partly the result of the loss of cattle through warfare, animal diseases, and land expropriation by whites.[33] The declining numbers of cattle owned by individual families meant that beer made from grain

gradually replaced soured milk at feasts and celebrations, a substitution that
contributed to the drinking of excessive alcohol. The trend of beer replacing
soured milk continued well into the twentieth century.[34] If we accept contemporary observations that drunkenness exacerbated many fights, then the pro-
liferation of beer drinking may have led to more fighting; that, in turn, could
explain the increased concern expressed by both white and African observers
about the levels of drinking and fighting in the early decades of the twentieth
century.[35]

But while beer drinking may have spurred some expansion of fighting in
the 1880 to 1920 period, it does not provide an adequate accounting for the
sharp increase in violent incidents reported in the 1930s, 1940s, and 1950s, by
which time beer drinking had long been a feature of rural life. We must look
to other factors for an explanation of that change. Some of these other factors
have more direct connections to the effects of government policies, as we will
see in the next section.

Faction fights also sometimes erupted from stick fights that suddenly drew
blood, as several observers noted in the 1930s. These observations need to be
understood as reflecting African societies as they stood at that time rather than
as descriptions of timeless, unchanging traditions. Two scholars writing in the
1930s, Monica Wilson and J. H. Soga, each described fighting as an ordinary
part of the lives of African boys growing up in the countryside. Wilson wrote
that "fighting with sticks is as constant an occupation of the Pondo [boy] as
is playing with a ball of the English [boy]. I have seen a mother playing with
her son of 2 or 3, pretending to hit him so that he put up one arm for defence
and tried to hit back; boys of 4 and 5 have their knobkerries, and begin to
scrap."[36] While Wilson described stick fighting as play, she acknowledged that,
among older youths, a recreational bout of stick fighting could shift in an
instant to open combat: "Often two neighbouring districts are in such a state
of war, that if a boy from one enters the other he is immediately attacked. The
border-line between a game and a serious fight between districts, in which
several may be killed, is undefined."[37]

J. H. Soga's published observations of Xhosa society date from the same
decade, and his descriptions of fights among boys are similar. He wrote that
"these fights are often very serious affairs, and it is quite a common occurrence
for one or more boys to be killed in the course of them, or to die later of
wounds. Serious wounds are the order of the day, but these are regarded with
pride by the sufferer."[38] Both Wilson's and Soga's remarks accord with the description given by Nelson Mandela of the type of stick fighting he practiced
during his youth, which, given that he was born in 1918, would have also

occurred in the late 1920s and early 1930s.[39] The three accounts taken together show that, by the 1930s, boys and adolescents commonly enjoyed stick fighting as a game, but that game could easily explode into wider combat that drew in older men and resulted in serious casualties.[40]

The Rise of Lethal Faction Fights in the Twentieth Century

Wilson, Soga, and Mandela all acknowledged that stick fighting among boys often turned into more lethal battles, but beyond that they offered little discussion of the larger, more deadly faction fights that were becoming frequent by the early 1930s. The records of rural magistrates document that faction fighting was on the rise, and white officials were alarmed. In 1931 the Native Affairs Department asked the South African Police in the Transkei region to report the number of faction fights over a span of twenty-eight months from 1929 through 1931. In this period, there were a total of 1,514 fights, or an average of 54 fights per month across all the twenty-seven districts.[41] Given that these fights typically involved more than ten people and sometimes as many as two thousand, the total number of participants was substantial. My research has included over 256 trial records that involved faction fighting from twenty-one Transkeian districts in the period between 1900 and 1963.[42] Such fights were a consistent feature of rural life over that period, and there was a jump in the numbers of fights that came to trial and a shift in the types of weapons used in the fighting. These new weapons included battle axes and knives, weighted knobkerries studded with nails, and occasionally guns, all of which contributed to graver injuries and higher numbers of deaths. The combination of more fights and deadlier weapons contributed to widening concerns over the social causes and consequences of these battles.

A case from Tsolo in 1924 showed both the characteristics of a "boys" fight turning into something more serious as well as the impact of more lethal weapons. The police reported that this fight developed among older boys from two different groups, whom the police identified as belonging to separate ethnic groups—Mpondomise and Mfengu. The fighting began with "young boys" who had encountered each other at the local trading store that straddled the line between the two groups' "locations" (wards). A quarrel had sparked a stick fight between the groups, and over the next few days the fighting grew more intense and drew in larger portions of the communities. By the third day, "the fighters were young men and when one side was driven back . . . an appeal was made to elders to come and help. The women then (Thursday night) gave the war cry and the real trouble commenced." The police report estimated that about three hundred women and seven hundred to one thousand men were ultimately engaged in the battle. The men carried guns and assegais as well as fighting sticks, and women in both groups burned huts and stole livestock. At least seven people died and multiple others were injured.[43] This case showed the complex social web that underlay many faction fights. Newly available weapons turned a local contest initially between adolescents into a much more serious battle that engaged entire communities. The fighting then refreshed and redefined people's identifications with particular social or ethnic groups, a process that heightened the potential for additional violence. The active participation of women in the fighting also calls into question claims about strong connections between fighting and masculinity made by some scholars.

A 1935 court case from Willowvale provides a second example of a fight where casualties were aggravated by the use of new weapons. Two groups of older adolescents, each including twelve to fourteen "boys" (as the court records described them) between the ages of eighteen and twenty, were accused of culpable homicide for a fight that ended in two deaths. The groups had squared off against one another, armed with both plain fighting sticks and weighted knobkerries studded with iron nails. After the fighting was over, several lay injured and two had died from crushed skulls. The presiding magistrate at the trial noted that studded knobkerries had become a particular problem in the district. He blamed these weapons for the deaths and for the serious and growing problem of fighting. He convicted all the defendants and sentenced them to between six and eight months of imprisonment.[44]

The impact of new weapons became even greater in the 1940s and later. A selection of court cases shows the escalation of weaponry and violence in fights and the corresponding escalation of official concerns. For example, a fight in 1944 involving thirty men (whose ages ranged from twenty-one to forty-three) broke out in Ngqeleni. There had been a large party with beer and dancing. As the event wore on, one faction at the party attacked a second faction with whom they had previously fought. Both groups carried sticks and battle axes. As one participant stated at the trial: "At a big function [party] axes are always carried. . . . People come from all directions and it is necessary to be armed with axes to fight with if one is attacked." This statement suggests that, by the mid-1940s, there was an almost constant threat of fighting at any social gathering that involved young men, many of whom considered carrying battle axes to be essential. In this case, at least two people died in the fighting, and several were injured.[45]

Another case, this time from Willowvale in 1946, involved more than twenty-five adolescents and men between the ages of nineteen and twenty-six. Most were armed with iron-studded knobkerries, although one combatant wielded a sword.[46] In 1948 a large fight in Mount Frere involved seventy-eight men and resulted in two deaths after heavily armed factions fought at a wedding. The magistrate lamented that "the crimes of fighting and assault have been increasing rapidly in this District." He admonished the defendants: "You have been repeatedly warned that your actions will bring severe punishment upon you— you have been warned—you have failed to take heed and now you have only yourselves to blame."[47] By the early 1960s, men were more commonly carrying guns as well as axes and knobkerries: several faction fights in Libode in 1960 and 1961 involved firearms, with as many as one thousand people participating in each battle.[48]

Weapons such as battle axes became as common as fighting sticks for men, and they also became objects to be admired. In 1961 the Bantu Affairs commissioner (the new title recently taken by magistrates) of Mqanduli noted that "the battle axes used in this district are for the most part well, and in many cases beautifully, made and finished with brass and silver ornamentation. Obviously, they are made on the Rand and sold to boys [*sic*] working on the mines."

"Xhosa men dressed in traditional clothing, Transkei, South Africa." Photograph by Anne Fischer, islandora 8276. Used with permission of Iziko Museums of South Africa.

Owning and carrying weapons became fashionable, a fashion that extended across age groups: "It has now developed into a recognised custom that until a boy is circumcised he should carry a battle axe. Even boys of 10 years of age can be seen with small 'hand-made' battle axes."[49]

The fact that men and boys invested time and money in crafting and buying beautiful weapons that they carried to parties and around town was evidence of the militarization of youth culture. The aestheticization of weapons suggests how normalized fighting had become. Older boys and young men may have engaged in armed contests partly as a sport, but for many older men, the carrying of weapons and their willingness to use them was a defensive strategy for navigating a perilous landscape: the rural environment that had become routinely more dangerous.

Poverty, Manhood, Fighting, and Land

We have seen above that faction fights increased in numbers and in lethality from the late 1920s onward. In that same period, poverty and land shortages also became more common in the region. Some of the landlessness was driven by population growth, and it is possible that demographic factors contributed to rising levels of fighting.

The African population of South Africa in the first half of the twentieth century swelled dramatically (the census figures suggest that it almost tripled), meaning that there was a significant rise in the proportion of the population under the age of twenty-five.[50] In many societies the rate of violent crime is strongly correlated with the proportion of young men under twenty-five years old.[51] These population increases in South Africa, at a time when most of the African population lived in the countryside, meant that there was greater competition for land, especially because the South African state had dramatically restricted African land ownership. Younger men in particular were affected by the state-created land shortage because they were sometimes forced to postpone marriage and a family, both of which were gateways to adult social status.[52]

The need to acquire land to marry and become a full adult may have led to increased conflict and fighting over land. The anthropologist Jonathan Clegg analyzed a series of faction fights that broke out within the Msinga district of Natal in the 1930s. He suggested that the proximate cause was the development of an "ideology of vengeance" among Africans, but that the longer term, underlying cause was the insufficiency of land. Clegg concluded: "Finally 'faction fighting' must be seen as an active attempt on the part of the traditionalist to maintain the infra structure [*sic*] of his rural economy. The threat to this economy, is diminishing land created by overpopulation. The colonial government gave the reserve an external boundary but left the people in the reserve to sort out their own internal boundaries, paving the way for the emergence of an 'ideology of vengeance.'"[53] Clegg's analysis countered the ideas that young African men who battled each other were engaging in purely beer-fueled brutality or blood sport. Instead, his analysis portrayed the fighting as displaced resistance to the policies of the white-controlled state.

In analyzing the complex and combative atmosphere of the period between the late 1920s and the mid-1960s, there is a closer connection between fights that arose from local rivalries and those that erupted from broader political and economic issues than there was in previous decades. Discussions of fighting that see it as an outgrowth of the difficulties young men faced in achieving full adulthood through marriage and farming rely on strong evidence for the economic decline of rural life by the mid to late 1930s, a decline that continued through much of the twentieth century. Before the 1930s, fighting had not been a significant marker of masculine identity. Instead, the full achievement of adulthood had rested on one's success in maintaining a thriving household.[54]

In this vein, Anne Mager's study of life in the eastern Cape region in the 1945–60 period concluded that fighting resulted from "thwarted masculinity."[55] As the old historical markers of elder status—becoming the head of a thriving household and presiding over family and farmland—became difficult to attain, young men sought to use their proficiency at fighting as the defining element of the complex transition to adulthood. Mager suggests that the violence was fueled by the desire to control access to both land and women.

There is a lot of evidence from the 1940s and later that a significant number of young men fought regularly. Many of these battles emerged from rivalries over land, even though they were not about control over specific plots of farmland. For an example, we can look at a series of massive fights that took place in Ngqeleni in August 1947. There had been a beer drink and a fight broke out between seventy members of a group from one ward and forty men from another. (The people who fought were not identified as belonging to different ethnicities but rather as having allegiances to different headmen). Combatants wielded assegais, battle axes, and studded knobkerries; one person died on the first day of fighting. Both groups rearmed the next day, and according to the police report, a huge number of people turned out to fight: "An impi [military formation] estimated at about 2,000 armed men and women appeared from the Konywayo ward and raided about 40 kraals [homesteads] in the Matshezi ward. Doors of the huts were damaged and belongings removed, about 30 head of cattle, 50 sheep and several pigs and fowls driven away to Konywayo ward where the majority of these animals . . . were killed and eaten by the Konywayo section." People from the Matshezi ward fled temporarily into the neighboring district to escape.[56] Over the next three years, more fights between the two wards broke out. One erupted from a dispute over a headman's daughter: she was found having sex with a man from the other ward who refused to pay the usual fine of cattle for the "damages" done to the young woman. Another fight was in retaliation for an assault on a herd boy, and a third broke out at a dance for young people.[57] In the same district but involving different wards, more faction fights occurred in 1949 that were provoked initially by a fight between groups of adolescents. The original fight generated several subsequent battles between adult men armed with "guns and assegais and other weapons" after one adolescent sustained serious injuries.[58]

These battles in Ngqeleni (and there were similar rounds of fighting in several other districts in the same decade) were not fights that confronted the white-controlled state directly. In fact, when relatively small numbers of lightly armed police showed up at some of the fights, the combatants dispersed quickly and then resumed fighting once the police had left. Nor were the combatants trying to gain immediate control over land to be farmed. These battles were primarily local disputes that involved insults, control over family members or girlfriends, and the protection of the broader vicinity or turf. But it is important to note that these local disputes erupted along boundaries constructed by the state and the individual factions were led by headmen chosen as traditional leaders by the state. Thus, while these were local disputes, they were also framed and exacerbated by broader state policies. The fights resulted in loss of property, injuries, and deaths and then often developed lives of their own as they fueled retaliation.

While most battles sprang from local troubles, by the 1940s and 1950s, many fights either targeted or were led by headmen and chiefs. Headmen and chiefs had positions as both traditional leaders and appointees of the state, and their participation in the fighting suggests a stronger association with political motives. As we shall see in the next section, by the late 1950s and 1960s, anti-apartheid political pamphlets identified many of them—sometimes individually by name—as agents of the state, and police and magistrates were quick to see threats to headmen and chiefs as threats to the state. An analysis that captures the volatile mix of locally based rivalries and broader political grievances is more likely to capture the reality of the choices that people made about whether to participate in or condone violence in this period.

While land was an important source of rivalry, so was love and the potential for marriage. Fights could also develop over love affairs and jealousy, which then went on to spark larger battles. One example emerged from a fight in Libode in 1954. A twenty-three-year-old man attending a party had argued with another young man over a woman who was also attending the party. The argument blossomed into a full-scale fight involving several people, during which the man hit his rival in the head with a knobkerrie, killing him.[59] A similar fight developed in Elliotdale in 1960. The police reported that "the fight was started by one youth of the one party who had been away at the mines and on his return from the mines found that his girl friend had been going out with a youth of the other party. These youths first argued about this and then fought. The groups then took sides and a general fight with battle-axes then took place between them."[60] Fights over girlfriends, like those over territory and group identity, were about establishing control and protecting personal claims.[61] These fights could also ignite broader battles beyond the personal claims of jealous young men as larger social groups rallied behind them.

A third example, from Mqanduli in 1955, shows the confluence of several factors, including competition over girlfriends and "turf," a desire for revenge, the quick escalation of fights between younger men into larger battles, and the normalization of violence. In November an adolescents' dance quickly turned into a fight between two groups of rivals. The police report stated that one group ("the Mjikweni boys [*sic*]") "had battle-axes with them, this is their custom, as they dance with their axes and they carry them at the dances to show off." Another armed group challenged them, and in the ensuing fight two people died. A retaliatory fight took place a few months later, in early April 1956, at a local trading store, where the two groups of young men engaged each other once again with battle axes; four people died in this fight. Three weeks later, one of the groups ambushed a member of the other group along with the woman he was with. Both suffered severe wounds from the ax blows and the man died. On the following morning, there was a counterattack against the homes of several of the group who had committed the ambush: the attackers set fire to fifteen homes and killed livestock. These acts precipitated another raid on the same day as 350 people attacked a group of 60 people commanded by a local headman. This confrontation resulted in general fighting and then the burning of seventy-three more homesteads. The magistrate eventually intervened directly by meeting with the different groups. He managed to prevent another attack, but hostilities continued to simmer.[62]

These large, lethal fights that developed at parties and morphed into wider combat share some characteristics with urban gang violence of the same era. There is little evidence, however, that members of urban gangs (*isitshozi* or *amalaita*) were involved in rural faction fights.[63] Instead, individuals, most of whom were not gang members, did bring experiences of urban brutality home to the rural areas with them and they also brought weapons that made fighting more lethal. The effects of this reverse migration were exacerbated by the fact that white mine officials and city administrators often deported men who had been involved in fights on the mines to their home districts in the rural areas rather than putting them on trial and imprisoning them in the city.[64]

Although rural factions were not derived from urban gangs, they often acted on similar concerns about controlling territory and access to girlfriends. Beyond these local and specific concerns that motivated individual fights, participation in the fighting may have contributed to the longer term development of group identities, even if they were not necessarily motivated by a search for a more generalized masculine identity.[65] These group identities were sometimes associated with wider ideas about belonging to a specific "tribe" or ethnicity, or they could be local and specific to a particular ward under one headman. At least until the late 1950s, police, headmen, chiefs, and other state officials were rarely singled out as targets of fighting. But the greater incidence of fighting resulted from broader political and economic stresses caused by state policies, and the fighting itself threatened the stability of rural social structures. By the late 1950s, the adolescents and young men who were veterans of fighting became available for attacking state officials and policies.

Fighting and Confronting State Policies

Some rural fighting took root in state policies designed to foster identities based on "tribe." These identities were consequential because they emerged from and fed back into significant facts about people's lives, such as where they lived, whom they considered to be their chief and headman, and where they could farm and graze their livestock. The fact that chiefs and headmen were appointed by white administrators and ward and district boundaries were drawn by state policies reinforced these identities and give them additional meaning. When disputes arose over who should be the headman or chief, or who had the right to farm what land, government policies promoted intergroup conflict rather than fostering outright political unrest directed at the state.

From the onset of white rule, state officials had devolved power on local, tribal authorities as a way of grasping control over the rural population with the smallest outlay of state manpower and money. The retention of African chiefs in positions of local power also spread the responsibility or blame for the policies enacted by the state and channeled whatever dissent developed into localized and more easily containable unrest.[66] Thus, the question of whether individuals who participated in fights had political intentions may be less important than the structural distribution of political power that fostered and influenced the violence. This ruling arrangement reconfigured certain types of violence that took place in the countryside as traditional and made its political content less visible.

One of these conflicts with roots in the early decades of white rule in the twentieth century occurred in Qumbu in 1912 and 1913. Historian William Beinart describes these clashes as revolving around ethnicity, since they involved people who self-identified as Mpondomise who fought others who self-identified as Mfengu. But Beinart notes that the cultural meanings of these ethnic and tribal designations were constructed by white administrators and, crucially, by Africans themselves within the confines of the administrative system. The specific structures of colonization in the district shaped the formation of ethnic consciousness among Africans, and this in turn shaped the way that Africans interacted with the world around them.[67]

A similar, simultaneous development of ethnic identification and local conflicts occurred in Umzimkulu in the Transkei, on the border with Natal. There were two major ethnicities in the region, the Nhlangwini, a Zulu-speaking group, and the Bhaca, who spoke a Xhosa dialect.[68] By the 1920s there were regular fights among the young men of the two groups. A 1930 fight, for example, that involved 189 men broke out at a wedding. Many of those who began the fight rejected the legitimacy of the local headman who was attending the wedding. The tensions between those who supported the headman and those who opposed him led to insults that escalated into fighting. The battle ultimately resulted in the deaths of six people, including one woman.[69]

But these two tribes of Umzimkulu had not always been enemies. In the late 1890s there was an attempt by the two chiefs and their followers to join forces to rebel against the white-controlled state. Africans and the Afrikaans-speaking "Coloured" population known as the Griqua claimed that the colonial state and white settlers had unfairly seized some of their land as well as destroyed their political independence.[70] A rumor spread rapidly that local African groups (including both Bhaca and Nhlangwini) and the Griqua would bridge their differences and together drive the white settlers and government out.[71] In official circles in 1897, there was enough fear that a revolt was imminent that the chief magistrate of East Griqualand, Walter Stanford, rode out to the region to defuse the situation.

Stanford addressed the local chiefs in harsh tones. He stressed the military force that the state could bring to bear to crush a rebellion. He told the assembled Africans that they were foolish if they thought a rebellion could succeed. He commented that he had arrived with an armed force in Umzimkulu and was prepared to shoot any rebels, demanding that "all this [rebellious] talk must cease at once." Stanford held up as proof of the futility of armed resistance the example of the recent defeat of the Zulu kingdom to the north: "The Zulus and others talk [of rebellion] like that; and who are you—you are nothing, just little paltry tribes. . . . The Zulus cleared you out of your country and drove you before them and where are the Zulus now. Don't let me hear any more of this talk; you are the children of Government."[72] Stanford's bluster worked and the revolt fizzled out. But to ensure future political quiet, subsequent government policies nurtured the divisions among the groups whom Stanford had disdained as "paltry little tribes." Chiefs and headmen who were willing to accept the white-controlled state and work with white officials gained authority within the system, and their followers often benefited. But these benefits usually came at the expense of other, less-favored groups, a fact that both reshaped and entrenched competing ethnic identities.

These rivalries resurfaced in subsequent decades in the form of faction fights. There was, for example, an immense fight in Umzimkulu in late October 1923. Members of the local police had heard rumors that Nhlangwini and Bhaca men were preparing to attack each other and were stockpiling arms. Police reports traced the hostilities to an "old feud" that had been revived by the murders of two Bhaca men earlier in the year and fears among the Bhaca that the Nhlangwini men who had been arrested for committing the murders would either be released without trial or acquitted. The more immediate spark was an altercation at a wedding feast attended by people from both groups. A quarrel broke out that exploded into broader fighting with assegais and knobkerries. The local police (consisting of a couple of constables) were warned by combatants that they had better stay out of it or else they might be killed, and the police withdrew.

On the first day of fighting, about one thousand African men in total participated. The police reported that "before fighting commenced many women and children left their kraals and took refuge at the trading stations, [white-owned] farms, etc., in the vicinity, [with] approximately 100 women accompanied with their children going to Ibisi store and taking with them their possessions." The report noted that the movement of women and children out of the area was an indication they anticipated, "a rather bad time in the way of having their huts burnt, etc. and I am told by local authority that had the fight not been interrupted [by the arrival of the police] considerable burning would probably take place."[73] The local police called in reinforcements from other districts, who managed to quell the fighting in subsequent days, and they arrested 170 men. Two men had been killed and more than 50 wounded.

The police and the magistrate treated the fighting as entirely rooted in long-standing ethnic rivalries unconnected to state policies. In his report on the incidents, the magistrate wrote that 169 men had been charged with various offenses relating to the fight, with 120 ultimately convicted. He sentenced the 49 convicted Nhlangweni men (whom he considered to be the aggressors in the case) to pay £3 each or else serve one month of imprisonment with hard labor; he sentenced the 71 Bhaca men to pay £2 each or else serve two weeks of jail time. (All but three of the defendants paid the fines rather than go to jail). "I am satisfied," the magistrate concluded, "that there is nothing political in the trouble which arose, and so far as I can see, there is no reason to suppose that we will have any more trouble with these people."[74] The relatively low fines and short terms of imprisonment aligned with the magistrate's confident assertion that the fighting had not been politically motivated. They may also have indicated that he, like other officials, saw fighting between tribes as "natural" to the local population—an expression of an inherent African identity that the state simply had to accept as the norm.

Despite the official description of these events as "nothing political," the fight did have its roots in the political divisions that were fostered and reinforced by government policies. Moreover, the magistrate's description of it as a dispute rooted in ethnic rivalries went on to become a self-fulfilling prophecy: over the years, fights between the two groups broke out in 1930, in 1935, in 1936, in 1947, and then every year between 1947 and 1962.[75] White officials described these fights as tribal clashes and suggested that the only way to stop them was to keep the groups segregated by district or by wards within districts, a "solution" that only deepened the development of ethnic and territorial rivalries.[76]

The motivations behind many conflicts labeled as "faction fights" in the 1950s and 1960s straddled the line between local disputes and reactions to state policies. By the 1950s, conflicts in Umzimkulu had become openly about land, and in the context of the policy ambitions of the apartheid state, officials began to recognize the disputes as political. To implement the homelands policy in the 1950s and later, the state redivided the land into specific locations and districts reserved for specific tribes, regardless of any competing historical claims that others made and regardless of how recently a particular "tribe" had been constructed or reconstructed by historical events. When a major conflict took place between the Bhaca and the Nhlangwini in 1962, the magistrate labeled it a "faction fight" between two tribes. Tellingly, he also labeled it as "Bantu Unrest."[77] By the 1960s, administrators labeled virtually all fighting between groups of Africans in the rural areas as both faction fights and political unrest. The state had worked hard during most of the twentieth century to create tribes to maintain control, but the fighting that resulted from state policies was fast becoming a political threat to apartheid's plans.

A second example reveals a direct link between local violence and resistance to state policies. In 1959 and 1960 there were at least fifteen separate fights that took place in the Flagstaff district of the Transkei. The Transkei by that time was slated to become a "self-governing homeland" under grand apartheid planning within the next few years. As part of those plans, the state enacted new policies that gave more authority to compliant chiefs and headmen and that also raised taxes and implemented new agricultural policies.

Police reports on the first three fights in Flagstaff concluded that they had erupted at various young people's dances, and the police described them as apolitical, that is, "ordinary" faction fights between youths. The first one, in late January 1959, involved nineteen men and resulted in one death and two people being seriously injured. The second fight involved thirty-one men, and the third saw thirty young men taking part in the combat that left one dead and several injured.

While the police dismissed the first three fights as local brawls, when the fourth fight erupted late in 1959, the police began to acknowledge a political motivation. The nature of the fighting took a sharply more serious turn on the day after a dance that had been attended by twenty young men from one of the factions. As they were on their way home, "they found that they had been way-layed [sic], . . . and a general fight took place, spreading to the older men of the location." The ambush resulted in three deaths and multiple injuries. The police subsequently arrested twenty-one men including the headman from the neighboring district of Bizana who had participated in the ambush.[78] The loyalties of the people living in the ward were split: one section wanted to secede from Flagstaff and become part of the adjoining Bizana district because the headman there was from the same clan and was supportive of their land claims, while the other group remained loyal to the Flagstaff headman.

At least ten more fights occurred in Flagstaff over the next few months, and some of these fights began to target state policies and officials openly. One fight in April 1960 resulted in the headman phoning the police to tell them that "his tribesmen had chased him away from his kraal [homestead] and location, stating that he is no longer the Headman as he is in favour of the Native Tribal Authority Act," the recent law that implemented several apartheid policies at the local level. The police report concluded that "the intention of the Bantu is to burn the kraals of the members of the Bantu Authorities," in other words, to attack African leaders who were going along with state policies. The report suggested that a wider plan for political violence was underway: "Meetings are being held in this Location as also the adjoining Ntelenzi Location for the purpose of sweeping tribesmen up against the Tribal Authorities and either burn the kraal of Sub-chief Vukayibambe or kill him."[79] Three months later, another politically motivated attack occurred when a group of men decided to drive two of their headmen out of the area and burn their huts down because the headmen supported unpopular government policies.[80]

In his summaries of these fights, the Flagstaff Bantu Affairs commissioner once again aligned the categories of "faction fighting" and "unrest." He believed that the political dimension to local fighting was a result of the influence of the rebel "Congo" movement that was active in the region. There had recently been waves of violence in the rural areas that targeted African government officials, with attacks often following complaints about higher taxes, agricultural interventions, and the devolution of authority onto chiefs and headmen who were widely seen as corrupt and evil.[81] White officials, however, depicted this unrest as the result of shadowy "outside agitators"—a code phrase for Communist Party organizers—and dismissed the possibility that the violence had a basis in legitimate grievances against state policies.[82] "The people were led to believe," by "outside agitation" according to the magistrate, "that the Tribal Authorities system was responsible for the increase in the General Tax, General Levy, the Labour Bureau system etc [*sic*] and that rehabilitation, stock reduction, fencing control of ploughing etc [*sic*] were going to be introduced by the Tribal Authorities. . . . In short every possible complaint was attributed to the Bantu Authorities."[83] Rebels began to target those people who supported the government and "threatened and intimidated" them into attending meetings. "Persons who did not carry out the instructions of the leaders of the movement were assaulted and their huts burnt down. The movement which was given the name of the 'Congo movement' infiltrated into the Flagstaff District and the majority of the Headmen were forced to flee from their locations."[84] "Faction fights" had metamorphosed into political unrest. But the political unrest was still firmly rooted in local conditions.

As fighting became more political in the late 1950s and early 1960s, African nationalist organizations stepped in to try to channel it into a more organized and directed form of political resistance. There were numerous pamphlets circulating in Flagstaff, Bizana, and other districts from various political groups who were engaged in the anti-apartheid struggle, including the Congress of Democrats, the All-In African National Action Council, and the African National Congress, all of which denounced the state's Bantu Authorities policies and the move toward the creation of independent homelands under apartheid. These pamphlets disputed the state's characterization of the violence as purely local and tribal in nature. Instead, they insisted that the violence was part of a broad-based resistance to apartheid policies and the white-controlled state. A pamphlet from the Congress of Democrats (a leftist anti-apartheid organization) argued: "After years of peace Pondoland is aflame with discontent. But the Government refuses to present the true facts to the public. Why is the Government creating the idea that the Pondoland affair had nothing to do with the rest of South Africa?"[85] The pamphlet went on to emphasize the connection between the localized violence and the broader struggle against apartheid and concluded that "UNITY [IS] THE ANSWER."[86] Nationalist organizations had not incited these events but hoped to use them to raise people's political consciousness and strengthen national organizations.[87]

Even without evidence that national political organizations were inspiring this violence, white officials worried that local people's actions were indeed part of a wider wave of African nationalism. In all cases, officials' proposed remedy was the same: bolster the traditional power of the chiefs and headmen to control the youth, separate the tribal factions when possible, and arrest any outsiders who might be sowing dissent. Bantu Affairs commissioners moved factions or redrew the lines of administrative regions so that Africans could be administered by headmen from their "own" tribal groups. This often meant dividing larger linguistic groups into very small subgroups: rarely were administrators separating Xhosa from Zulu for example, but more often they were separating the Xhosa-speaking Bhaca from the Zulu-speaking Nhlangwini, or the Xhosa-speaking Mfengu from the Xhosa-speaking Mpondomise. This subdivision of Africans into separate tribes, ethnicities, and clans was part of an explicitly political project of the apartheid state to "retribalize" Africans and place them firmly under the control of newly empowered chiefs. The devolution of power allowed the central state to pursue its larger scale objectives of geographical segregation while leaving the chiefs and headmen to deal with local distrust and political unrest.[88]

As far as white officials were concerned, the retribalization of Africans was the cure for faction fighting and for political unrest. The state threw its weight behind a particular sort of elder-based patriarchy in the rural areas to establish discipline. The chief magistrate of the Transkei in 1957 contended that faction fights were caused by "the growing lawlessness of youths who roam about, armed with battle axes and who have even, on occasions, attacked adult men." He saw these youths as directly challenging the authority of their elders in the countryside and stated that "parents seem to have lost control, probably owing to many fathers being away in employment and so unable to exercise discipline. Tribal control in this respect also appears to have broken down and responsible adults are actually afraid of reprisals from the gangs." This putative lack of respect was directly related, in his eyes, to a decline in the practice of the traditional circumcision ceremony. He concluded that the violence "seems to be part of the world-wide revolt of the young as exemplified by 'tsotsis,' 'duck-tails,' and 'teddy-boys.'"[89] By tying rural violence in South Africa to alleged global trends, the chief magistrate effectively absolved the South African state and its policies from any responsibility for causing the unrest.

Individual state officials continued to peddle this explanation of rising violence as an outgrowth of youthful disrespect. In 1961 the Bantu Affairs commissioner in Mqanduli complained that there was a "battle axe menace" in the region. He traced recent faction fights to groups of older "boys" who, in his words, "roam around in gangs disrupting peaceful beerdrinks, molesting girls on their way to or from school and generally causing disturbances in the locations. Because of superior numbers and arms they are feared and any opposition to their aims is met with violence often resulting in death."[90] The commissioner's comments captured the problem as white officials saw it: older adolescents and young men were out of control in the countryside and were disrupting the peaceful pursuits of a previously idyllic African rural life. These young men needed, in his view, to experience the discipline of "tribal" life imposed by their elders.

The particular form of traditional discipline that the commissioner chose to highlight was the discipline imposed by going through the ceremony of circumcision. He believed that if all young men went through circumcision, the ritual would restrain them and curb the fighting. He suggested that all older boys be forced to undergo circumcision at age eighteen, and that any youths caught carrying battle axes in public should be "caned publicly in the presence of their girl friends who usually spur them on to fight." This public punishment would, he thought, be more effective than the current version: "Corporal punishment in the seclusion of a police station is looked upon as acquiring honourable scars of battle."[91] In invoking the concept of honorable battle scars, this official accepted the idea that young men were trying to gain honor through fighting. But he was also suggesting that forcing young men to be circumcised would impose a reinvented form of traditional discipline and propel them back to some imagined past in which youths were firmly under the control of elders.

By 1963 some African officials were implementing these suggestions. In the aftermath of a large fight in Elliotdale, in which two adolescents died, the local headman "promised that he would round up his uncircumcised boys and get them done [i.e., circumcised] immediately, a promise he has kept to the letter, as 49 of his boys are now in [ritual] lodges in the location. This action of the headman has resulted in this Sholora location remaining neutral in the present disturbances, an outstanding effort on the part of the headman, as Sholora 'boys' in the past were always in the forefront of any fighting."[92] The forced circumcisions of young men became part of an active effort to rebuild and reinvent a set of traditions on rural Africans. Officials hoped to reimagine and impose reconstructed limits on traditional rural violence and prevent it from destabilizing the apartheid state's control.

CONCLUSION

Two dominant analyses were used to explain rural faction fights. One that was popular among white officials was that these fights were the result of entirely local and trivial quarrels, unconnected to broader political issues and policies emanating from white rule. The second interpretation, more common among recent scholars, was that violent clashes were a direct product of segregation and apartheid policies and resulted both from the ethnic and tribal categories constructed by state policies and by resistance to those policies. Each of these analyses tells a partial story, however, a fact that becomes clear when one looks at the longer history of fighting in the rural areas.

Fighting had a history that can be traced back to the nineteenth century. To point out this longer history of fighting is different from asserting that Africans were "warlike" or prone to "tribal conflicts," however. Instead, there were particular historical circumstances during much of the nineteenth century that tended to make fighting skills necessary for the protection of families and chiefdoms. It was in this context that herd boys trained for war through stick fights with their peers and that older adolescents and young men fought each other to sharpen their skills and protect their livestock, their honor, and their families. In the nineteenth century, it is likely that elders could control and direct much of the fighting, not through the surgical intervention of male circumcision, but through a social consensus on the impropriety of lethal fighting as a pastime. Other factors, such as the availability of land that enabled young men to marry and to become farmers and heads of households also made it less likely that men would engage in lethal fighting over resources within their communities.

In the beginning decades of the twentieth century, stick fighting continued as a game for younger boys, where they learned basic strategies and tactics. Violent fights (faction fights) among adolescents and young men became more common because of several factors, and the more lethal fights of the late 1920s and 1930s onward were responses to changing circumstances. The broader use of deadly weapons, such as iron-studded knobkerries and battle axes, made fighting more dangerous. In addition, the African population increased substantially at the same time that laws restricted the quantity of land available to them, heightening the competition for artificially scarce land. Ideas about masculine identities may also have been shifting toward more of an emphasis on the performance of fighting skills, but evidence for such a shift in the rural areas is not definitive. What does seem clear is that African men and adolescents used the idea that fighting was traditional to authorize their use of force in various ways. They fought strategically against rivals for love, territory, and political allegiance. They "shadowboxed" with the constraints imposed upon them by state policies and shifting cultural norms. They also inflicted blows on those who opposed them (or fell victim to the blows of others). Rural fights had roots in rural communities and exploded over local, rural issues for much of this period.

While there was a shift toward more fighting with more lethal weapons from the late 1920s onward, the shift toward fighting that had explicit political motivations was more evident beginning in the early 1950s. Much of the blame for fighting in this later period attached to apartheid policies of retribalization. Individual fights were not necessarily politically motivated, but people fought over resources and against people and policies associated with the state. The groups for which they fought were sometimes defined by geography, sometimes by ethnicity, sometimes by family, and sometimes by allegiance to a particular chief or headman. The presence of groups of young men who were willing to fight made them available to pursue political aims at particular moments. One such moment arose during the revolt that developed during the 1950s and early 1960s in the Transkei.

The meanings that fighters gave to the battles differed from the meanings that scholars and contemporary observers have imputed to them as they have analyzed the fights. Not all fighting, particularly in the 1920s and 1930s when the first documented surge in fighting took place, was a veiled form of resistance to the white-controlled state. The roots of the violence in the early period came from diverse local grievances and priorities. But this changed by the 1950s and later, as men with fighting experience were available to be recruited by nationalist political movements. These later political movements were also responding to local priorities, and people involved often tried to link local with national grievances and demands.

Focusing on the political content of fighting in the 1950s, however, obscures the changes in violence in the earlier periods. Perhaps the most notable conclusion about the increasing levels of violence was the broad normalization of fighting within rural spaces. By the 1940s, young men routinely carried battle axes with them when they attended parties or went to trading stores—they felt that they had to for self-protection. Women participated in many of the larger faction fights by assisting in arson and livestock stealing; they also sometimes were at the center of disputes over their affections. Women's engagement gave the violence additional social legitimacy: even if they did not actively fight, women encouraged men to do so. Entire households became involved as one way of surviving in a precarious economic, social, and political situation. Younger boys carried scaled-down versions of battle axes as fashionable accessories, and when they practiced fighting, they would have been aware of the lethal potential of those weapons. And older men stepped into the fighting with studded knobkerries, spears, and occasionally guns when they needed to turn the tide of these battles begun at weddings, parties, and trading stores. The attempt by nationalist movements to channel the violence was an attempt to turn it toward more politically productive ends. But ignoring the local roots of the violence and insisting that it was all veiled resistance to national policies ultimately misrepresented or misunderstood the deeply local histories that lay behind the fighting.

In this context, it is tempting to see the twenty-first century interest in stick fighting as a martial art for children, discussed at the beginning of this chapter, as an attempt to tame the violence and turn it toward more socially productive ends. The imposition of a supposedly traditional discipline and restraint upon the fighting might impose a different set of rules and meanings and dilute the potential for lethal violence. But this movement still claims stick fighting is part of a traditional African cultural identity even as violence continues to be part of the lived experience in South Africa, both in the cities and the countryside. This acceptance of fighting as a form of traditional violence is a product of the colonial, segregationist, and apartheid contexts in which faction fighting emerged.

2

"The Girl Is Not Consulted"

Abduction Marriages and Gendered Traditions of Violence

At a hearing of the 1883 Native Laws and Customs Commission in the Cape Colony, an African headman responded to a question posed by a white commissioner about whether parents conferred with their daughter before arranging a marriage for her. "She is not consulted," headman Toto replied. "She is called to the kraal [cattle enclosure] where the men are assembled, and they say to her, 'You must smear yourself with red clay today, we are going to send you to so-and-so,' meaning her intended husband." Toto emphasized that a dutiful daughter would abide by her parent's decision, but he made clear that even a reluctant daughter had few choices: "Even if the girl says she does not wish to go with the man mentioned, she will be compelled to do so." The commissioners probed further, asking about the headman's personal experiences with his own family. Toto replied that of his seven daughters, two were married—presumably in arranged marriages—to "old men," whom he found less troublesome than young men. He maintained that he was not concerned about his daughters' opinions about their marriage partners: "I merely say to the girl on the day she is leaving [to be married], 'smear with red clay, you are going today.'" All his daughters, he stated, "go without a word and live with their husbands."[1]

Headman Toto was describing his idea of traditional marriage practices and the commissioners were eager to listen. The commissioners wanted to learn about the traditions underpinning African families so that the Native Affairs Department could make appropriate policies to govern Africans in the Cape Colony. Commissioners asked witnesses, white and African—all of them men—about marriage practices and the status of wives and daughters in African societies. Most testified that arranged marriages were the norm for African families, and partly based on such testimony, the acceptance of arranged marriages became policy among Cape officials. But many witnesses, both white and African, also stated that coercion involving physical force played a role in creating some marriages. As a subset of arranged marriages, these coerced marriages were more problematic for several witnesses and many white commissioners, even though they acknowledged that they too might be traditional.

At the time, one form of coerced marriage was the practice of abduction marriage or *ukuthwala*.[2] In an *ukuthwala* marriage, a man who wished to marry a particular young woman abducted her, took her to his parents' homestead, and then reported to her parents that he had married her and that his family promised to pay bridewealth to formalize the marriage. Abduction marriages were probably not as common as either parentally arranged marriages or voluntary elopements, but they were an option available to young men in the late 1800s.

The African men who testified to the 1883 commission saw local marriage practices as essential features of their identities as patriarchs and defended not just arranged marriages but also *ukuthwala* as practices handed down from the past. Chief Ngangelizwe of the Thembu testified to the commission that "sometimes a young man steals a girl and runs off with her, . . . but whenever they come back we [the fathers] take the girls away and the man has to pay [bridewealth] for her."[3] Chiefs and headmen who spoke to the commission insisted that all marriage customs as currently practiced were the bedrock of African communities and should be retained. In 1883, however, abduction marriages were where white officials drew a line: in general, while white officials were willing to condone arranged marriages, they spoke against abduction marriages. Gradually, over the twentieth century however, white officials developed a greater tolerance for abduction marriages as long as they were accompanied by what white officials understood as the necessary and traditional rituals.

The shift toward official tolerance for abduction marriages over the twentieth century was part of the rebuilding of the "customary" that was essential to the white state's framing of Africans as essentially "rural," "tribal," and "traditional." Natasha Erlank, in her analysis of the 1883 Native Laws and Customs Commission, argues that Africans' ideas of gender and sexuality became metaphors in a discussion of more comprehensive differences between Africans and whites. "Treatment of women became a way (although obviously not the only way) to differentiate between European and African culture," Erlank writes. This differentiation was significant because, "through reference to social behaviour and arrangements, the Commissioners (consciously and unconsciously) could underscore racial difference without resorting to race as an explanation of difference. . . . Moral and sexual differences were, therefore, metaphors for racial difference."[4] As anthropologist James Ferguson has noted, rural areas in the colonial southern African context became synonymous with both "tribal" and "traditional," part of a colonial dualism that sought to legitimate white settler rule.[5] Under colonial rule, whites intended for Africans to reside in the rural areas, where they continued to perform traditional customs, while whites lived out their supposedly modern lives in the towns and cities, employing migrant labor as needed. By extension, African women and families who lived in the rural areas were supposed to embody the tribal and the traditional, while men became labor migrants for their working lives.

Young African men had reasons for participating in abduction marriages and likely benefited from the shift toward greater official tolerance of the practice. Elizabeth Thornberry notes that the custom of *ukuthwala* practiced in the late nineteenth century allowed young men "to gain leverage within marriage negotiations that they did not otherwise have," a point that emphasizes the generational tensions within rural African society at the time.[6] As the twentieth century progressed, the fact that many young men lacked the prospect of acquiring land on which to settle a wife, and perhaps also lacked the wealth needed to make the bridewealth payments, put them in an even more disadvantaged position in negotiations for ordinary, arranged marriages. At least in theory, abduction marriage allowed them to get around some of those disadvantages and marry.

Yet in looking at some of the criminal and civil cases that arose out of abductions, it is clear that fathers continued to control who could legally abduct their daughters. Fathers asserted the tradition of controlling their daughters and claimed the right to object to abduction marriages that they had not approved. The state's insistence on deferring to parental wishes by nullifying abduction marriages undertaken without parental consent undermines the conclusion that young men had gained an advantage. The state's deference to parental consent did not prevent the use of force in abduction marriages. In fact, claims about the traditional basis of coercion used in abduction marriages made it possible for state officials to uphold even quite aggressive use of force as a legitimate part of the tradition. Over the first half of the twentieth century, magistrates and the court system generally became willing to uphold abduction marriages as the state sought to fortify familial control in the rural areas.

And indeed, the reinvented practice of abduction marriage has proved resilient.[7] In 2009 the human rights organization Treatment Action Campaign (TAC) reported that abduction marriages continue to occur in parts of the Eastern Cape province. A case had exploded in the news headlines that year when a sixteen-year-old girl, accompanied by her young child, recounted her relatives' collusion in her abduction marriage in 2006 to a forty-two-year-old man. TAC's newsletter provided an explanation of the larger context of the practice of marriage by abduction: "The custom of *ukuthwalwa* is being abused in some remote areas of Lusikisiki. . . . Once a custom of arranged marriages, *ukuthwalwa* has become a violent practise. In many cases, parents are arranging for young girls to marry without the girls' consent." The newsletter stated that "more violent scenarios involve *ukuthwalwa* being used to legitimise the abduction of 14 to 17 year old girls for forced marriage. The victims are being abducted by strangers as well as by relatives. These young girls are being forced into unlawful marriages with widowed men who are 55 to 70 years old. The men are often HIV positive."[8]

The South African newspaper, the *Sunday Times*, commenting on the same incident that prompted the TAC report, suggested that *ukuthwala* was a "once-forgotten practise that is now being revived by poor, rural South African families desperate for money."[9] These reports are significant because they document that abduction marriages still took place in the twenty-first century. But the reasons they provide for the custom's longevity are also notable: They describe the practice as part of traditional African culture that in 2009 had become outdated in the context of modern South Africa where, according to the reports, it was being practiced only by the financially desperate and the culturally antiquated.[10]

There were other significant problems with the reporting of the 2009 episode. Both reports erred by implying that all arranged marriages among Africans were the same as abduction marriages. Moreover, while TAC's reporting asserts that *ukuthwala* had only recently incorporated violence, as we shall see below, *ukuthwala* historically has often involved physical coercion and outright violence to force young women to accompany their abductors. And while the *Sunday Times* opined that poverty was only recently a motivating factor in these marriages, a reading of the historical evidence on abduction marriages shows that, since the beginning of the colonial period, abduction marriages have frequently had an economic dimension.

The continuation of the practice in the twenty-first century's altered cultural context raises issues about its status as a traditional form of marriage and how African women and parents have sometimes upheld traditions even at a high cost to themselves and their children. It also forces us as scholars to look more closely at the ties between violence, sexuality, and ideas of proper gender roles. We need to examine the connections between changes in traditions and the broader changes wrought by a succession of state policies and enforcement mechanisms provided by the state's courts.

This chapter argues that abduction marriages were one way of inscribing violent practices into African families as elements of a reimagined tradition. In the colonial and apartheid context, "tradition" was the antithesis of "modern," just as Africans were the antithesis of white settlers. Men frequently migrated to cities to find wage labor, leaving their families in the countryside as government policies made it difficult for entire families to move with them. As segregationist and apartheid legislation framed the rural reserves as places where Africans lived traditional lives, maintaining rural families and upholding cultural traditions often became the burden of women.[11] But men continued to exercise control over their families even if at a distance. The rural family was one of the few places where African elders, including both men and some women, could exercise authority by invoking tradition's significance.

MARRIAGE, TRADITION, AND SOCIAL NAVIGATION

At the beginning of the colonial period in the Transkeian region in the 1880s, many white officials and missionaries criticized all arranged marriages, and they were even more adamantly opposed to abduction marriages. The practice of arranged marriages, combined with the payment of bridewealth, caused many whites to label such marriages as forms of slavery, a view sometimes echoed by Christian Africans. Quite a few whites deemed most arranged marriages and all abduction marriages as synonymous with enslavement.[12] By the early twentieth century, however, state policies, and most crucially the magistrates' courts, endorsed the legality of all arranged marriages and accepted the legitimacy of many abduction marriages, even if they included substantial physical force.

The change in official attitudes resulted from a complex, long-term negotiation between African elders—particularly men—and white administrators that occurred within the confines of official policies. White officials edged away from a policy of extinguishing African cultural practices that they saw as inconsistent with "civilization" and toward policies that reinforced differences, especially since these differences became the justification for continued political oppression and segregation. The differences between Africans' marriage practices and whites' marriage practices were signs of the supposedly essential differences between the races and made continued white rule seem like a moral choice.[13]

Marriage was the foundation of the family, and the family became the repository of traditions. The idea of elders claiming cultural traditions to bolster their authority within families accords with Ferguson's point that in colonized Africa, culture was a performance delivered under "a situation of duress."[14]

Living under the constraints imposed by white rule, people considered that both arranged marriages and *ukuthwala* were traditions rooted in the pre-colonial period and were therefore respectable elements of African cultural identity. Throughout the twentieth century, there was frequent debate within African households over what constituted a traditional marriage,[15] but there was consensus that arranged marriages were traditional and respectable. And as we shall see, over that same period, abduction or coerced marriages also came to be accepted and deemed traditional and therefore respectable.

The culture and context surrounding marriage were not static. People contracted marriages for many reasons, both social and economic. Families whose daughters married in traditional ways remained respectable; those families whose daughters migrated to town and had children out of wedlock lost both bridewealth payments and often their social respectability.[16] Marrying principally for love was the province of the aspiring middle-class of mission-educated Africans, while parents from other sectors of African society often disparaged the idea as naive. Simultaneously, marriage and bridewealth payments, or *lobola*, became a form of economic exchange, at least for some families. But the fact that marriages had an economic dimension did not lessen their respectability or their aura of tradition, in part because economic factors were part of a strategy for the family's survival over the long term. Thus, when young women refused to agree to parentally arranged marriages, parents sometimes colluded with suitors in planning their daughters' abductions. In doing so, they were engaging in social navigation to achieve family stability over the long term.

Women often faced obstacles in terms of their choices in marriage. They had to engage in social navigation through and around these obstacles to plot a course into a future. Henrik Vigh explored the concept of social navigation in Guinea and among African migrants in Lisbon who faced great uncertainty in their lives. "Social navigation" was his translation of a local term, *dubria*. Vigh explained *dubria* as people bobbing and weaving to "the push and pull of social forces—not as static constraints or positions of power in a social field but as social effects that engage social beings and bodies within the social environment."[17] Most of Vigh's informants were young men who found themselves without the economic means to marry and start a family. They adopted various strategies, ranging from social networking and street hustling to armed revolt, to advance to the next life stage of full adulthood.

While Vigh did not interview Guinean women, other scholars have applied his insights to analyses of women in other countries who faced a similar lack of options and used forms of social navigation to survive and achieve their own ends. Mats Utas, analyzing women's lives in Liberia during the extended civil conflict of the 1990s, suggests that scholars too often create a gendered opposition of agency versus victimhood that flattens the understanding of women's options. He notes that women, even those who find themselves in objectively dangerous circumstances, employ tactical agency to make use of what resources may be available to them to survive.[18] And Marjoke Oosterom has investigated how women and youth navigated life in the repressive Zimbabwean regime of Robert Mugabe between 2013 to 2016. She suggests that youth, in particular, normalized the violence and uncertainty that existed around them until they became the "background against which everyday life continues to be produced."[19] Sometimes they tried to use the violence to their own advantage. The rural South African context in the early twentieth century is not a direct analog to Guinea or Liberia in the 1990s or Zimbabwe in the 2010s, but South African women found themselves in similarly uncertain positions as the social and economic landscape shifted around them. There were some new opportunities for women, but there were also new constraints and real dangers. Women had to make their life choices against this background.

This chapter will use the records of court cases and other documents concerning abduction marriages to trace some of the connections between physical coercion in *ukuthwala* and the South African state's segregationist and apartheid policies. The court cases discussed in this chapter only tell a partial story about abduction marriage. These were cases brought either by the young women themselves as they tried to nullify their marriages or by their parents or guardians when the abductions took place without their approval.[20] But as partial as they may be, the cases provide evidence of how abduction occurred, their legal status, and what recourse young women and girls had if they objected. The cases also illuminate the official stance toward these marriages and how white magistrates determined which marriages were legitimate and which were not. The line between what was legally unacceptable and what was acceptable moved as the courts began to tolerate greater male control, including the use of force, over young women and translated into an acceptance of abduction marriages that followed traditional practices (as judged by the magistrates). Both African traditions and colonially administered customary law shifted over time, and certain kinds of violence against women became legal and was subsumed under the category of traditional. The courts actively shaped the legality of abduction marriage while they simultaneously reconfigured conversations among Africans on the use of violence to contract these marriages. Magistrates took active roles in deciding cases and framing which traditions and customs would be legally accepted and how they had to be performed to cross the legal threshold.

Early Colonial Development of Abduction Marriages

Scholars have documented how South Africa's geography became segregated along racial lines. From the earliest divisions of towns into white and black residential areas during the colonial period to the country's division into "white" South Africa and ten individual "Bantustans" for Africans under apartheid, whites and blacks often occupied different geographic spaces. Other scholars have pushed beyond the discussion of racialized geography to discuss how geography also became gendered. As South Africa industrialized through the 1960s, increasing numbers of African men and some women lived much of their adult working lives in the urban areas. Simultaneously, the rural reserves were where most women, children, and retirees could legally reside.[21] The processes that constructed this gendered and racialized geography rested on the violence of land expropriation and systematic political and economic oppression.

As male labor migration became more common, families who remained in the rural areas symbolized an ongoing connection to culture and the ancestors buried at the homestead. Thus, the rural family became the stewards of both the land and cultural traditions. However, the practices of these cultural traditions often changed even though many people, including both Africans and whites, defended the supposedly unchanging nature of tradition.[22]

The designation of rural life under segregation and apartheid as essentially traditional was an idea that retained tremendous resonance. The Comaroffs, writing about women in colonial cultures, noted that "in the signifying economy of empire, black women often came to embody rural tradition. Sometimes portrayed as the premodern counterpart of working-class European females, most of them remained, willingly or not, in increasingly impoverished domestic enclaves, far away from 'modern' centers of production and public life. . . . Here, in 'reserves'—later termed, literally, *homelands*—. . . they became the prime bearers of a cultural identity that fixed the place of their people among other peoples of color on the subcontinent."[23] Women thus bore the burden of upholding traditions. That task could be a source of respectability and power (at least within the family) as well as a significant constraint on their actions.

That women and particularly wives would become the icons of rural tradition was never a foregone conclusion, however. Instead, the role of the traditional rural woman emerged from cultural changes that resulted from many other changes to social and economic processes occurring within South Africa. These processes included legal limitations on access to arable land, the development of a predominately male migrant labor system, the creation of the colonial and then apartheid state, and the complex interactions of African and white colonial cultures. Many Africans and whites saw rural marriages as both the anchor of the African population in the rural areas and as the foundation of cultural identity.

Both whites and Africans, for different reasons, had an interest in maintaining some version of African culture in the rural areas.[24] For whites, reducing the number of permanent African urban residents and thereby stifling the political demands made by the African population meant preventing the migration of women and families to the urban areas. The resulting system of male migratory labor also meant that white employers could justify the low wages paid to laborers because women and children living in the countryside could produce food for the family and thus subsidize wages. The white-controlled government enacted laws that limited rural to urban migration for most women and family members. While these laws did not entirely prevent migration, they did make it risky. If women migrated to towns, they exposed themselves to the violence of state enforcement measures and the brutality of urban life.[25]

For African men and elders, keeping daughters and wives in the rural areas meant retaining control over whatever farmland was available to them. It also allowed them to live out, in an attenuated form, identities as homestead heads and social adults in a generational chain stretching from their ancestors to their descendants. The homestead's economics, including the payment of bridewealth, were indistinguishable from the broader social and spiritual meanings of the homestead. If the homestead survived economically, it represented an accomplishment of other goals as well. While daughters married into other families' households, daughters-in-law maintained the rural homes of sons, while grandchildren helped with farming and household chores. The interests of white administrators and African men and elders (including many older women) converged on the issue of control over daughters and their marriages as a necessity for the continuation of the rural African family.

Daughters often had other ideas. Sometimes, daughters' newfound independence resulted from exposure to Christianity and a desire to convert, especially in the early period before 1920. The records of missionary stations in Natal and Zululand in the 1880s and 1890s provide numerous stories of girls defying their parents to attend or continue attending mission schools.[26] If the girl's parents were not Christian, her conversion eroded the influence her parents could exercise over her and often made a marriage to a non-Christian man more difficult. And women who came into contact with missionaries were sometimes profoundly changed even if they did not convert. A Wesleyan minister from the Cape, W. Holford, testified to the 1903–5 Native Affairs Commission that when young women worked in white households, "the more they learn such domestic habits and acquire the money to feed and clothe themselves, the prospect of marriage is unwelcome." In his view, independence was not just a habit of mind. Young women became independent as a result of economic autonomy: "It is going further still when they have in their own hands the ways and means of living which render them independent both of father and prospective husband."[27] Mission education, wages earned, and a broader set of experiences provided options for young women. The parents' prospects of choosing whom their daughters would marry faded as their daughters' sense of independence sharpened. Marriage opportunities, and with them the promise of cattle paid as bridewealth, were sometimes postponed or foregone altogether. The loss of bridewealth payments for a daughter might then prevent her brother from marrying, thus posing an even more significant threat to the family's survival into the future. Some African elders felt that they had a duty to restrict their daughters' options for the good of the family across time and generations.[28]

The roots of these ideas about women's proper roles emerged from attitudes about marriage. Historically, people debated whether women should have a say in selecting whom they would marry. Young women frequently insisted that they should be able to choose, and for a time, at least until the early 1920s, the colonial state agreed.[29] The Native Code of colonial Natal, for example, required that all women attest at their marriages that they were marrying of their own free will.[30] Commissioners of the 1883 Cape Native Laws Commission repeatedly asked witnesses whether the Cape should impose similar requirements, although ultimately the Cape never imposed such requirements. In the 1880s and 1890s, many magistrates and some ministers believed that young women needed to be both liberated from their fathers' control and recruited for Christian conversion.[31]

In contrast, older African men who testified to the 1883 commission asserted the propriety of paternal control over the family. The "former king" (as the commission report styled him) of the Zulu, Cetshwayo, when asked about marriage customs, described a "father knows best" scenario. A father might consider his daughter's wishes when arranging a marriage. Still, he ultimately should follow his own judgment of who would make the best husband: "If the girl was allowed to go to any man she wished, she might choose a bad man, and that is why the father controls her, and sends her to the man he wishes to have her."[32] Cetshwayo acknowledged that the number of cattle a man offered as bridewealth could influence the father's choice. But he stressed that the daughter's welfare was paramount for most fathers and that the father's choice was best, even if the daughter disagreed.[33]

From the eastern Cape, the Mfengu headman Pambani echoed Cetshwayo's sentiments. In his testimony, he stressed that "we do not look alone to the cattle" given as bridewealth when selecting a daughter's marriage partner "but to the character and standing of the man to whom we give her. We do not allow a girl to choose a husband for herself, we choose for her." Pambani stated that "in former days we used to compel our daughters to marry the man we selected for them." He lamented that the influence of whites and particularly of missionaries was eroding girls' willingness to go along with their fathers' wishes: "Now the girls are giving us trouble in this respect, and this trouble arises through a thing called love."[34]

During the precolonial period, the family was a more dynamic and fluid social construction than the headman Toto, who testified to the 1883 commission (quoted at the beginning of the chapter), or Cetshwayo or Pambani allowed. But the picture of a father preserving a moral society based on the family, assisted when necessary by the judicious use of force, became a standard narrative about precolonial life. When a commissioner asked Chief Ngangelizwe of the Thembu about "what your custom of ukulobola [bridewealth] is," the chief responded, "Now you have hit upon the proper question, and we will answer it."[35] His answer emphasized the father's ultimate right to make choices about appropriate marriages for his children.

This picture of harmonious precolonial marriage practices was at odds with the often-expressed opinion among missionaries and magistrates in the period through the first decade of the 1900s that women and daughters were the drudges of African society who needed liberation from the demands made upon them by the men of the family.[36] Women could only achieve this liberation, they suggested, if arranged marriages and abduction marriages were outlawed. For example, the Reverend E. J. Barrett, a Wesleyan missionary at Kamastone, wrote in an 1883 article for his missionary journal that many African parents "will be on the look-out for rich husbands for their daughters." And he feared that "many a poor girl will be forced by cruel beatings and persecution to go and be the wife of a man whom she detests; perhaps some toothless, decrepit wretch, worn out with a life of sensuality; who already has wives in abundance, and plenty of cattle with which to pay for more."[37]

R. J. Dick, a "special magistrate" for Kingwilliamstown, gave a slightly more measured assessment of arranged and coerced marriages at the hearings of the 1903–5 Native Laws and Customs Commission. Dick stated that, since the 1850s when he first came to live in the eastern Cape, marriage had become a contentious issue partly because young women became aware of other options. One of the commissioners asked him, "Do I understand you to say that at the present time girls are forced to consummate marriages that they do not wish?" To which Dick responded, "Yes, occasionally, and not infrequently." The commissioner followed up and asked whether a young woman had any legal way to prevent herself from being married against her wishes, to which Dick replied that "there is no appeal as a rule. What happens is this. If a girl is forced into a marriage and she does not commit suicide—which happens occasionally— she runs away, perhaps to her people, but that is hardly likely to be the case where her father has sternly compelled her to enter into that marriage; but she goes to some distant relation. The husband then demands the restoration of his wife from the father, and on the latter's inability to restore her, the case comes into [the magistrate's] court, and in the majority of cases ends in a summary divorce." Dick further clarified his position that, as a magistrate, "I annul the marriage." When pressed to sketch out what might happen after such an annulment, he stated, "If the girl is here [in Kingwilliamstown] when the marriage is annulled the father takes her back again, but it frequently happens that the girl has never been found." He elaborated on how men dealt with a runaway wife: "Native law runs this way. If a man marries another man's daughter, and she refuses to live with him, or if she has escaped and run away from him, he is first of all compelled by Native custom to try and ascertain her whereabouts." If the husband found her and she still refused to live with him, "he goes back and says to the father of the girl, 'Your girl is living in such and such a district with so and so; go and bring her to me.' If the girl declines to obey her father, the husband goes to the court, and if it is found that the girl has left him because they could not live happily together, the marriage is annulled, and the husband gets a certain portion of his dowry back."[38]

In this extended discussion of compulsion in arranged marriages and young women's resistance, Dick did not address abduction marriages specifically. But his descriptions acknowledged that women did not always acquiesce to their parents' decisions. He also indicated that, as a magistrate, he did not automatically enforce a father's right to compel his daughter to marry. Dick was not attempting to prohibit all forced marriages, however. Only when a young woman ran away did he ratify her decision by annulling the marriage. Forced marriages continued to occur and occasionally had tragic consequences.[39]

The Expansion of Abduction Marriages

The official antipathy toward absolute paternal control over a daughter's marriage exemplified by Special Magistrate Dick shifted over several decades. Family life came under increasing pressure from labor migration and deepening rural impoverishment. As African families began to fracture under these stresses, official policies sought to hold families together and keep them in the rural areas. In setting up and maintaining the administrations that ruled their African subjects, white officials looked back to descriptions of rural African life in the 1880s as sources for the definitive version of African tradition. Drawing on these accounts, magistrates assumed that fathers had the right to enforce their decisions with coercion if they were acting within traditional norms recognized by the courts.[40]

Magistrates also began to tolerate abduction marriages even when accompanied by violence toward the women involved. This tolerance partly stemmed from opinions offered by African men who appeared as witnesses at government commissions. For example, Peter Mti wrote in his answers to the 1903–5 Native Affairs Commission that he believed most young women were quite happy to be abducted by prospective grooms. As an African clerk in a solicitor's office in East London and as the vice chairman of the Native Vigilance Association there, he believed that abduction of young women for marriage should not usually be prosecuted as a crime: "The crime of abduction amongst Natives should be clearly proved before a conviction is made, because abduction is generally resorted to by the Natives with the connivance of the girl's parents or her lawful guardian, and to those who are acquainted with Natives it is well known that it is a pleasure to a 'red' [i.e., non-Christian] Native girl to be carried away by a lover, as in her view it increases her marketable value."[41] In Mti's opinion, abductions were dramatic performances, in which women were either co-conspirators or willing participants, rather than crimes against women, and they were therefore morally and socially acceptable. Moreover, his suggestion that a young woman would approve of being abducted because it increased "her marketable value" provides insight into how entrenched economic considerations were even in the first decade of the twentieth century.

As Mti's testimony suggests, the lines between arranged marriages, abduction marriages, and elopements were already somewhat blurred. Many observers thought it hard to differentiate between coerced abductions and consensual ones (that is, elopements staged as abductions). J. H. Soga, writing in the 1930s, discussed abduction marriage and suggested that the term applied to two types of abductions: "to genuine cases of abduction by force, and also to faked cases of abduction." However, he also stressed "that there are real cases of forcible abduction" that families and the legal system should not condone.[42] Coerced abduction marriages posed legal and moral problems for all concerned in rural colonial society in the early twentieth century.

Some of these legal and moral problems played out in court cases heard in magistrates' courts. In determining whether a contested abduction marriage was legal, magistrates typically tried to discern several facts. First was the question of the girl's age: in the Cape Province, any woman twenty-one years or older could not be married off by her parents or guardians without her consent, nor could she be abducted without her consent. If the woman was under twenty-one, then the second question was whether her father or (usually male) guardian had consented to the marriage. If her father or guardian had agreed to the abduction marriage or retroactively condoned it, then the marriage was legal, at least in the Transkeian Territories.[43] The third question that the Transkeian magistrate would try to answer was whether the woman herself had conspired in the abduction. Typically, this meant that the magistrate had to determine if she and the abductor had a previous or ongoing sexual or romantic relationship. If the young woman conspired with her abductor, it did not make the marriage legal if her guardian disapproved. Still, it did protect the abductor from being convicted of kidnapping and rape. Instead, he could be fined as part of a civil proceeding for having "damaged" the young woman, with the fine for "damages" being paid to her guardian. In that case, the young woman returned to live with her parents, who might arrange a subsequent marriage between the woman and her abductor.[44] While these questions themselves were usually clear, the answers were occasionally less straightforward.

One 1915 case from Cofimvaba dealing with an attempted abduction marriage provides evidence about the practice and how it was tolerated and constrained by African family members and the magistrates' courts. A nineteen-year-old woman was walking on the road to Queenstown, intending to visit family. She met a thirty-eight-year-old man who talked her into walking with him for a while. Shortly after, when she tried to veer back toward her original destination of Queenstown, he grabbed her and, according to her testimony at the trial, he "began to beat me with a walking stick. I tried to run away but he caught me and again [he] beat me. My dress got torn. Being in fear of him I walked along with him. He said he was taking me to Mgwali, Engcobo district where he would make me his wife." At one point in the journey, the young woman appealed to some adult women who were passing by on the road; she asked them "to help me but they declined to interfere." Later, the man took her to "a certain kraal [homestead] where there was a wedding in progress. He made me sit down. Some women came up to me and asked me why I was crying and I told them that accused was stealing me. The men came up to me and I asked them to rescue me from him. These men took us to the Headman of Ngxwabangu. Accused was arrested and brought here."[45] In many of its details, this story was a common example of an attempted abduction marriage, but the woman in this case was quick to alert people she met that the man was abducting her against her will.

When the case came to trial after a complaint filed by her guardian, there were few differences between the abducted woman's story and the story told by the man who abducted her. The man stated at his trial that after he had forced her to walk with him: "I then told her that I wished to make it clear to her that I was not going to allow her to return [to her own home] as I was going to abduct her (twaala) for the purpose of marrying her in Tembuland. I took her shawl, and took her by the hand and forced her along. She wanted to go to Queenstown. She got away and ran away. I chased and caught her. She tried to run away again and cried. I caught her." In his version of events, there was even tacit approval of his actions from the women they met on the road: "We met women. I told them we were going to Tembuland. Complainant was crying and the women told her to go as all women have to be married in this way under Native Custom." While the women travelers perhaps saw nothing wrong with the man's actions, the older men and the headman at the destination homestead obviously did since they intervened and took the young woman to the police. These different reactions suggest a discrepancy between the women seeing the abduction as part of ordinary customs versus the headman understanding the abduction was possibly illegal.

At the trial, the magistrate's decision turned on the fact that the abductor had not sought the consent of the young woman's guardian (her brother) before grabbing her. The woman had no previous relationship with the young man, which indicated that the young woman had not conspired with her abductor. The magistrate ruled that there was no marriage and that the man had committed a crime for which he was sentenced to nine months in jail with hard labor. The magistrate's ruling was not in response to the objections of the young woman, however. Instead, it was rooted in the guardian's disapproval of the abduction and the magistrate's decision to uphold the guardian's claims.[46]

Another abduction case from Nqamakwe in 1916 showed how magistrates interpreted and partly reconstructed marriage customs as they endorsed the absolute authority of parents and guardians. Twelve men from the same family were accused of assault in an attempted abduction of a young woman named Martha. In this case, Martha's guardian, her brother Walter, had initially arranged for her to be married to Buti Swaartbooi, and Walter had even accepted the payment of eleven cattle as bridewealth. She, however, had rejected the prospective husband: "My banns of marriage were being published. I left my father's kraal before they were published. I was running away from the marriage. My guardian was annoyed and fetched me back." Martha's refusal put an end to the marriage plans, and the guardian had to return the bridewealth cattle. Walter was able to return some of the cattle but, unfortunately, seven had already died and he could not afford to replace them. At the trial, one of the accused men alleged that Walter had suggested that an abduction marriage might solve both of their problems. This allegation was an essential element of their defense—if Walter had assented to the abduction, it was not a criminal act, and the violence that took place could be seen as part of a traditional abduction marriage. Walter, however, denied that he had approved of the kidnapping.[47]

Regardless of who thought up the idea, the attempted abduction occurred one night after Martha and her family had gone to bed. It quickly turned into a melee. Swaartbooi and eleven members of his family burst into the hut, beat up several members of Martha's family, and grabbed Martha from her bed. She testified that, as she resisted, she was physically attacked: "No. 2 [accused] caught hold of me and bit off my fingernail. It was dark in the hut. I held to the bedstead. I was being held by many others and they beat me. Miriam [her sister] went outside and screamed. Cecil [one of her brothers] was trying to keep the people from taking me away. They beat him." She described that, in the attempt to take her, "I was choked and the bedstead to which I held got broken as it got across the doorway."[48] Once outside, her abductors blindfolded her and pulled her along the road to the groom's house. "On the way I was beaten with a sjambok [whip] when we started from my kraal. I was quite naked." They took her to the Swaartbooi homestead. Later the same night, her relatives attacked the Swaartboois with fighting sticks and retrieved Martha. They subsequently filed a complaint with the police, which led to the trial. The sheer physical brutality of the abduction, attested to by several witnesses, led to all twelve defendants being convicted of assault. Yet the magistrate sentenced all the defendants to only one month in jail.

The twelve defendants appealed the verdict, and in responding to the appeal, the magistrate had to justify the convictions. He stated that no one denied that the attempted abduction took place and that a fight broke out. But the magistrate did not believe the defendants' story that Martha's guardian had conspired in the attempted abduction because the abductors had physically restrained him in his hut as the abduction happened. The magistrate was also critical of the defense's claim that the abduction had been properly carried out according to custom: "To 'twala' or carry off a girl is a custom of the natives though it is not usual where the marriage is to be by Christian rites [both families were Christian]. It is done secretly by the lover assisted by perhaps one or two friends carrying off the girl when found alone, the girl offering little or no resistance."[49] From the magistrate's perspective, the problem with this instance of *ukuthwala* was not that the people involved were Christians, nor was the problem the practice of abduction marriage itself. Instead, the problem was that, in his eyes, how the abduction was carried out was not sufficiently "customary": "A 'twala-ing' in the manner it was conducted in the present case, even accepting the defence account, would certainly not be considered regular." The magistrate went on to suggest how a customary abduction should have happened: "If Walter [the girl's guardian] had consented it would have been the easiest thing possible to have arranged to carry off the girl secretly. The version that she was taken quietly by arrangement with Walter in the manner alleged by the defence is on the face of it highly improbable." The magistrate concluded that the accused abductors "were not satisfied to await an opportunity to 'twala' the girl in the customary way and decided to take her at all costs, hence the raid on the kraal."[50] Thus, the magistrate implied that his court would uphold the legality of an abduction marriage as long as it was carried out properly (in his view) and accomplished with the consent of the young woman's guardian. And this magistrate's opinion was the norm for magistrates at the time: the chief magistrate (whose court was the first court of appeal) affirmed the original judgment and the relatively light sentences.

The two court cases described above show that, in the 1910s magistrates tolerated abduction marriage as a legitimate form of customary marriage but with significant restrictions carved out. One limitation was that the woman's guardian had to have given consent. The second was that the abductors could only use limited violence to coerce the woman, while the woman provided only token resistance. The magistrate was the one who determined what constituted "limited violence" and "token resistance." Over time, as we shall see below, even these limits on violence faded as the question of the guardian's consent became the paramount concern for most magistrates. The increasing weight given to the guardians' consent and the proper performance of traditional marriage rites revealed the central concern that many white officials had—they wanted families to maintain absolute control over young women.

Abduction Marriage as the Exercise of Control over Young Women

Adolescent girls and young women frequently resisted the controls that parents and guardians tried to place on them. By the 1920s and 1930s, women began to migrate with greater frequency away from their rural homes to find wage labor at smaller urban centers.[51] By the 1940s women were expanding their options to include Johannesburg, Durban, Port Elizabeth, Cape Town, and

East London. Unmarried women living in urban environments usually were there without their parents and they often evaded the control of broader kin networks.[52] While individual women sometimes migrated as part of a family strategy to provide supplementary income for their rural kin, they often found it personally difficult to return to the rural areas and lose their autonomy.[53]

Colonial officials were eager to assist the family in maintaining control over young women. C. L. R. Harries, a native commissioner in the Transvaal, testified to the Select Committee on Native Customs and Marriage Laws in 1913: "If a woman is roaming about at large in the towns, we assist the guardian to recover her . . . because we regard it as an undesirable thing to allow this girl to roam at large about towns. They [*sic*] must be under control."[54] The need to restrict women's migration to urban areas was a position reinforced by the Stallard Commission, whose report led to the passage of the 1923 Natives (Urban) Areas Act. The act encouraged the development of uniform statutes on urban racial segregation and gave white municipal authorities the right to exclude African women from legally living in urban areas designated as "white."[55]

The 1923 law could not address all the difficulties that families faced in trying to keep control over their young women. Most significantly, when fathers migrated to work in the urban areas and to the mines, their prolonged absence from family life often resulted in the loss of direct control over daughters who remained in the rural areas. Fathers usually delegated their authority to other family members, and in addition, magistrates and colonial courts actively tried to bolster the control of absent fathers over their families.

White officials' fear about the rural family's disintegration coincided with similar fears held by African elders, both men and women. Officials wanted to keep African families in the rural areas; African elders wanted to retain whatever authority and power they had over their junior family members to ensure the longevity and the morality of the family and the homestead. Evidence of these concerns on the part of Africans can be seen in a survey sent by many African organizations (including the Native Advisory Boards Association, Native Interdenominational Ministers' Association, Native Mine Clerks' Association, Transvaal Native Teachers' Association, the Bantu Women's League, and the Joint Council of Europeans and Natives) to Transkeian magistrates to be sent on to local chiefs. They asked the chiefs to consider various proposals under several headings, including: "1. To clean the towns of disreputable women; 2. To prevent Native Women and Girls deserting their homes in the Native areas against their parents' wishes."[56] Several African men also testified to the Native Economic Commission in the early 1930s, commenting on the problem of "loose women" in the urban areas. The Kroonstad (Orange Free State) chapter of the Joint Council of Europeans and Natives—a relatively liberal social welfare organization—wanted all Africans living in town to register their marriages with the local municipal authority to "prevent desertion and the consequent evils and to prevent illegitimacy."[57] White officials and some older Africans hoped to keep unmarried African women from living in town at all. In 1931 a group of African civic leaders in Umtata in the Transkei passed a resolution stating that any African man coming to town and "bringing with him his wife must bring a letter from the Magistrate or headman of his district certifying that she is his lawful wife according to Christian rites or by native law."[58] These declarations clearly expressed anxieties about unmarried women living in town and the younger generation's alleged immorality as threats to marriage as an institution.[59]

Such anxieties were common in the 1930s and later among older Africans. Many African parents worried about what might happen to their daughters if they moved to town alone. A daughter's migration indicated that the family needed her financial contribution. If the daughter married an unsuitable man or, worse, became "spoiled" (pregnant without being married), the family's social respectability could suffer.[60] Arranged marriages and abduction marriages in which the parents colluded with the groom allowed parents to marry their daughters to the parents' choice of suitors.[61] A parentally approved abduction marriage addressed the problems of a daughter refusing an openly arranged marriage or an unmarried daughter moving to town.[62]

Throughout the southern African region, abduction marriages were common in the early twentieth century. Colonial law in Swaziland condoned marriage by abduction even if it involved significant violence to compel the women to submit. Historian Hamilton Simelane notes that laws encouraged Swazi men to see their wives and daughters as their property, and Swazi society began to see independent women as immoral. A Swazi woman who tried to avoid an arranged marriage might meet with physical violence either from her prospective husband or her own family. If she successfully escaped the wedding, she could suffer rejection by her parents and lose her reputation.[63]

In Zululand, magistrates reported that abduction marriages allowed parents to choose, against their daughters' wishes, wealthier and often older men who could pay a higher bridewealth. Coerced marriages were illegal under the Natal Native Code, but they occurred regardless.[64] In the 1930s the Native Economic Commission recommended that marriages contracted without the young women's consent be legally recognized and decriminalized, a step that the commissioner of Nongoma district deplored. "If this sort of thing [coerced marriage] can take place," he wrote in his comments to the commission, "whilst the Natives are under the impression that it is illegal, one may well imagine what will happen if they are told that the Government will not interfere, and that it is left to the parties concerned to come to a mutual agreement."[65] With the subsequent decriminalization of forced marriages and abduction marriages, Natal and Zululand's law became similar to the customary law enforced in the Transkei: An abduction marriage was legal as long as the young woman's father or guardian approved and as long as the groom's family followed through on the payment of bridewealth and the rituals associated with marriage. The woman's consent was no longer a requirement.

The Embedding of Violence in Abduction Marriages

Two cases in which an abductor faced rape charges in the Transkei provide evidence of the use of violence and the complicity of courts in abduction marriage from the late 1920s onward. The first case dates from 1929 in Cofimvaba. A young woman who claimed to be fifteen years old complained that she had been abducted when visiting with friends. During the visit, a woman had called her and one of her friends to come inside a hut in which a man also sat. The man announced his intention to abduct the girl, grabbed her, put her on his shoulder, took her to his own homestead, and then had sex with her. Both the abducted girl and her friend testified in court that the accused man threatened her with a sjambok (whip), and that she struggled and screamed. But the friend, Cabatana, added that "all girls scream when they are being 'twaalaed,'"[66] a comment that the magistrate understood as meaning that the friend saw the abduction as an ordinary example of *ukuthwala*.

The brother of the abducted girl, when he heard what had happened, arrived at the man's homestead and took his sister home; then he brought the matter to the headman. (The young woman's father was a laborer at the mines and her brother was in charge of the homestead in his absence). The headman advised him to bring the matter to the police. At the preparatory examination on the charge of rape, the attorney for the accused cross-examined the brother about whether he had arranged for his sister to be abducted for marriage. He denied it, although the defendant's attorney persisted in this line of questioning to establish that the sister and brother's household was relatively poor as compared to that of the abductor. "Accused did not ask me for my sister as a wife," her brother insisted. "He did not pay me cattle." As the attorney pressed, the brother responded, "I took my sister from accused's kraal because he took her without my knowledge or permission."[67]

Several circumstances in this case should have counted against the defendant. The first was that the young woman did not have a previous relationship with her abductor—she was not eloping with a lover. The second was her age: at age fifteen, she was too young to be legally married even in an openly arranged marriage. The third was that the brother, acting as her guardian in place of the absent father, swore that he had not consented to the marriage.

However, doubts about these circumstances were introduced by the testimony of the woman in whose hut the abduction had taken place. She claimed that the girl had gone along with the abduction and had not screamed or struggled, directly contradicting the evidence provided by the girl and her friend. She also stated that the defendant had told her that the girl's brother had consented to the abduction, thus contradicting the evidence provided by the brother. And the woman finally asserted that the abductor had told her that the girl was nineteen years old, and thus was not underage. (On the question of the girl's age, the district surgeon testified in the case that he believed her to be under sixteen years old). The doubts introduced by this witness were apparently sufficient for the magistrate to dismiss the rape charges at the conclusion of the preparatory examination; the case never went to trial.[68]

No written explanation for the magistrate's decision appears in the case file. What seems likely, however, is that he presumed that abduction marriages were commonplace and often involved force, including forced sexual intercourse. The magistrate also possibly believed that the abductor thought he had the consent of the girl's guardian or else could persuade the guardian to consent after the fact. If the magistrate adhered to the idea common among whites that women's families "sold" them to the highest bidder, he may also have found it easy to believe that a guardian from a poor household would consent to his sister's abduction marriage to a man from a wealthier household. Whatever his reasoning, the magistrate decided that there was no proof that any crime had been committed, and thus, abduction and forced sexual intercourse were legally rendered as something other than kidnapping and rape.[69]

A second case involving a violent abduction marriage emerged from Kentani in 1939. The facts in this case were significantly different in that the young woman was older (twenty) and her guardian actually did conspire with the abductor. Once again, the case showed how, in some cases, the state defined abduction and sexual coercion as something other than criminal kidnapping and rape. It also shows how willing this family was to subject their daughter to significant and repeated physical violence to accomplish an arranged abduction marriage.

The case itself involved two brothers charged with kidnapping and rape for abducting a twenty-year-old woman with the intention of one of the brothers marrying her. The two men accosted the young woman when she was alone and announced that they had come to "*twala*" her (marry her by abduction), with the brother named Kuleni being the prospective groom. During the circuit court trial, the woman testified that the two men had grabbed her, beaten her, and then taken her to their home. Once there, Kuleni tried to have sexual intercourse with her; she fought him off and bit his finger. His yelling brought his brother and another friend into the hut. The three men then beat her severely with a whip all over her body to make her submit sexually to Kuleni.[70] The following morning, the young woman managed to escape and flee to her father's homestead.

Two weeks later, the two brothers tried to kidnap her again. This time, she evaded them and fled to the nearby town to file a charge against them with the police. When she returned home, her paternal uncle upbraided her and, during their argument, she discovered that he had conspired with the two brothers to marry her off. (Her father was working in Johannesburg and had designated her uncle as guardian). She narrated their argument at the trial: "He [the uncle] caught hold of me. I said 'Leave me alone—Why do you catch me?' He then asked, 'Don't you know what I am catching you for?' I said I didn't and he then said 'I am taking you to Kuleni's.' I then asked him 'Didn't you hear that I have laid a [criminal] charge [against Kuleni]?'" At that point in their dispute, the uncle began hitting her with a stick, and she threatened to report him to the police and have him arrested for assault. According to her testimony, he responded: "I do not care about the Government. . . . The Government could 'voetsak' [go screw itself]. He then beat me again behind the left ear. I fell down. . . . He then pulled my arms behind my back and tied them up with a handkerchief. He said we must go to Kuleni's kraal [homestead]— he pushed me and I went." The pair walked to Kuleni's home, at which point the woman declared that she refused to marry Kuleni. Her uncle reportedly replied: "'If you don't want Kuleni [as a husband] go and drown yourself in the pools near the [cattle] dipping tank. Nkongolo [her uncle] then caught hold of me and . . . he directed that I should be bound with a rope."[71] Her uncle suggested that she not be given any food or water for several days and that her arms be kept bound behind her back to ensure she would be unable to run away again. The men then took the young woman into a hut where she was tied up and repeatedly sexually assaulted by Kuleni.

Despite the efforts to restrain her, the young woman managed to escape the following day and found refuge with a local subheadman. He reported what had happened to the police, and the magistrate conducted a preparatory examination on the rape and kidnapping charges. The case proceeded to a trial before a judge and an all-white, all-male jury in the circuit court in Butterworth. The two abductors were charged with rape and kidnapping; initially, her uncle was also criminally charged, but he died before the case came to trial.[72]

The legal issue at stake in the case was whether a customary marriage had taken place or whether the accused men might reasonably have *believed* that a marriage had taken place. If a marriage had taken place, then Kuleni's actions could not legally be charged as rape under the laws at that time.[73] An older male relative of the accused brothers testified at the trial that the woman's abduction and treatment were consistent with the custom of *ukuthwala*. He also stated that he, as head of the clan, had come to Kuleni's homestead on the occasion of the second abduction to slaughter an ox as part of the marriage ceremony: "There was a bride present. . . . I first saw this Complainant as a bride." The ox's slaughtering was a necessary part of a marriage feast, and the man's testimony supported the defense's contention that Kuleni had married the woman in a traditionally acceptable fashion.

The woman's father returned from Johannesburg to be a witness at the trial. He testified that, before the abduction by Kuleni, he had arranged a marriage for his daughter with a different man, but she had refused him. This experience led him to allow the girl's uncle to arrange another marriage and collude with Kuleni to kidnap his daughter. The father had known in advance about the arrangement: "My late brother Nkongolo informed me by letter while I was in Johannesburg of her proposed marriage to Accused No. 1 Kuleni. I agreed. . . . [The] girl was being asked for in marriage by Kuleni. He said he was satisfied with the suitor because he had paid dowry to him (Nkongolo)." Thus, the father confirmed that the uncle had helped arrange the kidnapping. He also noted that, because his daughter was a minor (at age twenty), they had the legal right to do so. The testimony of the woman's father and Kuleni's elder relative led the jury to find the defendants not guilty of kidnapping and rape.[74] In short, the jury effectively ratified the use of force and sexual violence to compel a young woman to marry because that use of force was supposedly traditional.

This case is distressing in its details of the multiple sexual assaults and the candid way that witnesses discussed what happened. Beyond the individual case, however, what is most disturbing is the apparent acceptance by the Cape legal system of this kind of violence against women in the name of customary marriage and tradition. The legal system in the 1930s tolerated and even endorsed violence against women if defendants could satisfactorily couch that violence in terms of "tradition" or "custom."[75]

Abduction marriages were common in the 1930s and later. For example, the anthropologist Monica Wilson noted that of twenty-six marriages that she investigated among the rural Mpondo population in the 1930s, five were marriages that parents had openly arranged; another five resulted from abductions; thirteen couples had eloped, and in three other cases the women involved had been married by their parents to men whom they did not like, and they had subsequently run away to live with their lovers.[76] Thirty years later, in the early 1960s, the Bantu Affairs commissioner in Libode (also in Mpondoland) reported that "only in a minority of cases does a public [marriage] ceremony known as 'umdudo' take place. The majority of customary unions result from 'ukugcagca' (elopement) and 'ukutwala' [abduction]."[77] While these comments are not conclusive evidence that abductions had become more frequent, they do show that abduction marriages had become legally and socially acceptable across the rural population, regardless of how young women felt about being abducted. They also show that the state had officially accepted *ukuthwala*—and whatever force might be entailed—as a legitimate, traditional form of marriage.

ABDUCTION MARRIAGE AS TRADITION

The frequency of abduction marriages suggests that there was a connection between official policy and traditional authority. Local officials condoned the practice as long as it followed rules that officials understood as part of the tradition. For their parts, parents and young men found *ukuthwala* to be a convenient way of contracting a marriage that got around any objections the prospective brides had. *Ukuthwala* became not just an acceptable but also a respectable and legal practice that many people saw as a legitimate element of traditional culture.

The violence that was associated with *ukuthwala* might simply have been an expedient way of carrying out abductions. Yet the use of violence against recalcitrant women may also have become one way of defining masculinity, as historian Anne Mager suggests: "Thus, for many, to be masculine was to assert male control over females, to extract feminine obedience literally through the wielding of sticks."[78] Men were allowed to use physical force to control women's bodies and they successfully mobilized the concept of tradition to assert their legal control over women in the state's courts. In contrast, women who tried to escape arranged and abduction marriages in the 1930s and later could not protect their autonomy in the courts. Women could not cite a tradition of a woman's right to be consulted, and the state had no vested interest in allowing women to assert their independence. The patriarchal elements of African traditional culture survived in the legal system because they could be retooled to achieve the state's goals of keeping African families in the countryside and maintaining control.

This reconstruction of the meaning of abduction marriage as an embodiment of tradition thus took place against the backdrop of official support for elders' rights over young women. Magistrates' acceptance of abduction marriages did not give young men free rein to take any young women they wanted in the countryside using whatever force was necessary: the state required the guardian's consent.

A case from 1951 in Libode provides evidence of the legal constraints on young men carrying out abduction marriages. In this case, two men kidnapped a teenage girl while she was at a stream drawing water in her home district of Tsolo. At the men's trial for kidnapping, the girl testified that she had never met them before. They approached her, knocked her down, and tied a rope around her neck. They then began to drag her: "While they did this I screamed and struggled but they overpowered me and I could not struggle [anymore]. Accused No. 2 started to hit me."[79] She was forced by the first accused to have sex with him, and then the abductors began walking her to their home in Libode. They spent the night on the road, and on the second day, she was again forced to have sex and was then taken to the young men's homestead. Finally, on the third day, she was able to escape, and she reported what had happened to the son of the local headman.

The headman took her to the police, and they began the investigation that ultimately led to the men's arrest and subsequent trial. The legality of the abduction depended on whether the girl's guardian had consented to the kidnapping. The girl's parents had died and left her brother as her guardian; however, he was away at work, leaving the girl's aunt as her acting guardian. The aunt testified that she had not arranged the abduction and did not consent to the marriage. The aunt's testimony as guardian sealed the abductors' fate: no marriage had occurred, and therefore they had committed a criminal kidnapping. The two men were convicted and sentenced to nine months in jail.[80] This outcome demonstrated that the state's overwhelming concern was to reinforce the authority of women's guardians to determine marriage partners and maintain control over the family. This authority made it more difficult for young women to leave their parents' homes for any reason, and it shored up the power of parents and guardians over both young women and men.

Allowing parentally approved abduction marriages may have been one way that state policies attempted to force African families, and particularly women, to remain in the rural areas. However, it was not the only response that state officials had to the problem of young women "roaming about town." In the late 1950s and early 1960s, the apartheid state extended pass laws to all African women, despite opposition by the African National Congress and other organizations.[81] The extension of pass laws to women were part of an attempt to implement "grand apartheid" in which Africans in the cities were "temporary sojourners" with no political rights.

The restrictions on women's migration also spoke to the anxieties held by many African men that they were losing control over their families. But it was not just African men who approved of controlling women through marriage. Some African women also condoned abduction marriages and the physical coercion that accompanied them. Thus, the persistence of *ukuthwala* was not simply about men controlling women with the assistance of the state; nor was it merely about trading young women for cattle as much of the commentary on the 2009 incident in Lusikisiki suggested. Women themselves, particularly older married women and those who had reconciled themselves to their own abduction marriages, were willing to uphold the custom as traditional and saw the resulting marriages as the glue that held rural society together. In describing *ukuthwala* among Mpondo people in the 1930s, Monica Wilson suggested that girls expected to marry when they were older teens and were often willing to reconcile themselves to abduction marriages. Wilson depicted a typical abduction: "She is seized when walking abroad, hustled along with much shouting and some blows, and taken to the groom's kraal [homestead]." Wilson explained that the girl's resistance was usually no more than a sham: "It is seemly that she should make a great show of resistance, even though she is pleased to marry the man who has taken her, and sometimes girls lie down and are dragged along the ground." Such marriages were, according to Wilson, "considered quite respectable" by African families, and the girl's weeping and active resistance were commonly understood as indications of her modesty and proper upbringing and not as evidence of real despair or outrage.[82]

This reading of abduction marriage as more or less benign and accepted by African women was echoed in another observer's writings. Joan Broster, an author who grew up in the Transkei, described the *ukuthwala* custom as she understood it in the 1950s and 1960s: "No girl will be captured without a fight, and she must make the men extend themselves even if only for show, for no one must be allowed to think that she brazenly wants to be taken in marriage. As soon as she is caught she sets up a peculiar ululating wail known as the *thwala* cry."[83] The force the abductors used was often considerable and Broster witnessed a few abductions that upset her. On one occasion, a young woman who had worked in Broster's family-owned shop was abducted. An older African woman who also saw the woman dragged away tried to allay Broster's worries by telling her the story of her own abduction experience many years before. Her paternal uncle (her father being dead) had conspired in her abduction. He

"Young Xhosa man and women, Transkei, South Africa." Photograph by Constance Stuart Larrabee, 1947. EEPA 1998-061092. Used with permission of the Constance Stuart Larrabee Collection, Eliot Elisofon Photographic Archives, National Museum of African Art, Smithsonian Institution.

had let the prospective groom's family know when they could grab his niece. This young woman had struggled against the several men who took her, even taking a large stone and successfully striking one of her abductors on the forehead hard enough to draw blood. But when she picked up a second stone, "a young *mfana* [adolescent boy] hit her over the head with his [fighting] stick, cutting open her scalp so that the blood ran, and today she carries a two-inch scar." On the day following the kidnapping, her uncle counseled her to accept her fate, saying, "We wish you to stay here [with the groom's family] and not to be a silly girl" by trying to run away from the marriage. [84]

When another young woman whom Broster knew was kidnapped for marriage by a middle-aged man, this same experienced, older African woman remonstrated with Broster over her visible distress. She said to Broster, "*Sukubabuhlungu—linjalo isoko.* (Don't hurt and upset yourself—it is our custom)." And she continued: "He is a good man and will be a kind husband. Old men make the best husbands. . . . They have learned *Induku ayinnamzi'*—the stick destroys the home."[85] Broster did not comment on the irony inherent in this statement: the man was using the stick literally to create the home by beating the woman into marriage.

As Broster recounted the conclusion to this story, some weeks later, she saw the young woman who had been abducted and described how "she had blossomed into a lovely young matron, and she was radiantly happy." Broster asked her if she was pleased with her husband, and "she giggled and said, 'Well it isn't too bad, although of course you know that I never wanted to marry him, but he is all right. I have no complaints.'"[86] Broster's ultimate conclusion about abduction marriages was therefore similar to that of Wilson: that abduction marriages were normal, often condoned and arranged by the young women's parents, and, crucially, that they were also commonly accepted by the young women involved. Moreover, older women often approved of abduction marriages. They defended them as traditional, despite the resistance displayed by the women and the physical force used to complete the abductions.

What possibly bothered Broster as she witnessed these abductions (although she never explicitly stated it), and what is troubling to anyone in the twenty-first century reading about abduction marriages, was how much these cases sound like narratives of sexual assault. And in fact, abduction cases that ended up in court sometimes became rape cases (when sexual intercourse occurred) if the women's guardians did not consent to the marriages. Both Wilson and Broster played down the violence involved in the practice because several African women told them that they had experienced these marriages and saw them as a matter of custom. As part of everyday life, physical coercion and *ukuthwala* were something they expected and accepted, and other young women should also expect and accept. There is support for this point of view in one of the court cases discussed earlier in this chapter: the young woman who was kidnapped on the road to Queenstown in 1915 cried for help when she and her abductor met some older women on the road. These women advised her "to go as all women have to be married in this way under Native Custom."[87] The young woman in that particular case successfully enlisted her family to contest and annul the marriage, but not all women had the same resources available to them.

Abduction Marriages as Domestic Violence

The fact that some women seemed to accept physical coercion as an element of an abduction marriage resonates with evidence collected in several recent studies on violence among sexual intimates. Adam Ashforth notes that many Africans living in Soweto in the late 1990s discussed certain types of physical violence within the family as "discipline": "'Discipline' is something meted out to children by their parents and to 'comrades' by their leaders when they misbehave—and to women by their men."[88] Ashforth cites a survey on domestic violence conducted by sociologists at the University of the Witwatersrand that found that half of the women they interviewed said they were "beaten regularly or severely" by their intimate partners, but "96.1 percent of all respondents claimed that no one in their household had been 'attacked by someone known to them,' suggesting that domestic violence or spouse abuse was not thought of in the same way as violent crime."[89] The concept of certain types of violence being justifiable as "discipline" rests on the belief that African men are patriarchs motivated not by anger or selfishness but by a desire to maintain social harmony.

But this idea of justifiable male power over women can quickly transform into less specific assumptions of the right to control: Ashforth notes that "among young men, even those without strong ties to patriarchal forms of custom and tradition, the perception of wives and girlfriends as 'property' under their control is strong."[90] We saw evidence of men considering women as property in Peter Mti's testimony to the Native Affairs Commission in 1903 when he commented that women believed that abduction marriages increased their "marketable value." If men thought that they had bought the right to control their wives and that they legitimately kidnapped them, they might have felt greater autonomy to punish them at will.

Similarly, a study done by three anthropologists on women's attitudes toward forced sex in the rural Eastern Cape in the 1999–2001 period shows some acceptance by women of violence within the context of long-term intimate relationships.[91] The study found that young women were very unlikely to describe forced or coerced sex as rape or assault when committed by men with whom they had ongoing sexual relationships. This unwillingness to label forced sex as rape resulted from women's assumptions that it was normal for men to use coercion and physical force to obtain sex, even with women who were their regular intimate partners. Also, women saw their involvement in ongoing relationships with men as heightening their own social status even if the men sometimes forced them to have sex. Women's reluctance to call such forced sex "rape" was also partly owing to their unwillingness to see themselves as "rape victims," a label that entailed a loss of self-esteem, identity, and possibly social status.[92] Thus, not using the term "rape" for forced sex was part of a complex social and psychological calculation made by the young women. They saw forced sex as "normal," and they backed away from the possible consequences to their self-esteem and social status of taking on the label of "rape victim."

Sociologist Deborah Posel has discussed women's reluctance to label various types of forced sex as "rape" as one way the topic of the sexual victimization of Africans, particularly women, was marginalized during the apartheid years. She writes: "The prism of race also had a powerful effect on the apartheid state's limited sightings of sexual violence. . . . Recognition that sexual violence was widespread became exactly the basis on which the issue was ignored."[93] What is interesting, though, about the cases from rural South Africa discussed above is that it was not only the state that had "limited sightings" of sexual violence: it also seemed to be many Africans themselves. Posel acknowledges that this blindness existed among Africans and analyzes it by suggesting that the African family's economic and cultural logic made it less likely that women would want to label forced sex as rape because to do so might jeopardize family cohesion.[94] Posel does not directly tie this insight to a discussion of abduction marriage, but she does show that certain types of violence by men against women became widely accepted in the African population. The routine nature of violence in sexual relationships has also been analyzed by Memory Mphaphuli and Letitia Smuts. They conclude that "sexual violence in intimate relationships occupies an unusual social space, as, although hidden, it is also an example of the everyday."[95]

The current problem of sexual violence in South Africa may have its roots in the official treatment of sexual violence as a traditional element of marriage in the late nineteenth and early twentieth centuries. By the 1930s to 1960s, the white-controlled state's official position toward *ukuthwala*, accepting it as a customary form of marriage, was part of the broader refusal to see sexual violence as criminal when that violence occurred to African women. Traditional marriage practices, including abduction marriages, thus continued under the reimagined form of customary law practiced in the rural native reserves, areas that later became homelands under apartheid policies.

But the state was not the only relevant actor in the historical process that constructed abduction marriages as both traditional and legal in the twentieth century. Prospective husbands performed the abductions and often did so with the collaboration of parents and guardians; they sometimes did so with the ultimate acceptance of the abducted girls. Many women, both as mothers and as brides, apparently went along with these marriages and encouraged other women to go along with them too. Not all women consented to these marriages, but the daughters' wishes were rarely considered relevant: if they were under twenty-one and their parents or guardians condoned the wedding, then the claims of tradition trumped the daughters' personal preferences.

The use of force in completing these abductions raises significant and complicated questions of its own. Was the violence used by abductors and young women's resistance to that violence usually just a form of performance, as some sources suggest? Or were they significant evidence about the women's states of mind and, more specifically, of their reluctance to marry? Was outright violence commonly a part of all abduction marriages or just of those that became criminal cases? The evidence here is, at best, equivocal and hard to interpret.

On the one hand, there is evidence of certain young women putting up much more than token resistance and of women running away repeatedly from their abductors and reporting the abductions as crimes to headmen and police. On the other hand, some older African women told young women who were being abducted that these marriages were simply part of the culture and something that any woman of marriageable age might expect. Despite these contradictory possibilities, the state from the 1930s onward usually sided with the abducted women's parents or guardians. If the parents condoned the abduction and marriage, then the marriage was legal; if the parents were against the kidnapping, then it became criminal, and any forced sexual acts became legally prosecutable as rapes.

And some women did reconcile themselves to their abduction marriages. These women took apparent pride in becoming both the stewards of tradition and the stalwarts of the family in the rural areas; they also saw themselves as the bearers of a certain kind of toughness for having endured the abductions that created their homesteads. The fact that at least some women physically fought the abductions or resisted by running away or notifying the authorities indicates that not all women were willing to go along with the ritual, no matter how customary it may have been. Resistance carried its own hazards, however, as women who resisted were open to even greater levels of coercion and physical violence, as well as social stigma, all legitimated in the name of tradition.[96]

Some additional questions remain. Does this reading of abduction marriages as essentially violent tell us anything about African women's political consciousness living in the rural areas? Did individual women's decisions about whether to consent to their abductions or to resist by either fighting back or by reporting them to the authorities, or indirectly by preemptively eloping with a lover or running away to town, reflect either social conditions or broader political choices? Did the violence of the kidnappings and their aura of tradition cause or inflame more generalized violence against women in later decades?

In suggesting some answers to those questions, it is essential to remember that African women were not a uniform community. Their responses to the problems raised by abductions were conditioned by their ages and educations, their families' social and economic status, their religious beliefs and broader life experiences, and undoubtedly by their personalities and individual family dynamics. Moreover, a young woman who objected to her abduction had either to run away or else she had to find an advocate willing to support her in court. The latter strategy usually meant finding an older male family member who endorsed her objections and had the legal standing to bring the case. If a woman with such support took her abductor to court, the abduction could be prosecuted as a crime; without such support, it was a marriage. Under such circumstances, women's acceptance of *ukuthwala* could have been a performance delivered under "a situation of duress."[97] Young women often had to engage in social navigation, making choices between difficult options. Some African women assessed the dangers and possibilities of their situations in the rural areas and chose to accept *ukuthwala* as their best path into the future.[98]

Regardless of the many individual differences among women though, violence became a legally and socially accepted way of forcing girls and women into marriages in the name of social continuity and tradition. To some degree, this forging of abduction marriages was part of what Ferguson has called a "new customary" that helped to defend some space for African familial autonomy from erosion by white-dominated social and political values.[99] Yet limited autonomy for the African family frequently came at the direct expense of a woman's right to consent to a marriage partner. Women's acceptance of physical violence or even social coercion in marriage had more to do with the gendered political and legal structures of the twentieth century than it did with adherence to an unaltered tradition transmitted directly from precolonial society. The acceptance by some women of their forcible abductions was part of a strategy of survival within a system that was stacked against them.

Coda

The 2009 case of abduction marriage in Lusikisiki described earlier in this chapter provoked a great deal of controversy among South Africans, with the debate largely—if somewhat misleadingly—framed as a binary contest between "modern" laws and "traditional" customs. By 2009 the legal system had changed: women's legal rights were better defined, although the idea of tradition playing a significant role in determining women's rights and social status, especially in the rural areas, persisted.[100] The *Sunday Times*, in a follow-up story on the abduction marriage at the heart of the controversy, interviewed a retired African academic who "descried the unorthodox revival of ukuthwalwa, saying it did not fit the modern world. 'Children are literally being sold, almost to the highest bidder. This is paedophilia. . . . In the old days men abducted women who were of marriage age, not minors. This is not culture,' said the academic who added that 'in the past, girls who were abducted were not raped. The girl was kept safe until she accepted the love proposal from the man.'"[101] This academic criticized the ongoing practice of abduction marriage as being out of step with the modern world. Yet the idealized description he gave of how people practiced the custom in the past suggests that he attached a good deal of nostalgia to the idea of traditional culture, particularly regarding gender roles.

The legal system in the twenty-first century has changed from the old colonial and apartheid legal systems. Under customary law in the colonial and apartheid eras, white magistrates might well have deemed the 2009 abduction case legal. The case satisfied at least some of the criteria that such magistrates used to determine if a valid marriage had occurred: in collaboration with the girl's guardians, the older man abducted the girl and subsequently paid a bridewealth of three cows to the girl's family. A magistrate from an earlier era might have thought her too young at age fourteen to be married. Still, he might just as easily have overlooked that detail had the girl escaped and reported the marriage to the authorities.

While no one quoted in any of the press reports openly defended this particular abduction marriage when it came to light in 2009, certain African authorities defended the broader practice of abduction marriage as an element of tradition. A BBC reporter quoted Prince Xhanti Sigcawu from the Eastern Cape, who commented that "'ukuthwalwa like all our other customs was and remains an important part of who we are as people,' he says. 'There is nothing wrong with the practice when it is done in the right way—which is when the girl is at the right age and the parents are involved and agree.'"[102] It is worth emphasizing that Sigcawu's objection to the girl's abduction stemmed from her being only fourteen years of age at the time of the marriage. He was not concerned about a lack of consent on the girl's part as long as the parents "are involved." The same news report framed the essential tension within abduction marriage as a conflict between modernity and tradition. It quoted a spokesman for the Congress of Traditional Leaders of South Africa, Chief Pathekile

Holomisa, who thought that the practice "has been corrupted by greed for material purposes. It has no place in today's society."[103]

Discussing the persistence of abduction marriages as an issue of modernity versus tradition obscures some essential characteristics of intimate partner violence and sexual violence that persist in twenty-first-century South Africa. Women have been more often successful in exercising their independence and avoiding abduction marriages. However, violence and sexuality still seem to be linked in common expectations, whether that sexuality encompasses the violence inherent in abduction marriages or physical violence against intimate partners. And women's families still have a strong voice in determining their fates. The young woman whose abduction was at the heart of the 2009 controversy noted that she had begged her aunt and brother not to allow the man to abduct her, but they felt that her wishes were irrelevant. In an echo of headman Toto's statement in 1883 to the Cape's Commission on Native Laws and Customs, she told the BBC reporter that "they told me that I didn't have a say in the matter."[104] The girl was not consulted, and it was the laws and policies of the white-controlled state in the first half of the twentieth century that had carefully cultivated the roots of this forceful silencing.

3

Deaths in the Family

Supernatural Harms and Violent Remedies

In 1935 a murder took place in Butterworth district in the Transkei. The death became the subject of a preparatory examination in the magistrate's court before going on to a judge and an all-white, all-male jury in the circuit court. The prosecution's case accused a sixty-year-old woman and her twenty-year-old daughter of murdering the younger woman's baby boy shortly after his birth.

From witness testimonies, a story emerged that the baby's young mother was an unmarried woman who had returned to her rural home after spending some time living in East London. It became evident to the neighbors that the young woman was pregnant, and shortly after returning home to live with her mother, the young woman gave birth to the child. The two women hid the fact that the younger woman had delivered the child and the child died—the victim of a deliberate killing—shortly after. Suspicious neighbors investigated and called the headman in, who then brought the case to the notice of the white authorities. Interwoven in this story were accusations of witchcraft and immorality made against the women and of incest against the local headman.[1] While this family's story was both tragic and extreme, it illuminates the hardships of rural life that had become common for African families in the context of white rule and the occasionally desperate actions people took to try to navigate their circumstances.

The history of forced and abduction marriages discussed in the previous chapter highlighted the legal and social opportunities permitted to African elders, particularly men, in choosing marriage partners for their daughters during white rule in the rural areas. These opportunities allowed for the use of coercion and violence in creating marriages in the name of preserving tradition. Beyond the control of sons and daughters, however, the broader history of rural family life also reverberated with conflicts over gender roles, cultural norms, and morality that sometimes resulted in physical violence.

Much of the existing literature on familial violence in South Africa has focused on the violence committed by men and adolescent boys against women and girls. Yet Africans have historically understood women to be powerful and potentially disruptive. People believed that women could call upon their ancestors to protect them and use various familiars or supernatural medicines to harm enemies and rivals.[2] Beyond their putative magical powers, women had moral and economic power in the household. Women maintained the homestead, raised children, and often tended livestock and crops, particularly when men were away as labor migrants. These duties gave women a great deal of control over the daily lives of their families. Yet with greater control came the possibility of greater blame if there was illness or death in the family or if the homestead did not thrive.

This chapter analyzes several specific cases of violence within rural African families in the Transkeian region from the 1880s through the mid-1960s, as documented in the court records of magistrates. The relatively small number of events and cases discussed in this chapter illustrates common conflicts and the significance of beliefs in supernatural powers in framing local disputes. They also allow us to see women not primarily as victims of violence but as people who exercised different types of authority within households and within African society in the countryside. Women helped revise and hold together African traditional culture during a period of flux in the social, economic, and political structures of broader South African society. They often had to use social navigation to maneuver through various older social practices and colonially constructed constraints to protect themselves and preserve their families. While these social changes were substantial and frequently disadvantageous, a few women could pursue new opportunities, such as becoming diviners, that combined traditional norms with innovations. However, the maneuvers and options that women adopted generated additional strife within their families and among neighbors.

The evidence presented in the court cases below demonstrates the frequency with which violence within the family stemmed from beliefs in supernatural actors and witchcraft. These supernatural beliefs also linked to conflict between neighbors and sometimes to the resistance people mounted toward state policies. In this chapter, I argue that one can understand both violence and witchcraft accusations within rural families and communities as attempts to gain control over precarious social and political circumstances. People used witchcraft accusations and violence, sometimes together, sometimes separately, to isolate and eradicate causes of social disruption and punish the instigators. In making these accusations, people hoped to stabilize their own positions and preserve a way forward for themselves and their families. The connections between allegations of witchcraft against a specific family or community member and the broader feelings of insecurity forged by the colonial and apartheid states need an in-depth investigation in the rural context.

Framing Family Violence: The Scholarly Background

Most analyses of violence within rural South African families have looked at broad political and economic factors as causes, including the effects of male labor migration, the decline of the rural economy, and the political powerlessness of Africans within the colonial and apartheid systems. One common explanation is that violence resulted because responsible adult males were not routinely present to exercise their social authority and discipline younger men.[3] A second explanation is that men generally, frustrated by their loss of authority, vented their frustration by dominating other family members, sometimes violently.[4] The literature on masculinity, in particular, has put forward the idea that violence became an essential element of masculine identities.[5] Robert Morrell notes that "while hegemonic masculinity generally operates without recourse to violence, it is the case that the capacity for and threat of violence underpins it. On occasion, violence becomes brutally visible."[6] In a similar vein, Clifton Crais concluded that men's infliction of violence—both on other men and women—in the political unrest that erupted in the 1950s in the Cape Province was an attempt to recapture their masculine identities while also engaging in political resistance.[7] This literature has located the underlying causes of violence in the broad social and economic system of inequality and oppression and in the performance of masculinity; there has been much less emphasis on contributing causes within the particular households affected.

But while it is clear that social and economic oppression created underlying tensions, these analyses do not completely capture the nature of violence within families.[8] First, they imply that men were either the only ones capable of violence or that only men's violence was socially significant.[9] Second, they indicate that men have historically taken out their frustrations stemming from structural oppression on their immediate family members, who had even less power than they did within the system developed by colonialism and apartheid. Moreover, in the South African context, many of the scholarly analyses of family violence have focused on the apartheid and postapartheid periods, thus leaving unexamined the earlier historical changes in domestic tensions and gender identities that may have precipitated violence within families.[10]

Finally, many of these scholarly accounts give scant attention to tensions within families as precipitating causes of the violence and to the ways that certain beliefs in the supernatural may have affected the outcome. In particular, witchcraft accusations frequently were at the root of familial violence, with family members and neighbors suspected of causing harm through supernatural means. Historian Katherine Luongo has elaborated on the necessity for considering witchcraft accusations in the context of acts of domestic violence in colonial Kenya as one way for scholars to gain a broader perspective about intimate violence.[11] Violence arose within the context of cultural norms, and some of these norms included beliefs in the supernatural powers available to women. Suspicions about women's capabilities, including the capacity to be violent themselves or unleash the violence of supernatural familiars, reveal the instability of gender roles and deepening social crises in the rural areas particularly. These suspicions often led to witchcraft accusations. Women responded and adapted to these accusations by using whatever resources they had available. These included mobilizing family networks to protect themselves, defying accusers, and increasingly, enlisting the assistance of state policies that criminalized witchcraft accusations. Women's use of these resources helped protect them as individuals and were evidence of how they employed social navigation to survive. Yet over time, their reliance on the state for partial protection may have heightened suspicions about women's propensity for violence.

Supernatural Beliefs, Violence, and Criminal Courts

Beliefs in witchcraft and the supernatural have a long history in the region. The turmoil created by the colonial takeover in the 1880s and its overthrow of precolonial ruling systems combined with the intrusion of new economic forces and threats to make witchcraft accusations common. The Reverend J. A. Chalmers testified to the 1882–83 Cape Native Laws and Customs Commission that allegations of witchcraft seemed to increase at the time of "the cattle sickness" in the 1850s.[12] And Major Henry Elliot, then chief magistrate of Thembuland (part of the Transkeian region of the Cape), testified to the same commission that, shortly after the colonial takeover of the area, accusations of witchcraft within families had become "a very common offence." Women were often the focus of these suspicions. Continuing his 1882 testimony, Major

Elliot asserted, "It is not unfrequent [*sic*] that a woman is smelt out [accused of using witchcraft], and that she is driven away from her home on a charge of having caused the illness of a beast [cow] or child."[13] Testimony from a group of Africans, including the chief of the Thembu and several headmen, echoed this view: "It is a very common thing among ourselves for a doctor [diviner] to smell out a woman, and say she has bewitched her husband, and the people believe it, and the husband as well."[14]

One reason why married women were vulnerable to witchcraft accusations came from a wife's status as an outsider within her husband's family. However, it was not only their marginality that made them vulnerable: women's significant power within families also made them liable to such accusations.[15] People's suspicions of women related to their social power within families as well as their outsider status. Beliefs in supernatural powers had long been part of African cultures in southern Africa. These supernatural powers included both the relatively benign powers used by the ancestors as well as the more malevolent powers of witches and supernatural familiars. Witchcraft familiars were often mythical figures, such as the *thikoloshe* (a "small, hairy being, having the form of a man,"[16] who performed evil deeds for the person who controlled him), *icanti* (a magical snake that could assume the form of any animal), and *impundulu* (the lightning bird that brought lightning strikes to the huts of enemies and who also caused illnesses). Witches were also assumed to use various substances, including herbs and animal fats, to create charms that would harm their enemies. Thus, calling a person a "witch" was not a casual insult. Instead, it labeled the person as evil and carried an implicit and sometimes explicit threat of violent punishment suitable for such an antisocial person.[17]

An analysis of witchcraft accusations immediately faces the question of what we mean by "witchcraft." T. O. Ranger has suggested that scholars have too often collapsed various beliefs into the one category of "witchcraft."[18] He concludes that this flattened concept of witchcraft evokes an idea of African "otherness" that ultimately puts Africans outside historical understanding. Yet the word "witchcraft" appears repeatedly in the testimony of court cases. In Transkeian districts from the 1880s onward, most of the court clerks who transcribed this evidence were Africans, literate in both English and isiXhosa. Their translation of various Xhosa words for supernatural actions as "witchcraft" was undoubtedly conditioned by the law and particularly by the criminalization of a range of actions emerging out of "witchcraft" beliefs. White officials in many African colonies tried to stamp out spiritual beliefs and practices that they lumped together as witchcraft.[19] This flattened notion of witchcraft, therefore, was the contemporary product of colonial rule. The term reflected the views of white officials that these practices were an immoral and dangerous holdover from the precolonial past.

Far from being static precolonial holdovers, however, witchcraft beliefs and accusations proliferated as colonial rule advanced. Africans faced numerous problems created by white rule, and as state policies and officials became increasingly oppressive, supernatural malevolence became part of a common explanation among Africans for those problems. J. H. Soga, writing in the 1930s about Xhosa culture, has an extensive chapter on beliefs in the supernatural, as does anthropologist Monica Wilson in her study of Mpondo culture. Soga wrote that the priest-diviner, often misleadingly called a "witch doctor," was a revered figure who mediated between the ancestors and their descendants and divined people who had committed evil. "It is an accepted axiom," Soga suggested, "among Xosas [*sic*] that no serious illness or death can take place except through the evil influence (*u-poselo*) of some individuals, usually termed *igqwira* (witch or wizard)."[20] More specifically, Wilson noted that "accusations of witchcraft and sorcery are reflections of the quarrels and tensions between wives and their husband's relatives, between co-wives, lovers, and neighbours, but they are also an aggravating cause of these quarrels."[21] Soga's and Wilson's observations provide evidence that Africans themselves discussed various malevolent events as resulting from witchcraft, even though they also had other isiXhosa words that made distinctions about different types of supernatural powers. The meaning of "witchcraft" thus became polysemic, as Africans themselves used the word in English to denote a number of different practices.[22]

Witchcraft allegations surfaced in trials relating to violence in domestic settings dating back to the early colonial period in the Transkei and Natal. Witnesses, defendants, and complainants often testified how witchcraft accusations had sparked confrontations that resulted in assaults, arson, divorces, and occasionally murders. Family members and neighbors frequently accused women of using either supernatural powers or familiars for their own malign purposes. Ancestors could also intervene to protect their own kin from others or punish their kin if they felt neglected; these interventions also fell under the rubric of the supernatural if not always included in the category of witchcraft. The willingness of ancestors to meddle in family life was another reason why people suspected wives of causing disasters, since wives brought their ancestors into their in-laws' homes.[23]

Some Africans consulted diviners to sort out the possible supernatural causes for problems, especially ones that persisted or were catastrophic.[24] A diviner was supposed to help in the process of healing the family and allowing

"Xhosa men building homestead, Transkei, South Africa." Photograph by Constance Stuart Larrabee, 1947. EEPA 1998-061174. Used with permission of the Constance Stuart Larrabee Collection, Eliot Elisofon Photographic Archives, National Museum of African Art, Smithsonian Institution.

the family to rebuild the homestead. When the diviner decided that a family member or a neighbor had used witchcraft, it could lead to a physical assault against the "witch" or to a divorce after the accused wife was driven away from her husband's home. If an assault against the named witch occurred, the state considered it a crime; if a divorce resulted, the wife's family had grounds for not returning the original bridewealth if they could prove that their daughter had been singled out as a witch and driven away by her husband's family.

However, even having a consultation with a diviner could be a crime under Cape law. The 1895 Witchcraft Ordinance made it illegal for someone to "impute the use of non-natural means" to another person, that is, accuse another person of witchcraft. White state officials used the terms "supernatural" and "non-natural" as synonyms for witchcraft and considered witchcraft beliefs to be both harmful and imaginary.[25] They saw diviners as frauds even though they accepted the fact that many Africans believed in their powers. Thus, diviners could also be prosecuted for fraud if their clients were unhappy and decided to file a complaint against them.

Walter Stanford, who in 1893 was an influential magistrate in the Transkei, described his understanding of the categories of witchfinders and witchdoctors: "The witch-doctors are a distinct and powerful class. . . . [A diviner] learns to detect and counteract by communication with supernatural powers, and their aid, the spells, enchantments, poisons, or other concoctions of a material kind, used by wizards and witches in spreading disease or other evil among the people and cattle. He thus becomes a guardian and protector of life and property, and when fully qualified, emerges from his seclusion with a certain sacredness about his person and calling, which has led to these men being called priests as well as doctors."[26] Stanford thus acknowledged that diviners helped people understand why catastrophic events occurred and what steps they might take to remedy them. When diviners found themselves criminally indicted in colonial magistrates' courtrooms for having practiced their professions, it pitted one form of morality and justice against another.

The state's criminalization of witchcraft accusations was rooted in its denial that witchcraft was real. But in trying court cases, magistrates had to walk a fine line: they knew that people who assaulted a named witch were acting on their sincere beliefs. Thus, even though magistrates did not believe in the reality of witchcraft themselves, they understood that many Africans believed it and took actions based on those beliefs.

Many Africans who came into contact with the judicial system understood the official attitude toward allegations of witchcraft, particularly after the first two decades of colonial rule in the region. As a result, they may have tried to keep them out of the official eye. Nevertheless, specific episodes came to the magistrates' courts. For example, people accused of being witches sometimes reported their accusers to headmen or magistrates, particularly if they had been physically attacked or threatened. Under these conditions, caught between competing notions of morality and justice, witnesses who provided testimony had to weigh what they said carefully. Yet even after considering the potential problems with the testimony in cases about allegations of witchcraft, the trial transcripts provide some remarkable evidence of the intimate nature of most witchcraft accusations and their connections to violence within families and communities.

Witchcraft accusations were often gendered and threatened violence. Many of the people accused of witchcraft were women, and during the twentieth century, many diviners were also women. People accused of witchcraft regularly suffered intimidation or direct physical harm, such as having their huts burnt down, to drive them away. The state's attitude toward witchcraft accusations did not dissuade everyone from making accusations and, by the 1950s, the state itself became the focus of some witchcraft allegations. Chapter 5 will discuss witchcraft allegations that crossed into the realm of anti-state politics in the 1950s and 1960s, but we will continue this chapter by returning to the tragic death of the baby in Butterworth.

A Baby's Death: Gender, Law, and Witchcraft Allegations

The death of the baby recounted at the outset of this chapter unleashed a series of accusations and counter-accusations that revealed tensions in rural African society. What started as a domestic tragedy—the young woman's secretive birth and her baby's untimely death—led the local headman to investigate the circumstances as a possible crime. Ultimately, the headman brought the case to the magistrate, who opened an inquiry.

The week before the magistrate opened the preparatory examination, a tense episode had unfolded at the home of the two women. Their neighbors confronted them about their suspicions regarding the baby's birth and subsequent disappearance. Initially, both women vigorously denied that any child had been born, even though neighbors knew the younger woman had been pregnant and it was clear at the time of the confrontation that she was no longer pregnant. When the local subheadman and headman arrived, summoned by a female neighbor who suspected that the baby had been either killed or deliberately exposed, the headman demanded that the younger woman be examined physically to confirm that she had given birth. As the headman's son (who was present at the confrontation) recounted, both women objected to the exam, and the younger woman tried to run away to escape it. He stated that "we went and brought her back about sunset then father told the [other] women to go and examine her."[27] As both of the women selected to do the physical exam recalled, "We examined [Accused] No. 2 by force."

The examination indicated that the younger woman had recently given birth even though her mother continued to deny it. According to witnesses, however, after the questioning continued, the young woman provided a new account of what had happened: "She said she had gone to the Kei River [nearby] and had there given birth to a child which she threw into the river."

No one believed this story. Instead, they searched the women's huts, especially the kitchen hut because a perceptive neighbor had noticed that its floor was freshly smeared with dung. The neighbor recollected: "We dug up the floor of the hut and found the dead body of a newly born child. . . . When the earth floor which covered it had been removed we called to No. 1 [the older woman] to take it out and she took it out and laid it down outside. I noticed a cut on the neck of the child. . . . [Accused] No. 1 . . . was again questioned and she said she did not know anything about this child and that her daughter must have done this without her knowledge." The condition of the body suggested to the district surgeon, who arrived at the scene after being summoned by the headman, that the baby boy had been born alive several days previously and had died because his throat had been cut.[28]

During the confrontation at the women's home, the subheadman asked the younger woman to identify the father of the child. She replied that the father was the headman of a neighboring location, who was her cousin and was also present. Then the daughter accused her mother of having killed the child.[29] The evidence of the baby's body and the conflicting stories and accusations surrounding his death led to both women being arrested and subjected to a preparatory examination in the magistrate's court. (All cases involving capital crimes first underwent preparatory examinations before being tried in the regular circuit court).

Questioned in court, both accused women stated that they had been beaten by the men present at the confrontation to force them to answer questions. They alleged that it was after the beating that the younger woman had changed her story and accused her cousin of being the dead child's father and her mother the child's killer. The older woman stated that one of the men had also accused her of being a witch. In court, that man denied that he made the allegation of witchcraft, but the confrontation was volatile enough that such a denunciation might have occurred.

The headman, for his part, denied that he was the father of the child and that he had ever had sexual relations with the younger woman. He testified that he had previously questioned her about her pregnancy. Noting that the young woman's brother had moved to East London and that she had gone there to visit, the headman continued, "I asked her why she allowed herself to be made pregnant by town boys whereas there were boys in the [rural] location [whom she might marry]. I made this statement as she had come from East London and there was a rumour current that she had been impregnated there." An East London friend of the younger woman confirmed that story and said she knew that the father was an Indian man with whom the young woman had been "sweethearting."[30]

At the end of the preparatory examination, the two accused women were held for trial in the circuit court. By the time of the actual trial, the older woman had changed her story. When asked to answer the charge of murder formally, she replied, "I admit I did this. I killed the child as I was exasperated against the father because he was a man with three wives and without any property or means to pay the damages to my daughter" for her pregnancy.[31] In this statement, the grandmother of the dead child continued to implicate the headman as the child's father, perhaps to shift the immorality of the child's birth and subsequent death onto him. In the ensuing murder trial, the all-white, all-male jury accepted the older woman's confession and found her guilty of murder. The jury recommended mercy for her, but the judge sentenced her to death. The jury acquitted the younger woman of any crime.

This case was both shocking and complex. Yet it captured the impact of broader social issues and beliefs, particularly some of the fears that swirled around women living independently, as these two women were. The older woman had been born in Kingwilliamstown, and it seems likely that she had moved to Butterworth when she married. However, no witness mentioned the older woman's husband; presumably, the marriage had either dissolved many years before these events or, more likely, the husband had died. Meanwhile, the son had migrated to East London, leaving the women living on their own.

Africans in this region often regarded women as needing male supervision to control them and believed that women were more likely to be witches. Witchcraft accusations could divide a family and turn violence inward toward family members. Widows and married women living on their own were often targets of witchcraft allegations, while at the same time, they suffered economically from having no close male family members to help them farm.[32] In this case, three of the men who participated in the confrontation at the huts were directly related: one was an in-law, another a cousin, and a third was a nephew. If one of these men did accuse the older woman of being a witch, as she alleged, it might have emerged from latent suspicions within the family about her status as a widow.

The confrontation also functioned as an assertion of patriarchal control over this household of women, although the conflict was not strictly one of men versus women. The men took charge of the interrogation, but a female neighbor had initially alerted the community that the younger woman might have given birth in secret. The neighbors used physical force to get the women to respond to their questions. When the younger woman initially ran away to avoid a physical examination, the witnesses all agreed that the men captured her and then had her forcibly examined by female neighbors. The two women also alleged that they were beaten as part of the interrogation, a deployment of coercion and violence to restore the moral order that had been upset by the women's actions. The child's killing was a stark indication to her neighbors of deceit and the presence of evil in the household. The men, who were both neighbors and kin, entered the homestead as investigators and judges. When they elicited a confession, they enlisted the state, in the form of the district surgeon, to complete the investigation and, in the form of the judicial system, to convict and pass sentences.

Violence and patriarchal authority were evident in the courtroom as well. The women faced hostile questions posed by the male prosecutor and the male judge, while white male lawyers managed their defense. An all-white, all-male jury convicted the older woman of murder, and a white judge pronounced the sentence. In this narrow reading of the case, the interests of the African men and women who initially investigated the child's death and those of the white judge and jury aligned as they came to the same conclusion that the child was murdered. In a broader reading of the case, though, the interests of Africans and whites did not align so neatly. For example, the question of whether women were more liable to be socially disruptive and violent was one on which the opinions of white state officials and Africans diverged. The Africans who investigated the matter believed both women were capable of violence. But in court, the jury was more merciful toward the younger woman. The Cape judicial system and the system of native law followed by magistrates had a history of leniency toward women whose newborn children had died, sometimes under suspicious circumstances. The judicial system also had a tough stance regarding witchcraft allegations and actions linked to them, as discussed below.

For their part, the neighbors held both women responsible for their actions. The fact that one of the men allegedly called the older woman a witch points to a fear that she was harboring an evil supernatural familiar and posed a threat to the community. A grandmother killing her grandchild was undoubtedly the root of this accusation, but beyond that, the fact that she buried the child beneath the floor of the kitchen hut most likely struck African observers as an intimation of the older woman's intent to use the baby's body for witchcraft or sorcery.

There was a history of Africans believing that people used body parts to create powerful medicines.[33] In 1881 Charles Brownlee, then chief magistrate of Griqualand East in the Cape, cited a particular episode in his answers to the Native Laws and Customs Commission. He noted that an older man had killed his three-year-old granddaughter: "The body of the child was eventually found concealed in a gully with some portions of the flesh cut away" to concoct a particular medicine.[34] Fifty years later, drawing on her research among the Mpondo, Monica Wilson described a belief that witches who killed people sometimes resurrected them to enslave them.[35] Wilson also reported a suspicion that some women had supernatural lovers known as *izulu*. An *izulu* had vampiric habits that required infanticide: "An *izulu* is said often to turn on its owner, demanding to suck the blood of her relatives. If she refuses, it kills her. When a mother is accused of having killed her own children it does not mean that she wanted to kill them, but 'she had an *izulu*, and she loved her own body better than her children.'"[36] This kind of selfish exercise of supernatural power was the hallmark of a witch—someone who would sacrifice her child to fulfill her desires.

Aside from the suspicions the neighbors may have had about the older woman's use of witchcraft, they knew that the circumstances surrounding the birth and death of the baby threatened the larger society. There were prescribed rituals connected to birth and death that involved neighbors, kin, and friends—practices that had not been followed with this child. Correctly performed rituals reaffirmed the community's connections with the ancestors and protected it from enemies; their nonperformance posed a threat by leaving the community exposed to angry ancestors or evil spirits.[37]

In sentencing the older woman to death, the white judge presiding at the trial may have responded to the hint of witchcraft practices surrounding the baby's death and the concealment of the body. Typically, courts had a complicated method for dealing with witchcraft-related crimes. A person convicted of murdering another to use the body parts for witchcraft usually faced the harshest punishment possible—death.[38] The fact that the judge imposed the death penalty on the older woman may have indicated that he had concluded there was some witchcraft-related reason for the child's death and strange burial.

Although the trial acquitted the younger woman of murder, the prosecution could potentially have charged her with a lesser crime: concealment of childbirth. It was a crime for women to give birth in secret, although in practice, the only women ever charged with this crime were those whose children died shortly after birth. Determining whether a baby had been born alive and then killed or had been stillborn and the body then abandoned or buried was difficult, particularly in rural areas where finding a baby's body might occur several days after the child's birth and death. The crime of concealment of childbirth was thus far easier to prove than murder and typically carried a much lighter penalty. Even so, concealment of childbirth was an uncommon charge brought against women in the Transkeian region: in Umtata district, for example, between the years 1887 and 1951, with the total population ranging from twenty thousand to fifty-five thousand, there was cumulatively a total of sixteen cases prosecuted for concealment of childbirth, and never more than three in any single year. Those cases that did go to trial demonstrate some of the stresses common in rural families.

Several concealment of childbirth cases across multiple rural districts provide examples of the kinds of circumstances that led to women harming their children. In Umtata, the magistrate in 1910 convicted a nineteen-year-old, unmarried woman of concealment and sentenced her to eighteen months' hard labor. The father of the child was a migrant laborer in Johannesburg. The young woman, who was described by her aunt as "a respectable girl," gave birth alone and then abandoned the baby.[39] A 1925 case from Butterworth resulted in the conviction of a woman for concealment, even though she admitted in court that she had covered her newborn child, intending to smother her. The accused woman was married, but her husband had been away in Cape Town for two years continuously and the child was not his. Despite the mother's confession, the district surgeon, who had examined the baby's body, did not think that the child had been born alive. The magistrate sentenced her to two and a half years in prison.[40]

One common trait of these concealment cases was that the accused women were either unmarried or had husbands who had been away as migrant laborers for extended periods. Most of the women expressed a sense of personal shame and despair when they testified at their trials and suggested that economic and social circumstances had precipitated their actions. In all cases, the women were reported to the authorities either by family members or neighbors who had carried out initial investigations independently. For example, in a 1939 case from Engcobo, a young woman convicted of concealment of childbirth was fined £10 or sentenced to six months in prison. She was a student who was engaged to be married, although her fiancé was not the baby's father. The fiancé broke off the engagement because of the pregnancy. She gave birth to the baby in secret and the baby died soon after, but the district surgeon could not determine why the baby had died.[41] In another Engcobo case, a sentence of nine months' imprisonment imposed by a magistrate in 1946 was significantly lessened on appeal to six months because of the absence of any evidence of violence on the deceased baby's body.[42] A woman in Tsolo in 1958 was convicted of concealment of childbirth after she admitted giving birth to a baby she had then deliberately exposed by placing it outside her home. The child's body disappeared and was never found. She stated in court that she had intentionally abandoned the baby because her husband had been at work in Johannesburg for several years, and the baby was not his. However, without the child's body to provide evidence of a live birth, the magistrate convicted her of concealment of childbirth and sentenced her to nine months' imprisonment with hard labor.[43]

These cases of the deaths of children demonstrated disturbing facts about the impact of male migrant labor on some families.[44] Much scholarly work on the psychological stresses of birth has documented that mothers in any culture or historical moment may develop depression, causing some to abandon or harm their babies.[45] The pressures on many rural African women of the 1910 to mid-1950s era may well have been unbearable as they tried to hold homes and families together. Some were poor and living on their own. Other women may have feared that a child born outside of marriage would threaten their relationships with their husbands. In all cases, the pregnancies threatened to push them outside the bounds of locally accepted morality. But the relatively lenient treatment they received when the state convicted them of concealment of childbirth—instead of murder—may have distressed many Africans within the community. From their point of view, these women had performed profoundly antisocial acts.

In the initial case of the two women in Butterworth, it seems likely that it was the direct evidence of assault on the child's body and the burial of the body under the kitchen floor that led to the murder charges. The jury's conviction of the older woman alone stemmed from her confession. Despite telling conflicting stories about the child's father and what had led to the baby's death, the baby's mother was not convicted of any crime. By setting the case into the context of the differing interpretations of these events that were available to Africans and state officials, it is possible to see the distinct natures of their concerns. White officials wanted to punish crime, and they also wanted to suppress witchcraft accusations. The women's neighbors were alarmed by the immorality of the pregnancy, the child's killing, and the possibility that the killing was related to witchcraft. Although this child's tragic death in Butterworth was a single case, it revealed a spectrum of problems faced by rural families as they navigated both a white-controlled legal and economic system and the local suspicions of supernatural actors and unsupervised women.

The Death of a Mother-in-Law:
Adultery and Intergenerational Tensions

Allegations of adultery, like out-of-wedlock pregnancies, could also inflame family tensions and result in witchcraft accusations and violence. In Umtata in 1951, for example, a murder case arose from domestic tensions in a house-hold of two women. A woman was accused in the circuit court of having murdered her mother-in-law with whom she lived. During a beer drink hosted by her mother-in-law, the two women quarreled. The mother-in-law accused her of becoming pregnant in an adulterous relationship, and she also accused her of being a witch.[46] As they argued, the woman struck her mother-in-law with a heavy cooking spoon and then struggled with her. The older woman collapsed and later died of her injuries.

At the trial, the young woman provided some background in her defense. She explained that her husband had "absconded long ago," by which she meant that her husband had left the rural areas as a migrant laborer and had never returned. He had stopped sending money back to his family as well. The mother-in-law "has treated me badly," she continued, "for the last three years." The woman recounted some of the verbal abuse hurled at her: "She says that I am a witch and that I have killed her son and that is why he does not come back. She swears at me saying I have no home or people. This made me heart-sore and on this day I could not control my temper. . . . I did not mean to kill her."[47] In this case of assault and death, the absence of the woman's husband had a significant and detrimental impact on the lives of his wife and mother. Judging from the testimony at the trial, however, the deceased woman's inter-pretation of their problems had laid little direct blame on the migrant labor system and instead placed the blame on her son's wife. The mother-in-law had blamed her for his continuing absence and had insulted her further by stating that she had no family. The latter accusation implied that her own fam-ily had cast her out, either because they considered her inherently worthless or because of some transgression. Adultery was also an issue, with the older woman alleging that her daughter-in-law had slept with another man. More-over, she accused the young woman of witchcraft, a grave and potentially harm-ful accusation because the consequences could be so grim, including the loss of reputation and the possibility of being shunned by everyone in the com-munity. The daughter-in-law's violent response was probably a heat-of-the-moment act, and it came after an extended period of escalating tension between the two women. At the trial, despite the woman's confession, the presiding judge found the daughter-in-law not guilty of murder and discharged her.

Once again, the state had stepped in to judge a criminal case that had re-sulted at least partly from broader social and economic conditions constructed by state policies. The interests of the state and of Africans generally often con-verged in suppressing criminal violence, but their interests diverged when it came to the question of witchcraft accusations. For state officials, witchcraft accusations were a persistent and dangerous crime that they wanted to extinguish. For Africans, witchcraft itself was a real and immediate danger. The state's criminalization of witchcraft accusations left officials open to the suspicion that they were conspiring with and protecting witches.[48]

Thus, when it came to maintaining social order, Africans had a complex relationship with the state, especially if any suspicion of witchcraft existed. Africans needed to enlist the state's enforcement powers to restore social order. By law, they had to report crimes to the authorities and accept trials conducted in the magistrates' courts.[49] And Africans did make extensive use of the courts, both in civil cases and by reporting crimes and then participating as witnesses in the prosecution of criminal cases. On the other hand, their interpretations of the causes and effects of illegal actions could be vastly different from the interpretations of white officials. These differences emerged clearly in Africans' willingness to look for supernatural causes and effects. When the state's judicial system punished the "right" people, in other words, those considered guilty by both white officials and Africans, everybody's interests were served, at least in those particular instances. But when the state stepped in to protect certain classes of people, including those accused of witchcraft and women charged within the community of antisocial behavior, many Africans saw the state's actions in a more sinister light. In those instances, the state seemed to be encouraging social disorder by protecting immoral (and possibly evil) people.

In the case of the woman killing her mother-in-law, the presiding judge acquitted the daughter-in-law of any crime despite her confession. While the judge's reasoning is not documented in the case file, it seems possible that he saw the mother-in-law's harassment, and in particular her accusations that her daughter-in-law was both an adulterer and a witch, as provocative. Since the assault occurred at a beer drink, he may have assumed that both women were under the influence of alcohol. The judge's decision, therefore, to acquit the younger woman may have appeared to be morally wrong on several counts to African observers, perhaps leading them to question more deeply the motivations of state officials and their willingness to shield people accused of witchcraft, even when they had committed violent crimes.

Violence against People Named as Witches

Witchcraft accusations were more likely to harm the person named a witch than the previous case might suggest. But as in the Umtata and Butterworth cases above, it was common for the alleged witch to be a woman and for the initial suspicion of witchcraft to come from family members or neighbors. In looking at a few additional court cases, we can see the suspicions people had of a white-controlled judicial system that protected people identified as witches. We can also see the development of a willingness among Africans to use a kind of vigilante violence against people whom the state would not punish.

A case from Xhalanga in 1928 involved a man who suspected one of his wives of causing his illness. The diviner he consulted linked gender, literacy, and contact with whites together as sources of the woman's alleged malevolent powers. The trial testimony also provided a detailed description of the divination process that detailed the story of a woman trying to navigate the impact of labor migration, illness, and jealousy within the family to protect herself against such accusations. In the court case, the diviner was on trial for practicing as a diviner; the woman whom the diviner had accused of being a witch had made the criminal complaint that led to the diviner's arrest.

At the trial, the husband recounted how he had traveled to a diviner with his two wives because he was ill and wanted to find out if there was a supernatural cause. "He was complaining," one of the wives testified at the diviner's trial, "that he used to feel compression, shortage of breath, during his sleep." Initially, the diviner's young female acolyte attended to the family: "A girl came and started smelling out [divining]. She was dancing about and told us to clap our hands. She said we had come in connection with a sick man." They confirmed her statement and went inside the hut to meet the diviner himself. The diviner told the husband that he had been suffering from this complaint for quite a while. The man agreed and said that his symptoms had worsened while he was away working at the mines. The diviner then diagnosed the cause of the tightness in his chest—a letter sent to him by one of his wives had contained something harmful. The wife testified that, "Accused [the diviner] said it was something creeping in from the stomach and had hair on it, and after some time he said the thing was a letter. We agreed and asked from what person that letter came. Accused said my husband styled the person 'Mama' who wrote that letter. On being further questioned accused told my husband it was his wife, meaning me, who wrote that letter to him. We asked what was the trouble that could come from a wife sending her husband a letter." The diviner replied that the letter had enclosed the notorious familiar, the *impundulu* or lightning bird, that belonged to the wife and subsequently invaded the husband's body: "Accused said to my husband that the mpundulu [*sic*] (lightning bird) was jealous of him and that mpundulu had been sent to him through the letter." The wife was skeptical of the diviner's judgment: "My husband believed this but I asked about this mpundulu. The doctor turned on me and said he did not even wish to speak to me, he did not speak to witches or wizards, but if my husband had not been there he would beat me."[50] The diviner thus accused the wife of being a witch who had used her letter-writing ability to harm her husband. He alleged that both her co-wife and the "Europeans at Cala" (the largest town in Xhalanga district) "had saved" her. It is not completely clear what the diviner meant by this. One possible interpretation was that he thought local officials and her co-wife had protected her from being identified and punished as a witch. It was also possible that the "Europeans" to whom he referred were missionaries who had taught her to write.

The wife refused to accept his diagnosis, however. She asserted, "I said the Europeans did not come into it and I wanted to know what I had done." She testified at the trial that, when the diviner would not answer her, "I left but said my money [the diviner's fee] would go back home. My husband took it [the money] from me by force and gave it to accused." She was indignant about the accusation: "I didn't believe what the doctor had said, I knew nothing about the mpundulu." The wife openly challenged the diviner to prove his charges. He responded by suggesting that the wife had acquired the lightning bird from her mother. Thus, the diviner's accusation was a mélange of ideas about women's predisposition to commit evil deeds, the complicity of whites in the use of witchcraft or the protection of witches, and the magical qualities associated with letter-writing.

The belief that personal letters had magical properties was widespread. The practice of literacy was "a ritual to be harnessed,"[51] and it conveyed powers to those who used it, as historian Patrick Harries noted. Similarly, anthropologist Philip Mayer reported that many Xhosa people in the 1950s believed that a witch could send an *impundulu* over a great distance to harm an intended victim. The wife could be jealous, fearing that the husband was committing adultery, or the *impundulu* could be jealous of the husband's relationship with the wife.[52] The *impundulu* allegedly "sucks people's blood, or kicks them so that they have pains in their backs and chest, and spit blood," as Monica Wilson noted.[53] The symptoms of being harmed by the *impundulu* were thus also the symptoms of tuberculosis, a disease commonly contracted by African miners in South Africa so that accusations of supernatural harm may have arisen frequently from an illness contracted in the workplace.[54]

After the diviner's accusation, the husband drove his wife away from his household, telling her that he believed her to be a witch. She retreated to the home of a male relative and, with his assistance, reported the episode to the police. At the end of the trial, the magistrate found the diviner guilty of imputing witchcraft to her and sentenced him to five months in prison.[55] The outcome of the case may have reinforced Africans' ideas that the state was complicit in protecting witches and perpetuating witchcraft. But the case also shows the profound ways in which notions of gender fused with supernatural beliefs and labor migration. A man who became ill while at the mines consulted a diviner who ultimately blamed his letter-writing wife (and her mythical *impundulu*) for his sickness rather than the working conditions in the mines. The case also shows how the wife navigated through difficult life circumstances she could not fully control. She had written letters to her husband to maintain ties to him during his long absence, probably unaware of the suspicions these letters might later arouse. When the diviner accused her of witchcraft, she did not passively accept the charge but instead asked for proof. When her husband drove her away because of the witchcraft charge, she regrouped and enlisted the assistance of her male relative and the state. She used resources available to her—which included kin networks and the magistrate's court—strategically to rescue her reputation and improve her life chances even if her marriage had failed.

A 1931 accusation of witchcraft in Idutywa had more unfortunate consequences for the woman involved. A man's son had been struck and killed by lightning and he consulted a diviner to find the cause. The diviner asserted that one of the man's wives (who was not the son's mother) had an *impundulu* that she had used to kill the boy. When the man returned home after the consultation, he told his family the diviner's verdict. The wife then asked her husband if he believed the diviner. In the words of a witness at the diviner's trial, the husband "said 'Yes, I believe it.' She said 'Did you have me in mind that you did not cross examine the doctor [diviner] on my behalf?'" Before the husband responded to her question, the wife "said to 'please give me some money to consult a doctor because I did not do this [kill the child with an *impundulu*].'" The husband answered: "'I will not give you money because you are a witch.'" Later that day, the wife committed suicide. Her death and the inquest that ensued led to the trial of the diviner, who was convicted of practicing as a diviner and was sentenced to four months in jail.[56] In this case, the wife tried to refute the diviner's accusation and wished to enlist a different diviner to support her innocence. But she lacked the support from a male relative that might have enabled her to go to court to defend her reputation.

Witchcraft accusations against women posed threats not only to women's reputations and marriages but also to their property and lives. Women used whatever tactics they could to deflect the social and physical blows such accusations could bring. One case of arson that came to trial in Lusikisiki in 1931 illustrates the variety of threats leveled against women. A man set fire to the huts belonging to his widowed aunt because he believed she was a witch. She and her children had been asleep when she sensed something was wrong. She testified in court: "I took the children out of the hut. Outside I saw my dwelling hut was on fire. . . . The hut was then completely burnt to the ground."[57] Her daughter saw the woman's nephew lurking around their hut at the time of the arson.

The woman explained the background of family strife at the trial. A few days before the fire, she had been called to her brother-in-law's home (where her nephew lived) and found him and other family members waiting for her. The brother-in-law's wife had just had a miscarriage, and her brother-in-law "told me to go near the cattle kraal [enclosure]," a place of spiritual significance within the homestead. Her brother-in-law then said to her: "'I have called you as it is you who is causing the illness of my wife.' He said I was doing this by means of Tikoloshe and Canti," two malevolent familiars associated with witches. The widow claimed that her brother-in-law had accused her of witchcraft previously. On that earlier occasion, two other huts of hers had been torched, although the culprit was never caught. On the basis of the widow's testimony and that of her daughter, the magistrate convicted the nephew of arson and sentenced him to nine months in jail.[58] In a related case, her brother-in-law was convicted of having illegally accused her of being a witch and was sentenced to a year in prison.[59]

In this episode, the widowed aunt probably suffered from social contamination and suspicion surrounding her status as a widow. Monica Wilson quoted an African informant as saying, "A woman without a husband is often smelt out [accused of witchcraft]."[60] Wilson attributed this to a general predisposition to accuse women of witchcraft. She also saw witchcraft accusations as policing behavior: "Any who make themselves unpopular are liable to be 'smelt out' [accused of being a witch]. The woman who is lazy and bad tempered will soon be accused of witchcraft. . . . Any who diverge from the social norm are in danger."[61] Wilson wrote this passage in the 1930s when life in the rural areas was changing owing to labor migration, land shortages, and government policies. Alterations in social norms eroded families from within and made witchcraft accusations and resulting violence more likely. A woman who stepped outside the bounds of socially acceptable behavior risked the social sanction of being named a witch, and a woman who was widowed could face suspicions from her husband's family over his death or over other illnesses or misfortunes in the family. Sometimes in these circumstances, women took their cases to the magistrates' courts. The magistrates' courts could not (and did not want to) alter the broader social conditions that underlay familial strife. But they could provide limited protection to an individual woman who found herself in a life-threatening situation.

A court case from 1937 provides another example of how the larger political economy had eroded rural family life, resulting in witchcraft accusations and violence within the family. A widow living in Umzimkulu complained to the local police that a man who professed to be a diviner had defrauded her. Her grandson had summoned the diviner to investigate why his father (the woman's son) had committed suicide. The suicide had occurred shortly after the father had returned from the mines in Johannesburg. The widowed grandmother testified that the "accused said he was a witch doctor and could drive away tikoloshes and evil spirits from my kraal. Accused then told me why my son died. Accused said my son was killed by tikoloshes and said the tikoloshes were still about my kraal [homestead] and that if I pay him he will drive them away and I will see them." The fact that the diviner stated that there were malevolent familiars roaming her home was an implication that she was a witch. She paid the diviner by giving him all her deceased son's possessions, but she never saw any proof of the malevolent beings: "Accused obtained these articles from me under false pretences. I paid accused these articles because I was afraid he will bewitch me if I failed to do so. I wanted to see evil spirits that accused told me about."[62]

For his part, the man on trial freely admitted that he was a diviner. He claimed that he had done his job and deserved the payment he had received: "I am a well-known witchdoctor and at my home I told complainant there were evil spirits at her kraal and if she pays me these articles I will show them to her and drive them away. I told accused [*sic*] I drove the evil spirits and tikoloshes away from her kraal and thereupon she paid me the articles before the court." The diviner felt that he had done good work and had not committed any fraud. The magistrate did not agree: he convicted the defendant of fraud and sentenced him to six months of hard labor.

There were several intimations of violence in this trial: the son having returned from the mines only to commit suicide, the question about whether witchcraft familiars belonging to the widow were the cause of the suicide, the grandson's engagement of the diviner possibly because of suspicions he harbored against his grandmother, and the woman's fear that the diviner would harm her through his supernatural powers if she did not pay him. The driving force in this domestic tragedy, however, was the violence of the migrant labor system and the harm done to people's lives by that system. At the trial, the grandmother was trying to recoup some of the losses she had endured through her son's death. The court's intervention may have helped her recover some of what she had paid the diviner, and it also may have helped to restore her reputation: If the diviner proved to be a fraud, then his statement that she harbored *tikoloshes* at her home was also fraudulent. But another possible interpretation that some African onlookers may have drawn was that the court was protecting a witch (the grandmother) from a legitimate accusation made by the diviner.

These cases demonstrated how the system of male migrant labor and worsening economic conditions, with all the inequalities and social tensions it produced, widened rifts within African families and communities along gender lines. Witchcraft accusations continued into the apartheid era, even with the state's attempts to stamp them out, and even if diviners were not always involved. Isak Niehaus has argued that the institutionalization of segregation and the creation of Bantustans (or homelands) as an element of apartheid policies allowed beliefs in witchcraft to flourish. These beliefs helped the local population to explain both rampant social problems caused by the structural violence of the South African state and the more localized harms instigated by poverty and drought.[63] For many Africans, the most dangerous wielders of witchcraft were to be found within the family and among neighbors.[64]

In 1962 another court case illustrated the familial troubles that led to witchcraft accusations. Two men were charged with arson for burning the huts of their uncle and his wife in Lusikisiki. The men suspected their aunt of killing one of the men's sons, and they wanted to drive her away. Initially, when the uncle's wife had been "smelt out" by a diviner, she had returned to her own father's home. Her husband had paid a cow to her family to get them to release her back to him and restore the marriage. However, when she returned to live with her husband, the nephews burned down the hut at night. At the time of the arson, the wife was asleep inside the hut, and the husband just happened to be outside to witness the crime because one of his cattle had escaped the cattle enclosure. He watched as two people set his huts alight, and he recognized the perpetrators as his nephews. One of his nephews had previously accused the man's wife of witchcraft "when [his] child died."[65] His nephews denied that they were the arsonists, although, perversely, one admitted to consulting a diviner: "I consulted a witch doctor. Complainant's wife was pointed out as a witch. Complainant sent his wife away. She returned. This did not worry me. I do not know who would burn complainant's hut." The magistrate did not believe the nephews' denials of involvement in the arson and convicted them, sentencing them to serve 150 days in prison.[66]

Historian Karen Flint notes that, among Zulu-speaking people, feelings of insecurity deepened because of their contact with the white-controlled state: "Colonialism brought new economic, social, and physical challenges that often worked together in a synergistic way to compound people's increasing health problems and the fear of witches."[67] Apartheid policies imposed after 1948 exacerbated these problems and left fewer ways for people to build healthy families.[68] People who accused family members of witchcraft were trying to find intimate causes for personal tragedies. The death of one of the nephew's children in the above case might have resulted from malnutrition or an infectious disease. But even if they had knowledge of the biomedical causes for the child's death, the family could easily have suspected their aunt of using supernatural powers to facilitate the child's death. People used violence against witches out of fear and anger, but people also intended the violence to punish perpetrators and restore the moral order.

Women as Diviners

Women who became diviners also had to navigate the crosscurrents generated by the official version of native law, popular beliefs in witchcraft, and greater insecurity in rural life. Diviners were skilled professionals who had spiritual abilities to determine causes of misfortune.[69] Both men and women practiced as diviners, but by the 1930s, evidence suggests that women dominated the profession of divining. As women became more associated with traditional culture in the rural areas and more burdened with upholding those traditions, it may be that as a group, women took on both blame for supernatural harms as well as finding additional opportunities for diagnosing and righting them.[70] A couple of cases will show some of the conflicting risks that women diviners took and how they tried to navigate those risks.

A 1933 trial from Cofimvaba involved the prosecution of a woman for practicing as a diviner. A man had consulted her to determine why some family members had died and to ask her to treat a sick child. Together the diviner and the family went through the divination process. At the end of the process, the woman "said there was a witch bird [*sic,* probably an *impundulu*] at the kraal [homestead]. I asked her to whom it belonged. She replied it belonged to the wife of my younger brother. She said the husband of that woman had died. She said that witch bird killed the man and the children of that wife. . . . My brother referred to had only one wife—Noorange."[71] Noorange recounted a similar story. The diviner, she said, "indicated me as killing the people of the kraal. . . . She said it was a widow whose husband died at the mines. I am the only one to whom this description applies." Noorange expressed how deeply the accusation affected her: "My heart was sore for three days. I was greatly grieved about this [accusation of witchcraft]. On [the] fourth day I stabbed myself. I tried a big knife but that would not go in. I took a small knife." Noorange's attempted suicide did not succeed, but it was an indication of how few options she felt she had in the face of the family's suspicions and the diviner's accusation.

When the woman charged with being a diviner testified, she denied outright that she had done anything more than prescribe herbs for the sick family members. She knew that divination was illegal: Noorange quoted her as defiantly saying at the time of the divining ceremony that "she did not care about being imprisoned." The diviner pled not guilty, but the magistrate convicted her. He sentenced her to "six months hard labor, during the first two months of which accused is to be kept in solitary confinement with spare diet on two days each week in accordance with prison regulations."[72] The harsh sentence probably stemmed from Noorange's attempted suicide and the evident harm done by the divination. Noorange's despair might have originated in the deaths of her husband and children, but the accusation that she was the ultimate cause of those deaths no doubt deepened her anguish.

Another case from Ngqeleni in 1952 also involved a woman accused of practicing as a diviner. In this case, a man, his two wives, and another family member approached the diviner to determine why one of his children was sick. He stated at the trial that the diviner had gone through an entire divination ceremony and had then indicated that one of his wives had caused the illness: she had allegedly sent her snake familiar (an *icanti*) into the child's head. He paid the diviner, and then, as he and his party walked home, he strangled the wife identified as a witch. The man was tried, convicted, and sentenced to ten years of imprisonment for murder. It may be that the diviner's accusation only confirmed long-held suspicions against his wife or that there had already been strife within the family. But the man killing his wife was a tragic conclusion to the family's story.

The woman accused of being a diviner denied that she had "smelt out" the man's wife. She claimed to be an herbalist only and said that she had recommended that the man take his child to a "European doctor" to receive treatment. She asserted, "I do not believe in witchcraft. I do not know what the fee is for smelling out. I have never seen a smelling out ceremony or a witchdoctor." The magistrate found her guilty of imputing witchcraft to the murdered woman and sentenced her to twelve months of hard labor.[73]

While many Africans believed that women in general—and wives and widows in particular—were more likely to use evil supernatural powers, they were also willing to consult powerful women diviners who could diagnose evil. Women choosing to become diviners in the twentieth century was an innovative attempt to reconcile and retool older beliefs rooted in rural African life with the newer realities of social deracination and economic insecurity. Women who became diviners defended their access to esoteric knowledge and power against men's economic and social control in the South African context.[74] In doing so, they were claiming aspects of African cultural traditions to guard rural life. However, women diviners often accused other women of being the sources of local problems, accusations that occasionally resulted in violence, evidence of one more way that violence became embedded in tradition.

CONCLUSION

The realm of supernatural beliefs became a place where people used the traditional powers of diviners against the adverse effects of state policies. Consulting a diviner was a way to affix local blame for local harms, even if those local harms were related to the impact of the state's political and economic policies. Violent retribution against people named as witches sometimes challenged the local social order and other times challenged the state's control over the right to try cases and enforce laws. Accusing a person of witchcraft could also be an incendiary statement about immorality and evil.

This chapter's discussion of violence within families has shown that rural Africans often assumed that both women and men had access to various physical and spiritual forms of power. Women played vital roles in family life. When most or all the adult men in a particular family were away at work, women had effective control over the rural household. But this control carried with it the significant risk of being blamed if the family did not thrive or if neighbors suffered economic setbacks, illness, or death. A wife could be blamed for a husband's illness or death even if it happened while he was a migrant laborer at the mines. Women could be blamed for a husband absconding from his rural family. Women also occasionally inflicted harm and committed violence on others, as cases of concealment of childbirth and murder demonstrate.

Shifting cultural and social conditions created problems and enhanced anxiety about the causes of those problems. People often used witchcraft accusations and violence to address these broader social issues and structural violence in very intimate terms. They needed an explanation for why they could not establish and maintain a viable family homestead or why family members had died or absconded. In these stories, the connection between an individual's domestic problems and the problems created by state policies became evident. The state's intervention to punish those who were avenging themselves against witches did not prevent accusations of witchcraft. Still, it highlighted the state's complicity in the destabilization of African rural life. African families and diviners had to navigate laws imposed by the state as well as social norms to try to stabilize their own circumstances.

In the next chapter, we will see how people marshaled beliefs in supernatural powers to assist specific acts of political resistance and violence. The anti-state violence that ripped through the Transkeian region in the 1950s and 1960s had roots in the spiritual understanding of malice and power. People held state officials accountable for destabilizing rural life, but they also understood that local people bore some guilt. Historically, anti-state violence and violence within the family and local community were not always two separate phenomena. Instead, they were both strategies for navigating life in a rural context that had become increasingly unpredictable and unstable. People used violence and witchcraft accusations to recapture some stability, authority, and autonomy for themselves and navigate through dangerous social and political waters.

4

Sons and "Hooligans," "World-Destroyers" and Rebels

Traditional Violence Takes a Nationalist Turn

In 1961 an African man from Lusikisiki testified at the trial of another local man accused of inciting people to rebel. There were numerous attacks that year on government officials, projects, and policies, such as fencing and tax collections. The witness described the accused man as a leader of a local rebel group known as "Congo." He stated that he had been forced to attend Congo meetings "because it was said that anyone failing to attend would have his throat cut." In addition, anyone who refused to pay money to support the rebels "would be regarded as a traitor and would be killed." These were not idle concerns: "From my own personal knowledge . . . I saw kraals [homesteads] burnt and people killed."[1]

Violence and threats were common tactics of the rebels as they attempted to destabilize state control in the Transkeian region, and this case provides examples of some of the methods used. A second witness at the trial confirmed the rebels' use of arson against people who collaborated with the state: "I have personal knowledge of large-scale burnings. The people whose kraals [homes] were burnt were called traitors and traitors were those people who were loyal to their headmen and obeyed the Government. I attended meetings of the Congo movement but was not a member. It was said that if I failed to attend I would be killed."[2] The actions of the rebels reflected moral judgments as well as political ones. A third witness at the trial noted that the accused leader of the Congo movement had told him to take a message to the local headman. Congo leaders had charged the headman not only with being a state collaborator but also of "having rendered pregnant the wife of another man." They had imposed a fine on him and "if he did not pay he was to be taken to Ntsingisi Hill," where the rebels convened their own court of justice. There the headman's life would be in jeopardy. The headman opted to pay the fine to the rebels and avoid the risk of worse penalties.[3] In using arson and threats of greater violence, rebels tried to enforce a political decision to reject all government measures and reinstitute a moral order. But in this instance, someone had complained to the police, which had led to the arrest of the man on trial.

The trial provided a vivid picture of how the state and the rebels used violence to try to take control over an unstable social and political context.[4] The state was imposing a series of apartheid-related measures that would cement its hold on the political system. The rebels, as well as less militant opponents, saw these moves as immoral because they wrenched control over daily life out of the hands of ordinary Africans. The older ways that Africans had navigated around state controls were no longer viable. Instead, rebels determined that they had to undermine the central state by employing locally used techniques of fighting and witchcraft eradication.

Witchcraft accusations and the question of their political dimensions were central to the criminal case brought by the prosecution in this court case as politics mixed with supernatural concerns. The defendant at the trial testified that none of the local hut burnings had been instigated by rebels but instead had resulted from a spate of witchcraft accusations made against various people. By framing the arsons as responses to witchcraft, he signaled the use of traditional violence to take on the state. He was not alone in doing so. A local correspondent for the Liberal Party's news outlet *Contact* noted that the rebel leaders from their meeting place on Ngquza Hill had sent out "*tshisa-tshisa* (burning) gangs, now in twos and threes" to burn the homes of suspected collaborators.[5] In this particular case, the local Bantu Affairs commissioner evidently took the threat posed by the defendant's actions seriously: the court convicted him of one count of inciting people to violence and sentenced him to two years' imprisonment.[6]

Among white officials, the dominant explanation for the rural rebellion was that it was the product of two factors. One factor was the incitement of "outside agitators," the phrase used frequently to refer to members of the Communist Party and the Liberal Party with the implicit meaning that political unrest was not representative of rural African opinion. A 1961 speech given by the head of the South African Police in the Transkei, J. A. C. Reay, to the Transkeian Territorial Authority (a local legislative body made up of chiefs and headmen) captured this narrative. After saying that "Chiefs, headmen and others in authority have been murdered although they have only done their duty to the best of their ability," he accused outsiders of causing all the problems. "These tragic events," he stated, "have occurred because some of your own people have come under the influence of communistic agitators. Brother has been incited against brother, son against father, family against family and even location against location. The people in the Transkei had enjoyed a peaceful life for many years before this tragedy struck your land and your people. Then the agitators came from outside the Transkei and poisoned the minds of the people."[7] Although there was little evidence to support this allegation of outsider instigation, Reay and other officials broadcast the idea that they were suppressing a communist-inspired revolt. Authorities felt they were justified in using whatever force was necessary, or as Reay put it, "It was necessary for the Police to take firm action."[8] That "firm action" included extreme counterviolence—sometimes directed against people who were not rebels and not engaged in any political activity—and increased police surveillance in an attempt to regain control.[9] As African National Congress leader Govan Mbeki observed: "The government was out for vengeance and life became a nightmare for peasants in the troubled areas."[10]

The second factor invoked by whites and some Africans working with the state was what they called the "hooliganism" of older adolescents and young men who allegedly had little deference for white officials and African leaders. They also began linking the violence to nationalist organizations that they saw as guilty of channeling this supposed hooliganism into political subversion. One chief commented to the *Rand Daily Mail* that the organization Poqo—the armed wing of the Pan Africanist Congress—was the cause of all political unrest in the Transkei. Some Poqo members, he suggested, "were young hooligans who armed themselves with axes and revolvers." He continued, "We came to the conclusion that they want to destroy the world. However, they are our sons. All our young men have joined Poqo in Cape Town."[11]

This chapter will demonstrate how blurred the lines became between sons and rebels. For the sons, the violence sprang initially from local grievances. The state's implementation of new agricultural policies, such as fencing and cattle culling, threatened rural people and their livelihoods directly. Sons responded by becoming rebels, and the rebels were taking *dubria*, the concept of social navigation through an unstable environment, to the next level. They turned their social navigation to disrupting the state's control in the rural areas; they were *dubria-ing* with their lives.[12]

Henrik Vigh used these concepts of social navigation and *dubria-ing* with their lives in his discussion of young men who joined the rebel group, the Aguentas, in Guinea. In the context of Guinea's civil war (1998–99), mobilization in the Aguentas gave young men a way to "expand the horizons of possibility in a world of conflict, turmoil, and diminishing resources."[13] *Dubria-ing* with their lives was not tied to personal greed, revenge, or a love of violence; it was instead a way of navigating out of an increasingly hopeless situation. It was "a question of balancing social death with violent life chances."[14] Similarly, the men who joined the rebels in the Transkei were caught in a world of turmoil and diminishing resources. Their situation was a crisis borne of being stuck in a political and economic situation that amounted to a kind of social stagnation. They too opted to *dubria* with their lives. Many coalesced into the rebel group Congo and into Poqo, both of which tried to subvert state control. Their methods included threats, physical attacks, and witchcraft accusations directed at family members, individual state officials, and local people deemed collaborators.

Rebels drew upon techniques of traditional violence, such as hut burning and assaulting people identified as witches, to strike meaningful blows against state actors and policies in the 1950s and early 1960s. For their part, white officials repeatedly tried to dismiss the violence as either trivial or illegitimate. White and black officials also used physical assaults and violence to reimpose what they saw as social order. Using court transcripts, official reports, and contemporaneous stories from newspapers, I will argue that this political violence grew out of the more mundane traditional violence that had been fostered by white control of the region for several decades. Until the early 1960s, most of the violence used by rebels was focused on local targets associated with state policies. But in 1962 and 1963, violence initiated by rural men escalated to a couple of spectacular attacks against a major political figure and a family of whites in the Transkei. These two attacks, orchestrated by Poqo members, took rural forms of violence to the national level.

Homelands and the Emergence of Rural Violence Targeting the State

In an attempt to forestall African nationalist demands for the end of the white supremacist state, the National Party government from 1948 onward instituted apartheid as a more thorough version of segregation. Apartheid included a plan to create "homelands," or "Bantustans," that would provide a sham concession to African nationalist demands for independence from white rule. The homelands would gain political "independence" from South Africa while remaining economically dependent on labor migration to industries located in "white" South Africa. The Transkei was the first of the homelands scheduled for attaining self-government (in 1963) and then for independence (in 1976). From the white National Party's point of view, homelands would relieve the South African state of any responsibility for allowing Africans a political voice outside of the homelands. Homelands would also provide a convenient dumping ground for unemployed Africans deported from the cities in white South Africa. African families were to remain in the countryside and maintain the homes to which labor migrants ultimately were expected to return. The idea that Africans were "naturally" rural was part of the myth that underpinned apartheid even though, by the 1950s, many Africans living in towns and cities had resided in urban areas all or most of their lives. But apartheid was committed to the myth that Africans were traditional and traditional meant living in the rural areas under customary law.[15]

State control had relied in the rural areas upon finding African leaders willing to work within its confines.[16] This reliance on African chiefs and headmen was designed to make governance by a white-controlled state more palatable to a majority of Africans, and the South African government's policies strove to freeze African society in an amber of state-defined tradition to prevent Africans from making political claims at the national level. In practice, though, many Africans questioned the legitimacy of the state and of those African leaders who worked within it. By the 1950s, decades of migrant labor, social changes, and economic decline in the rural areas combined with reactions to the newly aggressive apartheid policies to intensify African political resistance.[17]

As part of the apartheid plan, the state devolved additional power on local chiefs and headmen who were still primarily selected by white administrators. The Bantu Affairs Commissioner of Bizana noted that the district's residents saw the Paramount Chief, Botha Sigcau, as "autocratic and unsympathetic." They disapproved of his implementation of many of the new apartheid policies because "he did not obtain the agreement of the people and he ignored their wishes and their customs."[18] Africans were thus trying to use the idea of the customary relationship between a chief and his people to undercut the authority of the apartheid state.

State officials also devised aggressive measures to "rehabilitate" or "stabilize" African agriculture to allow for the forced resettlement of African populations from urban areas. Many of these stabilization policies were unpopular, including limitations on livestock, the consolidation of grazing land and widespread installation of fences, and the reallocation of land in a way that (white) agricultural planners deemed "rational," all done without consulting local populations.[19] The Bizana Bantu Affairs Commissioner reported in 1960 that the rebel movement had drawn up a comprehensive list of grievances that included agricultural policies, taxes, influx control and pass laws.[20] The wholesale disruption of rural life struck deeply at the strategies that African communities had developed for the survival of their families over several decades of white rule, and that disruption provided a rich context for revolt.[21]

As rebels confronted state policies and local leaders, they often used language and actions associated with witchcraft eradication. Rebels named chiefs and headmen "traitors" and threatened them with the punishment often used for driving witches out of the community—arson and death. "At the height of the disturbances," the Bizana Bantu Affairs Commissioner wrote, "the rebels threatened all persons who were working for or . . . who had at any time in the past been connected with the Government. . . . The rebels drew up lists of the Bantu [people] whose kraals [homesteads] they were going to burn."[22] The use of the language of witchcraft was an indictment of the policies that had created stark inequalities and arson was a cauterization of the evil powers that had implemented those policies.

Political violence committed by Africans throughout this period often arose in concert with rumors about political leaders and their reputed supernatural powers. Rumors about the supernatural captured both the malevolence of state actors' intentions as well as their demonstrated ability to arrest and imprison people who opposed them. The supernatural precautions that Africans took and the violence that they used against state officials invoked beliefs not as a secret code about politics but rather as an analytic statement about the state's deeply immoral policies. The language of the supernatural had infused African discussions about and actions toward the white state and officials over the whole period in this region since the 1880s.[23] Discussions of the supernatural— including witchcraft, beliefs in the ancestors, and Christian beliefs—were not suddenly absent from political thought in the 1950s and later.[24]

South Africa's whites also had beliefs and stereotypes about Africans that they actively elaborated in the 1950s and 1960s. These stereotypes included ideas of African savagery and cultural "backwardness."[25] Acts of violence committed by Africans in the 1950s and 1960s fed into whites' stereotypes to stoke a fear among whites of a looming "black peril," or "*swart gevaar.*" Black peril narratives flourished in the international Cold War environment, as stories about anticolonial conflicts emerged from Algeria, Kenya, and the Congo.[26] Assumptions about the communist inspiration of African militants drew directly from Cold War anxieties about the spread of Russian and Chinese political and military influence in the colonized world. The rumors that developed and became mainstream among whites in the late 1950s and early 1960s depicted African political dissidents and activists as puppets manipulated by international actors in a global struggle for dominance.

Nebulous fears among whites informed official explanations of the real violence taking place in rural South Africa. They also stoked the urgency given to the enforcement of state policies, often with massive levels of force. The scale of the violence in the 1950s and 1960s and the threats that the revolt posed to the South African state were such that officials declared a state of emergency in the Transkei in 1960, granting extraordinary powers to government officials.[27] Special mobile police units swept through the rural areas in an attempt to stamp out the rebellion, provide protection to chiefs and headmen, and reimpose state control.

African resistance to state terror included explicit accusations against officials of witchcraft and sorcery and, when targeting African collaborators, the classic technique for expelling and killing witches—hut burning.[28] A pamphlet issued by the Port Elizabeth office of the African National Congress in 1957, at the height of the revolt, was filled with imagery of chiefs using supernatural powers to assist in the oppression of the rural population, calling them "wizards" and suggesting that "the people know how to deal with wizards."[29] The rhetoric of witchcraft allegations moralized violence against these powerful men. These attacks within communities showed most clearly the links between local violence and violence against state policies and officials. A telegram reportedly sent in 1959 from Duma Nokwe, the general secretary of the ANC, to Botha Sigcau, the paramount chief of the Mpondo in Transkei, tersely warned Sigcau: "Beware of happily co-operating with the oppressors of the nation."[30]

Not all the people who faced threats from rebels were chiefs, however. There were violent attacks on people who complied with government regulations to avoid legal trouble. Some of these alleged collaborators were women living on their own. In one court case in Umzimkulu in 1963, a twenty-seven-year-old man was charged with two violations of the Fencing Act and four acts of arson. The 1963 Fencing Act was one of the so-called stabilization measures enacted by the apartheid state to control African land use by fencing off and limiting grazing land; the act made any intentional destruction of fences a crime. The imposition of fencing was deeply unpopular among many Africans because of their economic dependence on livestock and the need to access grazing land. But people who had fewer animals to graze or who had weak legal claims to the land they farmed were not always willing to confront the state over the question of fences. Independent women, either widowed or who had never married, often lived on land registered to their deceased husbands or fathers or brothers and remained on that land mainly through the lenience of the local Bantu Affairs commissioners. The Bantu Affairs commissioners, if they wished, could legally evict these women and reallocate the land to other people. Thus, independent women had a significant personal interest in complying with the state's agricultural policies, even unpopular ones like the Fencing Act.

During April and May of 1963, shortly after the enactment of the Fencing Act, four different middle-aged African women awoke in the middle of the night to noises alerting them that their huts were on fire. Members of all four homesteads had found threatening letters wrapped in tin near their huts either in the days before or immediately after the fires broke out. In three of the arsons, the arsonist placed other items with the letters. In one example, the culprit put the letter beside a short length of rolled barbed wire, the material used for the hated fences. In a second instance, the woman's sixteen-year-old son found "an image of a Zulu warrior" tacked to the door of one of the family's huts and a miniature knobkerrie. At a third homestead, an African policeman investigating the arson found a "bunch of letters, a flag, a miniature image of a Zulu warrior, a miniature assegai [spear], a miniature knobstick [knobkerrie], a piece of tin, and a bundle of partly burnt grass. . . . The flag was stuck in the ground in front of one of the huts. The bunch of letters were contained in the folded tin and nailed to the wall of one of the huts. The image was placed against the wall with the miniature assegai and knobstick just below where the letters nailed [*sic*]."[31] The arsonist may have intended the letters and objects as additional threats of physical violence or to convey some supernatural threats, although there was apparently no direct allegation made that the women were witches. The women's only obvious shared attribute was that they were older women living independently who had complied with fencing regulations. The arsons and the placement of threatening letters and objects suggest a connection between political grievances and gendered fears of immoral or antisocial behavior.[32]

Women were not the only victims of arson and violence that straddled the line between local and national political strife. The magistrates' records for the late 1950s and early 1960s show connections between violence against people perceived as criminals or immoral actors within the community and the development of anti-state violence. For example, in the first five months of 1957, the Bantu Affairs commissioner in Qumbu held nineteen preparatory examinations relating to hut burnings that resulted in deaths, injuries, and property destruction. Most of these arsons were vigilante punishments for livestock thefts. The vigilantes also directly accused the stock thieves of witchcraft, and they alleged that the state was protecting the thieves from justice.[33] There were over four hundred huts intentionally burned in Qumbu in the first few months of 1957 and one hundred huts in the adjoining district of Tsolo.

According to the Transkei's chief Bantu Affairs commissioner, livestock theft and the difficulty of successfully prosecuting stock thieves were the root cause of the problem: "The stock losses in the two districts aggregate hundreds of head [of livestock, mostly cattle] per month." He continued, "It is reported that the stock thieves constituted themselves into a sort of aristocracy which did not mix with lesser folk and at beer drinks would sit apart. They blatantly called themselves stock thieves." The chief Bantu Affairs commissioner reported that victims of livestock thefts were taking the law into their own hands. However, he cautioned that the arsons were going beyond the punishment of local criminals and verging into broader political territory: "The general indignation against stock thieves is now being made use of to cover the paying off of old grudges and even endeavours to intimidate officials. A few days ago I received an anonymous letter stating that any attempt to introduce stabilisation [policies] into Sulenkama location, Qumbu, would result in the deaths of Chief Isaac Matiwane, the agricultural staff concerned, and the Magistrate of Qumbu."[34] However, the chief Bantu Affairs commissioner did not take the political content of the violence seriously. Instead of seeing the violence as an indictment of government policies, he regarded it as an expression of the "emotional instability" of the local population: "With a tribe as emotionally unstable as the Pondomise, there is no knowing how far this might develop."[35] Meanwhile, stock thefts continued, and officials and chiefs seemed incapable of either preventing the thefts or punishing the thieves, a fact that made people directly associated with the state an obvious next target.

LOCAL VIOLENCE TAKES A NATIONALIST TURN

For a short time in the early 1960s, South Africa seemed poised for a dramatic political shift as African nationalist organizations challenged the inequality inherent in apartheid rule. In rural Transkeian districts, regional political violence coincided with this national turmoil. The 1950s in South Africa saw growing popular participation in the best-known African nationalist group, the African National Congress (ANC), whose power base mainly resided in the urban areas, particularly Johannesburg, Port Elizabeth, and Durban. A new nationalist organization, the Pan Africanist Congress (PAC), emerged in 1959 and drew support from younger migrant laborers in the major cities, especially in Cape Town.

Both the ANC and the PAC were trying to build broad-based organizations. The ANC had been pushing greater grassroots participation since the early 1950s. The PAC was a breakaway organization that wanted to accelerate the process by confronting the state more directly. Both organizations began protesting more vigorously in 1959 and early 1960. But the Sharpeville massacre of March 21, 1960, during which police shot and killed more than seventy unarmed African protesters, signaled that the apartheid state was willing to use extreme violence—in full view of both national and international communities—to maintain its hold on power. ANC and PAC leaders regarded the Sharpeville killings as a turning point: leaders concluded that further attempts at peaceful resistance to the regime were likely to meet with violent repression from the state. Many leaders called for new and more militant tactics.[36]

At the same time, state officials feared the emergence of an energized mass political movement among Africans. They arrested many leaders and, shortly after the Sharpeville killings, banned both the ANC and the PAC.[37] The bans led the two nationalist organizations to activate plans for underground wings to use sabotage and other violent acts to destabilize the regime's hold on power and, they hoped, spark mass political action to overthrow the apartheid state.[38] The move toward a more militant nationalist strategy, coming on top of prolonged resistance to various apartheid measures in the rural areas, seemed to be part of a broader wave of nationalism throughout the colonized world.

As part of the strategy of mass mobilization, African nationalist organizations looked to the revolts that were already occurring in rural areas. The African National Congress reacted to the ongoing violence in the Transkei in a pamphlet titled "The Year of Blood and Tears—1960." The pamphlet circulated in the Transkei, and copies of it ended up in the reports of Bantu Affairs commissioners as an example of the dangers posed by African nationalist thought. The rhetoric of the pamphlet was bold and linked local violence in Mpondo districts of the Transkei to nationalist resistance: "Towards the end of this year hundreds of people in Pondoland have been put in prison. In Umtata and other places, the gaols are full of brave people who are fighting for FREEDOM." The pamphlet suggested that African collaborators with the state were holding back progress: "The work could have been easy if we were faced with the Europeans only. What continuously worried us, which sometimes put us in danger, is that the Europeans hid behind our people. In rural areas they put the Chiefs and some of the men whom we love and respected in front."[39] Thus, the ANC pamphlet designated chiefs and other African officials who worked with the white-controlled state as legitimate targets of the revolt.

The ANC was joined in its militancy by the PAC and its armed wing, Poqo. The PAC, only eleven months old as an organization when the state banned it in 1960, was firmly committed to confronting the state. Its creation had been an attempt to build a following among an increasingly militant generation of young African men who wanted freedom not just in their lifetimes but preferably within the next three years, as PAC leader Potlako Leballo had promised would happen.[40] PAC leaders charged Poqo with initiating a violent struggle against the white-controlled state. But while the PAC was ideologically committed to armed struggle, it lacked the resources and organizational depth to carry out tightly planned military attacks or strategic sabotage.[41]

What the PAC lacked in organizational depth, its members made up for in militancy. Three incidents within a brief, three-month period between late November 1962 and early February 1963 indicated that members of Poqo were taking matters into their own hands.[42] These three incidents included the storming of a police station in the town of Paarl in the western Cape; the attempted assassination of Chief Kaiser Matanzima at his home in the Transkei; and the murder of several whites, including a road engineer and his family, living at a roadside camp in the Transkei. These violent actions created a wave of white panic over the state's inability to maintain control over the African population. The attack on the police station in Paarl took place in a town near one of South Africa's capitals, Cape Town.[43] Although the Paarl attack was a hugely symbolic act for Poqo, it has been well analyzed by other scholars and will not be a central topic in this chapter. In the context of the connections between regional and nationalist violence, Poqo's second and third plots, which took place within the Transkei and directly challenged the homelands framework, were of greater significance. Migrant laborers from the Transkei formed a significant portion of Poqo's membership. Many had rural families and rural grievances against state policies, and these two Poqo attacks fused national and local political grievances and tactics.

The Attempted Assassination of Chief Kaiser Matanzima

On 12 December 1962, a group of about one hundred men set out to assassinate Chief Kaiser Matanzima, the state-designated leader of the Transkei, at his home at Qamata in Cofimvaba. This attack was the third attempt on his life that year. Matanzima was a hereditary chief and a lawyer, engaged in building a political career within the contours set by the apartheid state. He had taken the title of "Paramount Chief of the Emigrant Thembu," which placed him near the top of the hierarchy of traditional chiefs in the Transkei. Matanzima was solidly behind the apartheid state's plans to make the Transkei into an "independent" country, and that support made him a target of the opponents of apartheid.[44]

Other, lower profile chiefs had already suffered attacks organized by local rebels. In Engcobo in 1961, for example, rebels burned the hut of a prominent chief and then murdered him and another man. A group of twenty-four local men allegedly participated in the murder. According to the district's Bantu

Affairs commissioner, the murdered man "was a loyal supporter of government policy and it was gleaned from the evidence that the motive for the murder might have been the deceased's share in the establishment of Bantu Authorities in this district."[45]

In Umtata in March 1961, the Bantu Affairs commissioner reported extensive opposition to government headmen, land stabilization schemes, forced livestock culling, and fencing. Rebels attacked those who supported the state, including one headman, Mqekela Dadeni, a "strong supporter of the government policy" who was "burnt to death together with a woman in a hut."[46] In Qumbu, which had seen extensive vigilante action against suspected livestock thieves in the 1950s, militants shifted their focus toward anti-state action: they threatened any chiefs or headmen suspected of colluding with the state. Qumbu's Bantu Affairs commissioner reported in 1961 that "Agitators against the rule of the white man are constantly circularising Chiefs and other Bantu exhorting them to prepare for the '*eventual and inevitable*' overthrow of the white man. Expressions such as 'sticking' and 'white pigs' are used. Some roneoed [mimeographed] circulars request the recipients each to ensure that ten other people are apprised of the contents of the letters. These letters are always anonymous."[47] The Bantu Affairs commissioner hinted at broader conspiracies and the involvement of outsiders: "Other agitators are said to drive into locations by motor car during darkness and late at night from places such as Cape Town, Port Elizabeth and East London and to disseminate anti-Government propaganda, and then they disappear again."[48] Although the official did not make this analogy, the language used by the Bantu Affairs commissioner was reminiscent of the language used by people who made witchcraft accusations involving the use of familiars who worked under cover of night.

In Cofimvaba, the district in which Matanzima resided, the Bantu Affairs commissioner had dismissed two headmen in early 1961 whom he suspected of sympathizing with the African National Congress. He replaced them with headmen more compliant with state policies.[49] In other districts, commissioners reported that vigilantes convened illegal meetings where they threatened and carried out violent actions against headmen and chiefs, much as Congo did in the case that opened this chapter.

By 1962 the multiple waves of rebel actions met with increasingly violent police responses. The support of chiefs like Matanzima for state policies invited sharper criticisms among those with political grievances. PAC leaders condemned collaborating chiefs in general and Kaiser Matanzima in particular. One PAC leader, Gilbert Hani, called Matanzima a "traitor" to his people. Another, Jacob Mpemba, declared at a 1962 meeting in Langa (outside Cape

Town) that "Matanzima is betraying his own people."[50] The PAC's fiery rhetoric and aggressive recruiting efforts among labor migrants from the Transkei promised an organizational home for what had been up to that point locally organized resistance against low-level chiefs and state policies.[51]

These verbal attacks on Matanzima crystallized into a plan to assassinate him at his Great Place (or headquarters) in Cofimvaba.[52] James Funani, one of the plotters arrested in the aftermath of the assassination attempt, stated that he had been recruited by another Poqo member while living in Langa. The man who recruited him also had asked for money to support the organization. The recruiter told Funani that "money was needed to expedite the attack on the Europeans who were living in the rural areas of the Transkei, and Chief Matanzima."[53] The plot to kill a high-profile chief required the planners to shield themselves by employing extraordinary measures, including the use of supernatural protections. Funani noted: "The Europeans of the Transkei and Chief Matanzima had all to be killed, . . . [and] there was another plan in which they should employ the services of a witchdoctor and who will wash us and make incisions on the forehead and the back of the head. This will immunise us from European bullets."[54] In addition, the men acquired weapons, including knives, pangas, and fighting sticks, while a few were able to get guns.

On the day before the planned operation, the Poqo men bought train tickets from Cape Town to Queenstown, the town closest to Matanzima's home, and boarded the train in small groups. According to Funani, the men all had incisions on their foreheads, evidence of the supernatural doctoring they had received.[55] Some additional doctoring took place when they arrived in Queenstown, and the leader reassured the recruits that the medicine would help protect them during the mission.[56] From Queenstown, they all took a bus to Ntlonze, a hill that overlooked Matanzima's residence. A few members of Poqo who lived locally joined the group. They assembled on the forested hill, waiting for their chance to kill the chief.[57]

The mission did not proceed according to plan. A few local African men, climbing the hill to cut wood, saw the group and asked them what they were doing. The Poqo members answered truthfully about their plans to assassinate the chief, perhaps assuming that all Africans felt as they did: "We told them that we had no quarrel with them but we had come to kill their chief Kaiser."[58] The local men walked on but they alerted the police to the presence of the Poqo party.

Just before sunset, the police arrived along with local African supporters of Matanzima. A brief shoot-out took place.[59] The Bantu Affairs commissioner of Cofimvaba reported that after the initial exchange of gunfire, "I was informed that the Police had made contact with an Impi [regiment] on the mountain overlooking the Great Place and that because of the well-disciplined manner that the Impi displayed and the suddenness of the attack the Police force which numbered about 60 men and officers had to ["flee for their lives" is typed but then crossed out and replaced with] retreat. Three men were injured one very seriously and taken to hospital."[60] As the police either retreated or fled for their lives, the Poqo members quickly dispersed. It was not until the next day that police, bolstered by reinforcements, redeployed on the hill.[61]

During the subsequent police search of the hill, they found six bodies of Africans who had been killed and another badly wounded Poqo member who later died. The remaining Poqo members had retreated across the nearby Indwe river, and the following day they regrouped at the train station to board a train returning to Cape Town. Police heard of this fallback plan and launched an assault on the train station. The assault was indiscriminate—police attacked both Poqo members and unarmed bystanders as they boarded trains. The ensuing battle ended with the deaths of one white policeman and seven additional Africans and the arrests of "hundreds," although ultimately only a few were charged with crimes.[62]

The police initially released a story that the clashes near the chief's headquarters and at the Queenstown train station had resulted from random attacks unconnected to national politics. This narrative followed the same script as many official reports on rural faction fights that described them as dangerous but fundamentally unconnected to politics. However, the involvement of self-professed Poqo members and the apparent planning that went into the attack made the official narrative untenable. The day after the battle at the train station, according to the Liberal Party news outlet, *Contact*: "All pretence was dropped . . . and the police came out with their hair-raising story that 'Poqo,' which they identified 100 per cent with the banned Pan Africanist Congress, was 'launching a serious invasion of the Transkei,' with 'shock-troops,' Basutoland headquarters, and 'assault waves' from Cape Town."[63] The *Contact* report described the assassination attempt as a significant blow to the apartheid state's policies, concluding that "a somewhat dazed South African public took stock of the ruins of the government's facade of a contented African population."[64]

Despite the preceding years of unrest, state officials had been caught flatfooted by the assassination attempt. In retribution they launched an aggressive campaign to stamp out the broadening anti-state violence. White officials, with the assistance of Matanzima, searched for anyone involved in the assassination attempt and the subsequent fighting at the Queenstown train station: "In a pre-dawn swoop, a strong force of police, assisted by more than 1,500 of

Chief Kaiser Matanzima's followers, combed the area near where the clash occurred. Two South African Air Force helicopters were used for spotting," the *Rand Daily Mail* reported.[65] The resulting arrests and investigations led to the employment of secret police and informers throughout the rural areas to protect chiefs willing to work with the state.[66] The state provided weapons (often including guns) to chiefs and headmen considered loyal and dubbed them "Home Guards."[67] It also retooled the judicial system to deal harshly with political dissent. It convened special courts for trying those accused of participating in the attack and proposed the first of many laws designed to detain people suspected of political activities for ninety days without charging them with specific crimes.[68]

To recapture control and undercut popular support for the rebels, officials needed to breathe new life into the narrative of all rural violence being fundamentally either traditional—and therefore apolitical (and possibly irrational)—or inspired by Communists or other outside agitators. At times they suggested the violence was both traditional and inspired by outside agitators. In April 1963 the Bantu Affairs commissioner of Cofimvaba held a public meeting with Kaiser Matanzima and other chiefs. At the meeting, the official and the chiefs stressed "the origin of Poqo, what it stands for, the dastardly murders committed by it, its close association to communism, the part played by witchdoctors and herbalists and the most effective way to deal with this organization which has only been equaled by the mau mau of Kenya."[69] In addition to the stepped-up security precautions to combat the spread of violence, the chief Bantu Affairs commissioner suggested using propaganda that would undermine Poqo's legitimacy among rural people. "Full use should be made of Bantu superstition," he wrote. He then referred to the Xhosa cattle killing of the previous century as one possible way to threaten Africans: "The disaster of Nongqawuse (1857) and the horrible results that followed should be made to realistically indicate what will happen to the Bantu" who might try to overthrow white rule. He asked other Bantu Affairs commissioners to provide him with additional ideas for his "positive propaganda" campaign.[70] The propaganda would, he hoped, refurbish the idea that whites were unquestionably in control.

Poqo had not succeeded in killing Matanzima, but it had channeled the anger and dissatisfaction of some young men and identified a larger target for their violence. It had also effectively captured the headlines in white newspapers and provoked panic among officials. At the time, it seemed that Africans were seizing the political initiative rather than navigating a context controlled by the apartheid state. This sense of a potential political shift was heightened when, in early February 1963, another act of overt political violence took place.

This time, it involved killing a white road engineer and his family as they camped beside a roadside work site in the Transkei. Poqo members, most of whom were Transkeian labor migrants, were also responsible for these killings.

The Killings at the Mbashe River Campsite

Late at night on 4 February 1963, a road engineer, Norman Grobbelaar, and his wife and two teenaged daughters, were killed at the caravan camp where they were temporarily living. Grobbelaar was working on road improvements near the Mbashe River. An unrelated man, Derek Thompson, residing at the same campsite but in a different caravan, was also killed. The *Rand Daily Mail* reported that "Mr. Douglas Bridger who was sleeping in another caravan about three-quarters of a mile away was awakened at 2:45 a.m. by an African who told him that the Grobbelaars' caravan was in flames. Bridger aroused his staff of 40 African labourers and drove to the caravans. They found the bodies of the family lying outside their vehicle. 'They had been butchered,' he said, 'It was horrible.'"[71] A local white trader had already alerted the police. From the start of the investigation, it seemed likely that this attack had been planned: "Mr. Bridger said that his African watchmen had been told three weeks ago that the camp and its white inhabitants were to be 'burnt out.'"[72]

Police initially denied any political motivation for the roadside murders. Instead, the police suggested that local people opposed to the road building had committed the murders in a traditional fashion: "The attack bore signs of the traditional Xhosa method of settling grievances by burning huts and then killing the fleeing occupants."[73] The police official in charge of the investigation asserted that the attack was not part of a broad political strategy: "Police information was that the attack had been made by about a dozen and not by 100 tribesmen as had been reported. After such an attack, the attackers usually left their homes and fled into the mountains. The police believed that this was the case in the present instance."[74] The official police statement might have been an attempt to calm whites' fears of a potential revolt. At the same time, it also reflected a commonly held white belief that Africans living in the rural areas were all apolitical "tribesmen" who frequently resorted to traditional methods of settling grievances—hut burning and murder.

Over the next few days, however, the official story changed to an acknowledgment of the involvement of Poqo members in the attack. One news outlet asked in a story headline, "Poqo or Tradition?" and then answered its own question: "Reports from the murder scene blamed Poqo, the Bantu terrorist organisation."[75] Several days after the attack, the *Rand Daily Mail* reported in a follow-up story that police finally admitted that the attackers were Poqo members and not traditional (i.e., apolitical) tribesmen. The newspaper quoted Lieutenant General J. M. Keevy of the South African Police: "'There is, therefore, strong reason to believe that this secret organisation [Poqo] is implicated in the brutal murder.'"[76] The police investigation determined that as many as sixty people had taken part in the killings; eventually, twenty-three were arrested, tried, and sentenced to death for their roles in what was by then commonly understood as a Poqo operation.[77]

By early March 1963, Kaiser Matanzima was touting the official government line that Poqo members were the perpetrators of these violent attacks and that outsiders were manipulating them: "Poqo is communistically inclined—that is my view." The *Rand Daily Mail*, in a story titled "Transkei Chief Blames Liberals, Reds," quoted Matanzima's remarks: "'The target is the White man. They want him eliminated, eradicated, killed. If the White man does not want to leave South Africa, they must kill [him]. Poqo does not pay attention to passes. They are taught if the White man leaves, they will own the country.' Poqo members were illiterate and they used witchcraft and very brutal methods when they murdered people, Chief Kaizer [*sic*] said."[78] Matanzima's statement brought together the threads of the various explanations developed by the apartheid state and those African officials who supported it. In his view, traditional violence was brutal but apolitical, while all politically charged violence must be "communistically inclined." Matanzima's dismissal of Poqo's membership as illiterate and irrationally superstitious was an attempt to play down the reality of anger at state policies and officials, including himself.[79] Speaking to a newspaper with a predominantly white readership and promoting his own status, Matanzima also emphasized the potential threats to whites posed by Poqo's plots.

In a similar vein, the Bantu Affairs commissioner in Butterworth spoke against Poqo and its actions at several public meetings attended by Africans in his district in the aftermath of the attack. He depicted Poqo members as predatory outsiders, stating that they were from the cities and were demanding money from local people to support them. He stressed that such resistance did not stand a chance against the power of the state by pointing out Poqo's use of "the services of witchdoctors." He suggested that this was irrational "because they believed the witchdoctors could treat them so that they would be immune from arrest and prosecution." He also pointed out "that it was ridiculous to believe that such people could take up arms against the authorities which had the latest type of weapons and aircraft and that in any case large number of the Poqos [*sic*] had been arrested and punished, some with the death sentence. Apart from the arrests people who joined these organisations are being rounded up by the Police and even those who claim that they had been forced to join the organisation have lost their employment and are being removed from the cities. In this way they have achieved nothing and are suffering."[80] In essence, the Bantu Affairs commissioner was telling Africans to stop believing that they could liberate themselves and instead return to a life of quietly navigating the unequal political and social environment constructed by the apartheid state.

The attacks received banner headlines in the press. "Talk was of killing Whites:—Poqo witness"[81] blared one headline after the assassination attempt on Matanzima; another headline read, "Manhunt in Transkei: The Scene at the Engcobo Caravan Slayings" after the killings at the roadside camp.[82] News stories amplified the fear of widespread revolt. The editor for the influential journal *Drum*, Frank Barton, testified to the Snyman Commission, which was looking into Poqo's activities: "'My information is that there were many more murders committed by Poqo than have reached the Press."[83] Barton explained that, according to his information, Poqo's general aim was "to kill all the Whites and seize the country." He believed that Poqo's leaders had stepped up their planning for revolt because of "the Government's plan for the Transkei [which] became the bit against which Poqo strained."[84] White fears about Poqo were palpable and informed state actions. Similarly, Africans' fears about the powers of the state were well-founded, and their fears and resentments shaped resistance to policies and officials. With many of the PAC and Poqo activists either captured or in exile, rural Africans returned to a wary, defensive stance.

Despite attempts by officials to dismiss the significance of the violence, grievances among rural people were genuine. The Poqo adherents who committed the attacks were not young men fighting for respect and turf, nor were they beer drinkers out for a recreational battle; they were not disciplining family members, nor were they engaging in personal revenge. Instead, these were adults trying to achieve a political organization's aims using techniques of rural fighting and witchcraft eradication that had developed over the past several decades.

The fact that these two attacks by Poqo members did not ultimately subvert the control of the state in a lasting way resulted from two factors. One was the miscalculation that the PAC's leadership made about the immediate willingness of most Africans to engage in revolt. Poqo's attempt to use migrant laborers as guerrilla fighters drew on ideas about the political temperament of the African people—that "the masses" were poised to ignite a confrontation with the state.[85] But the number of people who participated in these actions was small—several hundred at most. The second factor was the brutality of the state's response that demonstrated its willingness to use disproportionate violence to maintain control. Ultimately, even the PAC leadership felt that the attempted assassination of Matanzima and the killings at the Mbashe camp-site had been premature and counterproductive because they provoked a massive state response against a small and fragile organization.[86]

Poqo's failures did not mean the end of opposition to state policies. Africans developed new critiques of Matanzima and other collaborating chiefs in the aftermath of the Poqo attacks and the state's brutal response. In Mbakweni township (outside of Paarl), a pamphlet circulated that derided Matanzima's collaboration with the apartheid state. The pamphlet questioned Matanzima's legitimacy as a political leader and painted a vivid image of him as an almost unnatural figure delighting in the devastation of his people: Matanzima was "flying with the Boers over the blood of the people in helicopters. He wants a seat which does not belong to him and his ancestors have sworn at him.'"[87]

State officials were aware of continuing African opposition. Press reports noted that state officials were shocked at the "deteriorating security situation" in the Transkei. A reporter posed a question to the minister of justice, John Vorster, about "a rumour about the time of the Queenstown incidents in December 1962 that Poqo was planning a limited invasion of the Transkei." The reporter asked whether the situation had deteriorated since the beginning of the year and the minister said: "Yes, certainly, quite fast." Vorster then linked the attacks to the Communist Party and suggested that they had been funded by "outside sources,"[88] even though all the people arrested and charged were Africans who had roots in the rural areas. Vorster returned to the old script about outsiders being the instigators of all the unrest as whites themselves tried to navigate a situation over which they had lost at least partial control. The only navigation tools they had to hand were brute force and a stale story.

In an attempt to sprint ahead of African political opposition and render grievances moot, the state advanced the timetable for granting self-rule to the Transkei as the first official homeland. "If the Transkei fails, so will apartheid," read a headline in the *Rand Daily Mail* in November 1962, shortly after the Poqo attack in Paarl. The story quoted Dr. J. E. Holloway, a member of a government commission on homelands policy: "If the Transkei development fails it means the failure of the whole policy of segregation," a conclusion with which the other members of the commission concurred.[89] Traditional violence had tried to take the political initiative and upset the plans for continued white dominance. Rather than reevaluating grand apartheid as a policy, state officials chose to push ahead with a sped-up timetable for creating the homelands.

Conclusion: If Transkei Fails,
So Will Apartheid

If Transkei fails, so will apartheid—this was the prescient assessment made by a functionary of the apartheid state at the outset of the homelands policy. The idea that the creation of homelands would somehow make the apartheid state legitimate to the majority African population was always a fantasy, although it probably seemed like less of an illusion to whites in the 1950s and early 1960s than it does in hindsight.[90] White policy makers imagined the homelands as a fundamental element of grand apartheid. In contrast, Africans like Matanzima, who acquiesced to working within the homelands framework, undoubtedly had several motives, including personal career advancement and self-enrichment.[91] Officials advocating the homelands policy stated that it was a form of decolonization. In reality, though, it was a reformulation of colonial rule under a different name. The violence that had gone into the creation of white power in the region was remaking that control. The Transkei was a test case for homelands policy, and it was also a test case for resistance to that policy. The prominent ANC leader Govan Mbeki made his own prediction about homelands policies: "The Transkei, show-place of the Bantustan scheme, could well be the first battlefield on which apartheid will be defeated."[92]

The dramatic attacks initiated by Poqo members in the early 1960s grew out of the regional violence that African rebels had used during the previous ten years against local officials and chiefs. The spread of that political resistance beyond the rural areas was a reaction to events, including the killings at Sharpeville and the aggressive implementation of apartheid laws affecting migrant laborers, rural African farmers, and African political leaders. Poqo's avowed focus on killing whites and African collaborators was particularly alarming to the white public and the state. The interim report released by the Snyman Commission signaled that alarm. The report warned that "terrorism and 'unlawful activities' by Poqo would increase on a national scale, with the object of overthrowing White rule in South Africa this year [1963] unless drastic action [is] taken immediately."[93]

The wave of armed resistance that the commission's report predicted did not occur. Still, the report's apocalyptic tone indicated how threatened whites and the apartheid government felt by the outbreak of political violence. Beyond shocking the white population, the violence was evidence of rebels' attempts to take control of their social and political environment and not simply try to avoid the worst blows delivered by state policies.

The organization of rural resistance remained loosely structured and dependent on older skills and regional networks, an indication of Poqo's roots among migrant laborers in the urban townships and farmers who were new to political organizing. Local rebels were still targeting headmen and lower level chiefs, while Poqo was also trying to kill people—like Chief Matanzima—with a higher profile in national politics. The move toward violence was an escalation of the long struggle for survival. But this violence also targeted ordinary people, particularly women, without much political power. The use of supernatural substances to aid both the local rebels and Poqo was also directly linked to the earlier violence against local targets. These techniques demonstrated continuing beliefs in the supernatural, but they were not evidence of a lack of rational aims. They were part of the attempt to enlist spiritual powers to reinstitute a moral and political order that Africans controlled.[94]

Whites and Africans depicted Poqo's violence as part of deeper but quite different historical narratives. For many whites, as seen in mainstream press coverage and official reports, this violence by Africans was either traditional—thus underscoring the longer term narrative of African culture as "savage"—or else incited by communists with ulterior motives. These explanations deflected blame for the violence away from the history of African dispossession by whites and placed the blame on African culture or on global communist conspiracies. Both white and African narratives captured some fundamental elements of the causes behind the violence. Still, they told only partial stories that did not examine how the more mundane violence of rural life deeply informed these events.

A significant aspect of the story of the nationalist turn that rural violence took was how enmeshed violence became in the lives of rural people. This rural resistance often stemmed from an understanding of state officials as evil forces who used supernatural powers and violence to maintain their authority. In the 1952–63 period, violent acts, which included arsons, murders, intimidation, physical assaults, threats, and sabotage of government projects, emerged from rural grievances and were rooted in older cultural understandings of the nature of state power and the threats to local communities. Rebels advanced the use of violence as a way of breaking through the restraints imposed on them by the apartheid state. As Henrik Vigh noted of the ex-combatants he interviewed in Guinea, they joined a rebel group as they sought "to survive when networks have contracted to a bare minimum and resources are barricaded out of reach."[95] For rural South African rebels in the 1960s, resources were out of reach and African chiefs and headmen were no longer responsive to their concerns. Similar to their Guinean counterparts in the 1990s, these rebels were willing to take violent life chances. They were no longer simply trying to cope with a harsh reality; they were instead trying to remake the social networks that might allow them to take greater control over their lives. The categories of sons, rebels, hooligans and world destroyers had collapsed into one another.

Conclusion

Rural Violence Reconsidered

In January 1963, a few weeks after the attempted assassination of Chief Matanzima, rebels in Engcobo burned the homestead of a headman. Three huts were destroyed, but the headman and his family had already vacated the home because, in the Bantu Affairs commissioner's words, he "had taken precautionary measures on the strength of information that his kraal was about to be burnt down." The commissioner noted that "headman Bernard Sigidi is a member of the Transkeian Territorial Authority and one of the best supporters of Government policy. He is a marked man, probably on account of his support of the Matanzima group."[1] The arson committed against the Engcobo headman's household was a clear case of rebels targeting him for his political stance. They provided a stark warning of what might happen if he continued to endorse government policies.

In late February 1963, shortly after the Grobbelaars died at their burnt-out caravan, rebels fatally attacked a headman in Cofimvaba. The headman, Jonginamba, had received a threatening letter from local residents who objected to state plans to move their homesteads as part of the agricultural policies known as rehabilitation. A group of twenty-five men decided to kill the headman, and in preparation, they sought treatment by a war doctor. Later that same night, the group surrounded the headman's hut: some threw stones at the door to break it down, while others set the thatched roof on fire. Jonginamba had a gun, and he fired shots from within the house, injuring one member of the attacking party. The headman and his family tried to run away as the house burned, but the attackers caught up with the headman and killed him with battle axes.[2]

These two attacks on headmen in 1963 were representative of multiple attacks on chiefs and headmen in the late 1950s and early 1960s. The attacks were violent and politically motivated. Some chiefs and headmen who refused to back down, like Chief Matanzima and headman Sigidi, survived, while others, like Jonginamba, died. Still other chiefs tried to navigate the newly dangerous situation. In February 1963, the Bantu Affairs commissioner in Willowvale asked the local chief, Zwelidumile Sigcau, to allow fencing and other unpopular agricultural measures to go forward in his ward as a show of support for the state. The commissioner found Sigcau's response "both startling and disquieting. The Chief said that if a Headman or chief accepted rehabilitation [agricultural policies] he would be killed. In the old days the chiefs ruled their people but not now—a rather startling admission." The chief pointed out that a headman in Kentani had recently been killed because he had accepted rehabilitation measures: "The Chief and his advisers went on to advocate that fencing should be postponed to a later stage to allow the Chiefs to regain control. I replied that they were asking the Government to allow the Bantu to do just exactly what they liked. Their opinions showed that the Chief had no control over his people."[3] The commissioner was not used to having an African chief tell him "No" when it came to implementing government policies. Yet the rebels' use of violence had forced Chief Sigcau into the position of saying no to specific government measures, and, to that extent, the rebels had succeeded in shifting "the unstable political landscape" in their favor.[4]

The political landscape did not remain favorable to rebels for long, however. Later in 1963, the Transkei became a self-governing homeland under the control of Chief Matanzima and ultimately became "independent" in 1976. The fake self-governance did not alter much of the routinized violence of rural African life. The South African state pursued rebels over the next several years, tried many for participating in the unrest, and executed several.[5] The ruling National Party and its proxies continued as the dominant political force in South Africa for the next thirty years. When the Transkei (and the apartheid regime with it) ultimately imploded in the 1990s, it left behind a hollowed-out system of ruling through a combination of brute force, bribery, and appeals to traditional authority.[6] It also left behind the rural impoverishment and stark gender inequalities created by the structural violence of the apartheid regime.

The rural areas of the Eastern Cape Province, which includes what was the Transkei, and KwaZulu-Natal have experienced continuing violence since the 1994 transition away from apartheid policies. Some of the violence is political, as people with claims to being traditional chiefs and headmen compete for power and the status and money that comes with it. For the most part, the government of the ruling African National Congress party has deferred to traditional rulers in the rural areas, even when the claims of these rulers contradict or undermine the ideals enshrined in the constitution. This point is particularly clear when discussing violence against women in the rural areas. The South African Constitution advocates gender equity, but in the rural areas under traditional headmen and chiefs, women often struggle to gain access to land or protect themselves against physical violence.[7] Women's subordination continues to be legitimated by references to traditions, and violence against women is styled as a type of discipline. More generally, access to land and the economic possibilities that come with it have sparked political mobilization and violence in the rural areas. These struggles are lineal descendants of the struggles of the first half of the twentieth century.[8] The violence of the years since 1994 remains outside the scope of this book, but it is fueling the research agendas of many scholars.

VIOLENCE, TRADITION, HISTORY

The historical study of violence in rural South Africa asks us to think about how violence was built into the ruling structures of the white settler state and then enfolded into Africans' daily lives. A monopoly on the use of violence is a defining characteristic of a state and thus the violence wielded by the South African state was not unique. Violence was a foundational fact of the colonial state throughout Africa. The South African strategy of devolving much of the responsibility of local governance in rural areas onto supposedly traditional authorities was also common.[9] However, what the South African state did so successfully was to embed violence into colonially reconstructed traditions derived from local cultures. By the 1960s the state had pushed this strategy to an extreme with the system of homelands. But even before the National Party came to power, state policies and modes of governing had ensured that Africans' traditions were encoded with violent practices. The state, its policies, and its enforcement systems allowed and encouraged certain acts of violence within families and communities and then legitimated that violence as part of traditional life. This reframing of tradition as violent was a process that took place over several decades as people's ideas about tradition interacted with government officials and policies and the legal system.

Traditional practices developed along untraditional lines during the twentieth century. The sparring among recently circumcised young men described by Ludwig Alberti in 1807 looked very different from the all-out battles among men of various factions in the 1950s. Alberti stated that, while using lethal weapons such as spears and fighting sticks demonstrated their new status as men, the "weapons have been placed in their hands for the protection of their chief";[10] they were not to be used as toys or to settle personal scores. This picture contrasts with the descriptions of faction fights common in the Transkei from the late 1920s in which groups of armed men, sometimes numbering in the dozens, sometimes in the thousands, challenged, ambushed, and assaulted each other. Occasionally they fought over smaller, more personal grievances such as insulting remarks or rivalries over girlfriends, but over time, grievances multiplied and intensified. Fighting became more lethal as men began bringing battle axes and guns bought with wages gleaned as migrant laborers. The police, representing an institution of white settler authority, were usually either not present for these battles or ineffective at preventing them; headmen, who acted as deputies for the state, sometimes actively engaged in the fighting. By the 1940s and later, officials became convinced that Africans were "addicted to violence," as one magistrate opined.[11] By the 1950s the magistrates who tried fighters in court saw them as "hooligans" whose violent acts could lead to widespread political unrest if the state and African elders did not step in to tame them. Equating fighting with dangerous traditions and social unrest allowed officials to justify using coercive measures to repress the violence. Thus, while lethal violence had become more common under white rule, magistrates persisted in seeing the fighting as traditional and inherent to African culture.

A similar trend was evident in the gradual acceptance by the legal system of violence in abduction marriages, or *ukuthwala*, as traditional. In the late precolonial period, parents had felt it was their right to order daughters to marry men of their parents' choosing. Abduction marriages in the precolonial period were arranged either by elders to marry off unwilling daughters or by lovers to avoid the choices of their parents. In either case, the earlier evidence suggests that such marriages were relatively rare if also commonly accepted as customary.[12] But during the twentieth century, abduction marriages became more common and often involved considerable force; magistrates and white juries accepted this use of force as traditional as long as the guardians of the young women endorsed the marriages. Legally, the young women themselves did not have to consent to the unions. Distinctions between consent and outright resistance became blurred as a narrative developed among Africans that a young woman who fought against being abducted was engaging in a performance of modesty and would ultimately submit to the traditional marriage as a matter of duty and pride. Marriage was such a foundational part of rural life that parents and prospective suitors were willing to use violence to achieve it. It was also so foundational that, apparently, many women reconciled themselves to abduction marriages even when they fought them initially. Violence was thus instilled into marriage more generally and written into the traditions of rural family life.

Family and community members also faced violence when suspected of witchcraft. The white state opposed and tried to subvert consultations with diviners and imposed criminal punishments on those who accused people of witchcraft. Magistrates lamented Africans' beliefs in witchcraft and saw them as evidence of cultural "backwardness." The state's opposition and the force of criminal prosecution did little to eradicate these beliefs and may have given them a politically subversive dimension. Africans consulted diviners to diagnose the causes of problems they faced, especially family deaths and illness. While many of these problems resulted from state policies and the impact of labor migration, people looked for more local and intimate culprits. Violence, in the form of arsons and assaults, were common punishments for witches. While people often identified women, particularly widows, as witches, women were not just the victims of such violence. They also participated in it and sometimes, acting as diviners, leveled the accusations. While the state prosecuted criminal acts that resulted from witchcraft allegations, magistrates were seemingly blind to how state policies and the reliance on migrant labor in the broader economy created the social harms that led to witchcraft accusations.

Violence became associated with many traditions. Africans often claimed that the use of physical force was traditional and necessary to protect the family and shore up the moral order in the countryside. For its part, the state also used the idea of African traditions as violent to bolster its claims to power and authority. But the violent acts committed by Africans in the countryside were directly tied to the shifting circumstances of rural life. Over the twentieth century, the shifts in the social environment imposed significant strains on families' lives. People found it more challenging to achieve their expectations as the gap between what they thought was moral and desirable and what was possible widened. People often tried to bridge that widening gap with the use of violence. Physical force became more associated with masculinity, and men increasingly used physical force to build and maintain families. But the use of violence was not confined to men. Women used coercion and physical force to protect households threatened either by childbirth out of wedlock or the use of witchcraft to achieve selfish ends. By the 1950s, people began to use violence against state officials and unjust policies that threatened people's livelihoods. The two categories of political violence on the one hand and intra-familial and community violence on the other overlapped on issues of land allocation, fencing, and the naming and punishing of witches.

In the 1950s and 1960s, rural violence took a nationalist turn. The revolt that rippled through the rural areas began in response to local grievances over the imposition of new laws regarding agriculture and land use. As the state increased its reliance on local chiefs, like Matanzima and others, and made plans to spin the homelands out of South Africa, rebels began to identify higher profile targets. In particular, members of Poqo, the armed wing of the Pan-Africanist Congress, launched a series of attacks directed against whites and against Africans who supported the state. These attacks combined nationalist aspirations and economic grievances with older rural methods of witchcraft eradication.

Whites, both officials and the wider public, responded to Africans' grievances by pretending they did not exist. Instead, they focused on the rebels' appeals to the supernatural and their presumed irrationality. In press accounts on the attempted assassination of Chief Kaiser Matanzima, for example, the supernatural doctoring of Poqo members received more attention than African political and economic grievances. Just after the police attack on the train in Queenstown, as a few Poqo members attempted to escape, a *Rand Daily Mail* banner headline screamed, "8 Dead in Panga Riot: Berserk mob surge off train." The article underneath stressed the dangers posed by allegedly "berserk" Poqo members—who killed one policeman—and not the dangers posed by the police who shot and killed seven Africans, most of whom were bystanders.[13] Many of Poqo's adherents were men from the Transkei who worked as migrant laborers in or near Cape Town. The dreadful conditions of life for African labor migrants received little coverage. Instead, press coverage played up the analysis of government officials: that Africans were superstitious, brutal, and open to manipulation by outside agitators, particularly communists.

The various attacks by Poqo in 1962 and 1963 helped put the homelands policy and the "independence" of the Transkei onto a faster track, as white officials hoped to solve the problems African nationalism posed by creating pseudostates. But African nationalist demands were not so easily sidetracked, and increasingly between 1963 and the ultimate demise of the homelands in 1994, violence by state actors or their proxies in the rural areas was a necessary component of maintaining state control.

VIOLENCE: RED AND GRAY

Many of the court cases and reports by magistrates and police discussed in this study have documented individual acts of physical violence. This violence was "red" in Donald Donham's formulation.[14] But the mundane, structural violence of the state and its enforcers was often a bureaucratic gray. As magistrates described their reasons for judgment in multiple court cases, they built up layers of judicial precedent that hardened into the system of customary law applied to many aspects of African life. Magistrates' ideas of what constituted the traditional use of violence, in abduction marriages for example, legalized intimate violence committed by women's guardians and prospective husbands. They judged that men had not committed assaults, kidnappings, and rapes when those men had followed what the magistrates deemed traditional practices. State officials' acceptance of rural fighting, to pose another example, as a manifestation of supposedly age-old tribal disputes, deflected responsibility for social disruption away from government policies and toward African culture. Magistrates caned, imprisoned, and fined offenders, and sometimes sentenced them to death, all of which were bureaucratically sanctioned punishments.

Africans' use of violence was not always "red" either. People's ideas about respectability, morality, and honor underwrote some of their violence to create and maintain a version of family life and rural culture. Violent acts were products of people's understanding of what was traditional and legally approved under the colonial and apartheid regimes. Abduction marriages fell into this category as the perpetuation of families was an important goal for many parents. Africans also saw some faction fighting as acceptable if they could gloss it as "boys' fights" that taught discipline or revenged wrongs. Violence within families and among neighbors, especially violence aimed at named witches, was often an attempt to discipline family members or neighbors suspected of causing illnesses, deaths, and economic disasters.

When at least some Africans accepted the reconstruction of traditions as violent, it gave an aura of legitimacy to the violence. At the same time, the state's acceptance and promotion of violence as traditional dovetailed with white officials' ideas about African culture. Magistrates in the late 1890s were asked to comment, as part of their annual reports, on whether Africans in their districts were "progressing" in terms of civilization. Magistrates often wrote about how slowly people adopted "civilization" and how frequently violence occurred, particularly under the influence of home-brewed beer.[15] In officials' commentaries in the twentieth century, fighting became evidence of an ongoing lack of civilization: As one police official remarked when reporting on a 1959 faction fight in Willowvale: "The cause of this matter is apparently the general hostility between uncivilized and uncircumcised youths of different locations in the Transkei. It is traditional for them to behave in this manner before attaining adulthood."[16] Thus, white officials marginalized the aspirations of rural people who were already deemed marginal in the colonial and apartheid periods. By disparaging rural culture and experiences, state officials could also distract from their own roles in fostering the violence.

The state's use of both "red" and "gray" violence against marginalized people was not unique to South Africa. Nancy Scheper-Hughes, in her study of state-sponsored violence in Brazil, questioned the idea that violent acts were always "extraordinary": "What if the disappearance, the piling up of civilians in common graves, the anonymity, and the routinization of violence and indifference were not, in fact, an aberration? What if the social spaces before and after such seemingly chaotic and inexplicable acts were filled with rumors and whisperings, with hints and allegations of what could happen?"[17] Scheper-Hughes was concerned with how routinely the Brazilian state used violence against ordinary people. She suggested that the state's definition of much of the population as "marginal" made it easy for the state to justify all sorts of violent enforcement actions against them by defining them as inherently "criminal" or "deviant." The ruling elite took so little account of people in the lower strata of society that they were in an official sense "disappeared" and rendered anonymous. In Brazil this structural disappearance of people translated into the physical disappearance of critics of the regime as well as into rumors of state actors kidnapping poor people and snatching their organs to provide vital medicine for the wealthy, events and tales that captured the "ontological insecurity" of the poor.[18] Whether directly perpetrated by the state or by others, the broader impacts of violence were not just the immediate, physical injuries but also included a deep sense of anonymity; of having one's experiences silenced in the historical record; of being someone of "no account."

Over the period covered in this study, the South African state "disappeared" the violence resulting from state policies by pushing much of it into the rural areas and defining it as traditional. Migrant labor, segregation policies, and apartheid altered rural life significantly, creating what Glen Elder called the "procreational geography of apartheid." For an adult man by the early 1900s, working in the mines was one pathway to masculine adulthood. Earning wages at the mines made it possible for him to marry and have a family, yet going to the mines also meant losing intimate daily contact with his household for long periods.[19] Upon his return, exercising his authority could mean using force to discipline his children or wife, coercing a daughter into an arranged marriage, or fighting to protect access to land or the homestead. He and other family members could justify this violence as a form of discipline that was necessary and moral because it was part of a strategy to maintain the family and survive. While this intrafamilial and intracommunity violence was rooted in colonial and white rule, the violence was interwoven with the daily practices and moral structures of individuals' lives.

Rural people thus used violence as a part of their strategy for social navigation. They used it to exercise local and personal control over circumstances that made their lives uncertain. They acted in much the same way as Henrik Vigh's Guinean informants who, in a West African, postcolonial context, had "to navigate an unstable political landscape."[20] Vigh's Guinean informants were young men with few opportunities who opted to go to war, not to seek thrills or loot, but rather to open doors to new possibilities. When they fought, Vigh writes, "their battle was not so much against an Other as for a process of social becoming and improvement of their life chances."[21] Vigh's continuing research, however, shows the longer term effects of young people using violence to achieve their ends. Some of his informants have subsequently engaged in drug trafficking and other organized crime, becoming "anti-social bandits."[22] Poqo adherents and other rebels did not follow an analogous trajectory into banditry in the late 1960s. In the late 1980s and early 1990s, Poqo's parent organization, the PAC, regained political energy as African violence against the decaying apartheid state increased.[23]

Beyond the Guinean example, other scholars have shown the utility of social navigation as a concept to understand marginalized people as both actors and acted upon even in societies that are not at war. The idea of social navigation captures people's intentionality, their focus on desired ends, and also their vulnerability to disruptive events outside their control. In the context of rural South Africa, the fact that people could depict some violent acts as traditional made those acts more acceptable and perhaps more honorable. However, they often deployed violence in a calculated way to achieve specific ends rather than performing it according to culturally scripted rituals. Africans were trying to improve their life chances in a colonized and unstable world.

NOTES

INTRODUCTION

1. Cape Province Archives, Cape Town, Records of the Magistrate of Ngqeleni (1/NQL) 1/1/1/11, Case 324 of 1936, R. v. Dli Mtsho, 4 September 1936.

2. Cape Province Archives, 1/NQL 1/1/1/11, Case 324 of 1936, R. v. Dli Mtsho, 4 September 1936.

3. Cape Province Archives, 1/NQL 1/1/1/11, Case 324 of 1936, R. v. Dli Mtsho, 4 September 1936.

4. South African National Archives, Pretoria, Records of the 1932 Native Economic Commission (K26), vol. 25, File 69B, Replies to Commission questionnaire from the Native Commissioner of Bulwer, Polela division, Natal Province, to the Secretary to Native Economic Commission, 27 January 1931.

5. South African National Archives, K26, File N.E.C. 68D, Letter from the Magistrate of Idutywa to the Secretary to the Native Economic Commission, 20 February 1931.

6. Henrik Vigh, "Motion Squared: A Second Look at the Concept of Social Navigation," *Anthropological Theory* 9, no. 4 (2009): 423.

7. Anna Hedlund, "Simple Soldiers? Blurring the Distinction between Compulsion and Commitment among Rwandan Rebels in Eastern Congo," *Africa: The Journal of the International African Institute* 87, no. 4 (2017): 720–37; Katie Kuschminder, "Before Disembarkation: Eritrean and Nigerian Migrants Journeys within Africa," *Journal of Ethnic & Migration Studies* (2020): 1–16.

8. Julie Soleil Archambault, "Cruising Through Uncertainty: Cell Phones and the Politics of Display and Disguise in Inhambane, Mozambique," *American Ethnologist* 40, no. 1 (2013): 90.

9. Vigh, "Motion Squared," 432.

10. Leroy Vail, "Introduction: Ethnicity in Southern African History," in *The Invention of Tribalism in Africa*, ed. Leroy Vail (Berkeley: University of California Press, 1991), 1–20; T. O. Ranger, "The Invention of Tradition in Colonial Africa," in *The*

Invention of Tradition, ed. T. O. Ranger and E. Hobsbawm (Cambridge: Cambridge University Press, 1983), 211–62.

11. Kristin Mann and Richard Roberts, eds., *Law in Colonial Africa* (Portsmouth, NH: Heinemann Educational Books, 1991).

12. Helen Bradford, "Women, Gender and Colonialism: Rethinking the History of the British Cape Colony and Its Frontier Zones, c. 1806–70," *Journal of African History*, no. 3 (1996): 360–62; Elizabeth Thornberry, *Colonizing Consent: Rape and Governance in South Africa's Eastern Cape*, African Studies Series (Cambridge: Cambridge University Press, 2019), 38–40; Heike Becker, "History: Colonialism, Christianity, and Tradition," in *Unravelling Taboos: Gender and Sexuality in Namibia*, ed. Suzanne LaFont and Dianne Hubbard (Windhoek, Namibia: Legal Assistance Center, 2007), 26.

13. Jill Kelly, *To Swim with Crocodiles: Land, Violence, and Belonging in South Africa, 1800–1996* (East Lansing: Michigan State University Press, 2017); Mbongiseni Buthelezi and Beth Vale, "Collisions, Collusions and Coalescences: New Takes on Traditional Leadership in Democratic South Africa: An Introduction," in *Traditional Leaders in a Democracy: Resources, Respect and Resistance*, ed. Mbongiseni Buthelezi, Dineo Skosana, and Beth Vale (Johannesburg: Mapungubwe Institute for Strategic Reflection [MISTRA], 2018), 1–20; Jo Beall, "Cultural Weapons: Traditions, Inventions and the Transition to Democratic Governance in Metropolitan Durban," *Urban Studies* 43, no. 2 (2006): 457–73.

14. Murray Leibbrandt, Ingrid Woolard, and Christopher Woolard, "Poverty and Inequality Dynamics in South Africa: Post-Apartheid Developments in the Light of the Long-Run Legacy," *South African Economic Policy under Democracy* 10 (2009): 270–300; Geoffrey E. Schneider, "The Post-Apartheid Development Debacle in South Africa: How Mainstream Economics and the Vested Interests Preserved Apartheid Economic Structures," *Journal of Economic Issues* 52, no. 2 (2018): 306–22.

15. Jeremy Seekings, "The Social and Political Implications of Demographic Change in Post-Apartheid South Africa," *The Annals of the American Academy of Political and Social Science* 652, no. 1 (2014): 70–86; Robert Mattes, "The 'Born Frees': The Prospects for Generational Change in Post-Apartheid South Africa," *Australian Journal of Political Science* 47, no. 1 (2012): 133–53.

16. Jean Comaroff and John L. Comaroff, *The Truth about Crime: Sovereignty, Knowledge, Social Order* (Chicago: University of Chicago Press, 2016), 143–80; K. Durrheim, X. Mtose, and L. Brown, *Race Trouble: Race, Identity and Inequality in Post-Apartheid South Africa* (Lanham, MD: Lexington Books, 2011), 86–96.

17. Dineo Skosana, "Traditional Leadership and the African National Congress in South Africa: Reflections on a Symbiotic Relationship," in *Traditional Leaders in a Democracy: Resources, Respect and Resistance*, ed. Mbongiseni Buthelezi, Dineo Skosana, and Beth Vale (Johannesburg: Mapungubwe Institute for Strategic Reflection [MISTRA], 2018), 50–74.

18. Shireen Hassim, Tawana Kupe, and Eric Worby, *Go Home or Die Here: Violence, Xenophobia and the Reinvention of Difference in South Africa* (Johannesburg: Wits University Press, 2008); Belinda Dodson, "Locating Xenophobia: Debate, Discourse, and Everyday Experience in Cape Town, South Africa," *Africa Today* 56, no. 3 (2010):

2–22; Jason Hickel, "'Xenophobia' in South Africa: Order, Chaos, and the Moral Economy of Witchcraft," *Cultural Anthropology* 29, no. 1 (2014): 103–27; Jonny Steinberg, "Xenophobia and Collective Violence in South Africa: A Note of Skepticism about the Scapegoat," *African Studies Review* 61, no. 3 (2018): 119–34.

19. Pumla Dineo Gqola, "How the 'Cult of Femininity' and Violent Masculinities Support Endemic Gender Based Violence in Contemporary South Africa," *African Identities* 5, no. 1 (2007): 111–24; Kylie Thomas, *Homophobia, Injustice and "Corrective Rape" in Post-Apartheid South Africa*, Center for the Study of Violence and Reconciliation Report (CVSR, 2013).

20. Comaroff and Comaroff, *The Truth about Crime*, 218–23.

21. Kelly, *To Swim with Crocodiles*, 189–218; Benedict Carton, "Locusts Fall from the Sky: Manhood and Migrancy in KwaZulu," in *Changing Men in Southern Africa*, ed. Robert Morrell (London: Zed Books, 2001), 129–40; Sindiso Mnisi Weeks, *Access to Justice and Human Security: Cultural Contradictions in Rural South Africa* (London: Routledge, 2018), 1–23, 83–101.

22. William Beinart, "Political and Collective Violence in Southern African Historiography," *Journal of Southern African Studies* 18, no. 3 (September 1992): 465.

23. David Chidester, *Wild Religion: Tracking the Sacred in South Africa* (Berkeley: University of California Press, 2012), 13–14.

24. Donald L. Donham, "Staring at Suffering: Violence as a Subject," in *States of Violence: Politics, Youth, and Memory in Contemporary Africa*, ed. Edna G. Bay and Donald L. Donham (Charlottesville: University of Virginia Press, 2006), 18.

25. Chidester, *Wild Religion*, 52–64.

26. Donham, "Staring at Suffering," 18.

27. Saul Dubow, "Racial Irredentism, Ethnogenesis, and White Supremacy in High-Apartheid South Africa," *Kronos: Southern African Histories* 41, no. 1 (2015): 254–56.

28. Gary Kynoch, "Urban Violence in Colonial Africa: A Case for South African Exceptionalism," *Journal of Southern African Studies* 34, no. 3 (2008): 629–45.

29. Glen S. Elder, "Malevolent Traditions: Hostel Violence and the Procreational Geography of Apartheid," *Journal of Southern African Studies* 29, no. 4 (December 2003): 922.

30. Neil Whitehead, "On the Poetics of Violence," in *Violence*, ed. Neil Whitehead (Santa Fe, NM: School of American Research Press, 2004), 65.

31. Peter Geschiere, *The Perils of Belonging: Autochthony, Citizenship, and Exclusion in Africa and Europe* (Chicago: University of Chicago Press, 2009), 104–12.

32. Anne Mager, *Gender and the Making of a South African Bantustan: A Social History of the Ciskei, 1945–59* (Portsmouth, NH: Heinemann, 1999), 133–36.

33. Mager, *Gender and the Making of a South African Bantustan*, 161.

34. Anne McClintock, "'No Longer in a Future Heaven': Gender, Race and Nationalism," in *Dangerous Liaisons: Gender, Nation, and Postcolonial Perspectives*, ed. Anne McClintock, Mufti Aamir, and Ella Shohat (Minneapolis: University of Minnesota Press, 1997), 89–100; Gayatri Chakravorty Spivak, "Preface to Concerning Violence," *Film Quarterly* 68, no. 1 (2014): 61–62.

35. Helen Moffat, "'These Women, They Force Us to Rape Them': Rape as Narrative of Social Control in Post-Apartheid South Africa," *Journal of Southern African Studies* 32, no. 1 (March 2006): 137–41.

36. Daniel R. Magaziner, "Pieces of a (Wo)Man: Feminism, Gender and Adulthood in Black Consciousness, 1968–1977," *Journal of Southern African Studies* 37, no. 1 (2011): 59.

37. Gary Kynoch warns against a depiction of township violence in the early 1990s as a "one-dimensional morality play" that ultimately "works against the emergence of a more inclusive, less partisan nation-building project." "Reassessing Transition Violence: Voices from South Africa's Township Wars, 1990–94," *African Affairs* 112 (2013): 285.

38. Mark Hunter, *Love in the Time of AIDS: Inequality, Gender, and Rights in South Africa* (Bloomington: Indiana University Press, 2010), 158.

39. Belinda Bozzoli, "Marxism, Feminism and Southern African Studies," *Journal of Southern African Studies* 9 (1983): 149–55.

40. Kynoch, "Urban Violence in Colonial Africa," 629–30; Jonathan Clegg, "*Ukubuyisa Isidumbu*—'Bringing Back the Body': An Examination into the Ideology of Vengeance in the Msinga and Mpofana Rural Locations, 1882–1944," in *Working Papers in Southern African Studies*, vol. 2, ed. P. Bonner (Johannesburg: Ravan Press, 1979), 164–98.

41. Clegg, "*Ukubuyisa Isidumbu*—'Bringing Back the Body'"; Jabulani Sithole, "Land Disputes, Social Identities and the State in the *Izimpi Zemibango* in the Umzinto District, 1930–1935," *Journal of Natal and Zulu History* 27 (2009): 60–82; Brian H. King and Brent McCusker, "Environment and Development in the Former South African Bantustans," *Geographical Journal*, no. 1 (2007): 6–13; Jennifer Beningfield, *The Frightened Land: Land, Landscape and Politics in South Africa in the Twentieth Century* (New York: Routledge, 2006), 121–26.

42. Clifton C. Crais, *Poverty, War, and Violence in South Africa* (New York: Cambridge University Press, 2011), 8.

43. Crais, *Poverty, War, and Violence in South Africa*, 17–19.

44. Crais, *Poverty, War, and Violence in South Africa*, 150–54.

45. Norman Etherington, "Putting the Mfecane Controversy into Historiographical Context," in *Mfecane Aftermath: Reconstructive Debates in Southern African History*, ed. Carolyne Hamilton (Johannesburg: Wits University Press, 1995), 13–15; Sam Naidu, "Three Tales of Theal: Biography, History and Ethnography on the Eastern Frontier," *English in Africa* 39, no. 2 (2012): 51–68.

46. In Natal, native commissioners adjudicated legal cases concerning Africans on the basis of a codified "Native Law," while in the Transkeian region of the Cape, magistrates adjudicated cases based on their understanding of what was customary. Africans involved in trials in Transkeian magistrates' courts had the right to appeal verdicts to the chief magistrate's court. In the case of capital crimes, such as murder, African defendants typically were tried under colonial law in the regular court system, but preparatory examinations on these crimes often took place in magistrates' courts before going forward.

47. Cape of Good Hope, *Report of the Government Commission on Native Laws and Customs*, 2 vols., Facsimile Reprint (Cape Town: Struik, 1968), 2:444.

48. Mahmood Mamdani, *Citizen and Subject* (Princeton, NJ: Princeton University Press, 1994), 18.

49. Isak Niehaus, "Witchcraft and the South African Bantustans: Evidence from Bushbuckridge," *South African Historical Journal* 64, no. 1 (2012): 41–58.

50. Thomas V. McClendon, *White Chief, Black Lords: Shepstone and the Colonial State in Natal, South Africa, 1845–1878* (Rochester, NY: University of Rochester Press, 2010), 21–46.

51. Cape of Good Hope, *Government Commission on Native Laws and Customs*, 1:42–47, 65–66.

52. J. W. MacQuarrie, ed., *The Reminiscences of Walter Stanford* (Cape Town: Struik, 1958), 1:98–106.

53. Lungisele Ntsebeza, *Democracy Compromised: Chiefs and the Politics of Land in South Africa* (Cape Town: HRSC Press/Brill, 2005/6), 46–52.

54. South African National Archives, Pretoria, Records of the 1903–1905 South African Native Affairs Commission (C17), vol. 6, written replies by J. C. Garner, Magistrate of Libode, 13 November 1903, 34.

55. Sean Redding, *Sorcery and Sovereignty: Taxation, Power and Rebellion in South Africa, 1880–1963* (Athens: Ohio University Press, 2006), 13–29.

56. Ivan Evans, *Bureaucracy and Race: Native Administration in South Africa* (Berkeley: University of California Press, 1997), 166–75.

57. Henrik Vigh, "Social Death and Violent Life Chances," in *Navigating Youth, Generating Adulthood: Social Becoming in an African Context*, ed. Catrine Christiansen, Mats Utas, and Henrik Vigh (Uppsala, Sweden: Nordic Africa Institute, 2006), 47–55.

58. Saul Dubow, "Holding 'a Just Balance between Black and White': The Native Affairs Department in South Africa c. 1920–33," *Journal of Southern African Studies* 12, no. 2 (1986): 228–34.

59. Franco Barchiesi, "The Violence of Work: Revisiting South Africa's 'Labour Question' through Precarity and Anti-Blackness," *Journal of Southern African Studies* 42, no. 5 (2016): 880, 886–91.

60. Evans, *Bureaucracy and Race*, 268–75.

61. Vigh, "Motion Squared," 432.

62. William Beinart, "Beyond Homelands: Some Ideas about the History of African Rural Areas in South Africa," *South African Historical Journal* 64, no. 1 (2012): 7–8.

63. The court case records after 1902 are incomplete because they were culled, usually by retired magistrates preparing the case files for the archives. For some districts' records, the culling was extensive; for other districts, a larger proportion of the records remain. The criteria that magistrates used for this process were not documented.

64. Ann Laura Stoler, *Along the Archival Grain: Epistemic Anxieties and Colonial Common Sense* (Princeton, NJ: Princeton University Press, 2009), 2.

65. Poppy Fry, "Re-Reading the 1835 'Fingo Emancipation': Women and Ethnicity in the Colonial Archive," in *Gendering Ethnicity in African Women's Lives*, ed. Jan B. Shetler (Madison: University of Wisconsin Press, 2015), 90.

66. Benedict Carton and Robert Morrell, "Zulu Masculinities, Warrior Culture and Stick Fighting: Reassessing Male Violence and Virtue in South Africa," *Journal of Southern African Studies* 38, no. 1 (2012): 53.

67. Carton and Morrell, "Zulu Masculinities," 43.

68. Kate Rice's detailed account of attitudes toward abduction marriages among Xhosa-speaking informants in 2008–13 discusses why Africans currently assume the practice has deep historical roots. "Ukuthwala in Rural South Africa: Abduction Marriage as a Site of Negotiation about Gender, Rights and Generational Authority among the Xhosa," *Journal of Southern African Studies* 40, no. 2 (2014): 381–99. Elizabeth Thornberry has discussed the connections between *ukuthwala* and the customary in the eastern Cape largely focusing on the 1860s through the 1930s: Thornberry, *Colonizing Consent.*

69. Karen Flint, *Healing Traditions: African Medicine, Cultural Exchange, and Competition in South Africa, 1820–1948* (Athens: Ohio University Press, 2008), 95–118.

70. Tom Lodge, "The Poqo Insurrection, 1961–1968," in *Resistance and Ideology in Settler Societies*, ed. John Lonsdale (Johannesburg: Ravan, 1986), 179–222; Brown Bavusile Maaba, "The PAC's War against the State, 1960–1963," in *The Road to Democracy in South Africa*, vol. 1, *1960–1970*, ed. South African Democracy Education Trust (Cape Town: Zebra Press, 2004), 257–98.

Chapter 1. Neighbors and Rivals

1. Nelson Mandela, *Long Walk to Freedom: The Autobiography of Nelson Mandela* (New York: Little, Brown, 1994), 11.

2. Mandela, *Long Walk to Freedom*, 12.

3. Alex Duval Smith, "South African Townships Take Stick-Fighting Tradition into New Future," *Guardian*, 30 January 2011.

4. A similar article, with video footage, appeared on the BBC online, and the video has footage of children fighting each other, including a match between two young girls. "South Africa's Ancient Art of Stick Fighting," BBC News, 3 March 2011, http://www.bbc.com/news/world-africa-12632447.

5. In this time period for most people in the eastern Cape, one of the socially accepted differences between boys and men was whether the individuals involved had gone through the full ritual of circumcision and initiation. This ritual could take place any time after puberty, but often parents might postpone the ritual because of costs or a desire to bring together a cohort of boys to go through the ritual together. See J. H. Soga, *The Ama-Xosa: Life and Customs* (Lovedale, South Africa: Lovedale, 1931), 248–49.

6. Soga, *The Ama-Xosa*, 312.

7. Soga, *The Ama-Xosa*, 313.

8. Cape Province Archives, Cape Town, Records of the Magistrate of Flagstaff (1/FSF) 1/1/1/30, Case 119 of 1944, R. v. Mkosana Dlepu and others, 6 March 1944.

9. Sithole, "Land Disputes, Social Identities," 63.

10. Clegg, "*Ukubuyisa Isidumbu*—'Bringing Back the Body,'" 164–98.

11. T. Dunbar Moodie with Vivienne Ndatshe, *Going for Gold: Men, Mines, and Migration* (Berkeley: University of California Press, 1994), 185.

12. Keith Breckenridge, "Migrancy, Crime and Faction Fighting: The Role of the Isitshozi in the Development of Ethnic Organisations in the Compounds," *Journal of Southern African Studies* 16, no. 1 (March 1990): 55–78.

13. Carton and Morrell, "Zulu Masculinities," 31–53; Robert Morrell et al., "Hegemonic Masculinity: Reviewing the Gendered Analysis of Men's Power in South Africa," *South African Review of Sociology* 44, no. 1 (2013): 15–16; Keith Breckenridge, "The Allure of Violence: Men, Race and Masculinity on the South African Goldmines, 1900–1950," *Journal of Southern African Studies* 24, no. 4, Special Issue on Masculinities in Southern Africa (December 1998): 669–93.

14. Vigh, "Motion Squared," 423.

15. Sithole, "Land Disputes, Social Identities," 65.

16. Hlonipha Mokoena, personal communication, August 2021.

17. See, for example, a trial that arose out of a stick fight among boys in which one boy was killed: Cape Province Archives, Cape Town, Records of the Magistrate of Nqamakwe (1/NKE) 1/1/1/26, Case 131 of 1897, R. v. Mafana and 28 others, 9 July 1897.

18. Ludwig Alberti, *Account of the Tribal Life and Customs of the Xhosa in 1807* (Cape Town: Balkema, 1968), 87.

19. Alberti, *Account of the Tribal Life and Customs of the Xhosa in 1807*, 41.

20. Timothy J. Stapleton, *Faku: Rulership and Colonialism in the Mpondo Kingdom (c. 1780–1867)* (Waterloo, ON: Wilfrid Laurier University Press, 2001), 17–29.

21. Carton and Morrell, "Zulu Masculinities," 45–47.

22. See Charles Brownlee's description of intermittent fighting between the Mpondo, Xesibe, Bhaca, and Mpondomise in 1840–1873 and the "deadly feud" between the two Mpondomise chiefs Mditshwa and Mhlonhlo and their followers. *Reminiscences of Kaffir Life and History, and Other Papers*, 2nd ed. (Fort Hare, South Africa: Lovedale, 1916), 102–8.

23. Timothy J. Stapleton, "'Him Who Destroys All': Reassessing the Early Career of Faku, King of the Mpondo, c. 1818–1829," *South African Historical Journal*, no. 38 (1998): 55–63; Elizabeth Eldredge, "Sources of Conflict in Southern Africa c. 1800–1830: The 'Mfecane' Reconsidered," in *The Mfecane Aftermath: Reconstructive Debates in Southern African History*, ed. Carolyn Hamilton (Johannesburg: Witwatersrand University Press, 1995), 140–61.

24. See the narrative of invasions and raids provided in "Historical Sketch of the Pondomise Tribe as Taken from 'Vete' the Son of Umziziba," in Cape of Good Hope, *Commission on Native Laws and Customs*, 2:404–5; see also N. J. van Warmelo, ed., *History of Matiwane and the AmaNgwane Tribe, as Told by Msebenzi to His Kinsman Albert Hlongwane*, Ethnological Publication 7 (Pretoria: Government Printer, 1938).

25. MacQuarrie, *The Reminiscences of Walter Stanford*, 1:20–186; Redding, *Sorcery and Sovereignty*, 31–56.

26. Carton and Morrell sketch out a similar set of causes for the rise of the Zulu warrior stereotype in "Zulu Masculinities," 45–46.

27. Testimony of Veltdman, a Mfengu headman from the Transkei, in Cape of Good Hope, *Commission on Native Laws and Customs*, 2:477. For an example of testimony

provided by whites about drinking and fighting, see the testimony of William Rafferty Donald Flynn, a former magistrate, to the commission: *Report of the Government Commission on Native Laws and Customs*, 2:279.

28. Michael R. Mahoney, *The Other Zulus: The Spread of Zulu Ethnicity in Colonial South Africa* (Durham, NC: Duke University Press, 2012), 97–101.

29. Cape Province Archives, CMT 3/679, File 175, Returns under the heading "Crime," from Umtata District Magistrate, Blue Book for Native Affairs.

30. Cape Province Archives, Cape Town, Records of the District Council of Umtata (1/UTA C1/1/3), Letter from Samuel J. Mkaula, Assistant Secretary for the Umtata Native Vigilance Association, to the Chairman of the Umtata District Council, 30 July 1907.

31. All but two of the accused men were found not guilty of culpable homicide, although several others were found guilty of fighting or public violence, and three were found guilty of assault with intent to commit grievous bodily harm. The sentences for culpable homicide were two years of hard labor for both men convicted; for those convicted of assault with intent, the sentence was eighteen months, and for public fighting the sentence was one year (Cape Province Archives, 1/UTA 1/1/1/78, Case 1062 of 1951, R. v. Xego Fokwana and 38 others, 9 April 1952.

32. Cape Province Archives, Cape Town, Records of the Magistrate of Xhalanga (1/XAA) 1/1/1/12, Case 311/48, R. v. Nzingo Dyariwe and 14 others, 24 November 1948.

33. Bradford, "Women, Gender and Colonialism," 361–63; Soga, *The Ama-Xosa*, 381–83.

34. Patrick McAllister, *Xhosa Beer Drinking Rituals: Power, Practice and Performance in the South African Rural Periphery* (Durham, NC: Carolina Academic Press, 2006), 25–30.

35. McAllister also documents the high levels of concern expressed about excessive beer drinking by African representatives in the General Council (the Bhunga) in the Transkei. *Xhosa Beer Drinking Rituals*, 28–29.

36. Monica Wilson, *Reaction to Conquest: Effects of Contact with Europeans on the Pondo of South Africa* (London: International Institute of African Languages and Cultures, 1936), 160.

37. M. Wilson, *Reaction to Conquest*, 160.

38. Soga, *The Ama-Xosa*, 41.

39. Jacob Tropp provides a long quotation from an interview with R. T. S. Mdaka. Mdaka was a boy in the rural areas in the 1920s, and he discussed the necessity of boys knowing how to fight with sticks to defend themselves. *Natures of Colonial Change: Environmental Relations in the Making of the Transkei* (Athens: Ohio University Press, 2006), 128–31.

40. Tropp remarks that "youth fights, often involving many boys and resulting in severe injuries, were a regular feature of life in the early colonial period. . . . Rather than simply reflecting what colonial officials neatly categorized as 'faction fights' between distinct 'tribes' or levels of 'civilization' . . . these confrontations involved a complex combination of changing cultural identities and economic situations." *Natures of Colonial Change*, 128.

41. South African National Archives, Pretoria, Records of the Secretary for Native Affairs (NTS) 7640, File 2/331, Reports on criminal statistics for the Transkei, compiled by the South African Police.

42. It is likely that magistrates only tried cases that involved fighting when they resulted in deaths or multiple serious injuries, a possibility that would tend to result in an under-reporting of the number of fights.

43. South African National Archives, Pretoria, Records of the Ministry of Justice (JUS) 188, File 2/62/14 (part 2), Letter from W. Taylor, Inspector, South African Police, to the Deputy Commissioner, South African Police, Umtata, 8 April 1924.

44. Cape Province Archives, Cape Town, Records of the Magistrate of Willowvale (1/WVE) 1/1/26, Case 292 of 1935, R. v. Sololo Pakati and 23 others, 28 August 1935. The fact that some of the defendants were listed as "boys" on the trial record probably indicated that they were not circumcised and thus had not passed through the ritual that gave them adult status.

45. Cape Province Archives, 1/NQL 1/1/1/12, Case 559 of 1944, R. v. Ngcingi and 29 others, 18 October 1944.

46. Cape Province Archives, 1/WVE 1/1/26, Case 25 of 1946, R. v. Mboli Gudlani and 24 others, 27 March 1946.

47. Cape Province Archives, Cape Town, Records of the Magistrate of Mount Frere (1/MFE) 1/1/1/40, Case 673/47, R. v. Maxoki Maroyi and 77 others, 13 January 1948. The sentences ranged from six months of imprisonment with hard labor to monetary fines of £15 for several of the accused.

48. Cape Province Archives, Cape Town, Records of the Chief Magistrate of the Transkei (1/CMT) 3/1478, File 42/8, Letter from the Bantu Affairs Commissioner, Libode district to the Chief Bantu Affairs Commissioner, 14 March 1961.

49. Cape Province Archives, 1/CMT 3/1481, File 42/15, Letter from the Bantu Affairs Commissioner of Mqanduli to the Chief Bantu Affairs Commissioner, 18 January 1961.

50. According to the census, in 1904 the total African population of South Africa was 3.4 million; in 1960 the total African population was 10.9 million. Even if the exact population figures are inaccurate, they still indicate substantial population growth. For a discussion of the problems of relying on census data, see A. J. Christopher, "The Union of South Africa Censuses, 1911–1960: An Incomplete Record," *Historia* 56, no. 2 (2011): 1–18.

51. Steven Pinker, *The Better Angels of Our Nature: Why Violence Has Declined* (New York: Viking, 2011), 312–13, 684–89; Henrik Urdal, *A Clash of Generations? Youth Bulges and Political Violence*, Expert Paper Series No. 2012/1 (New York: United Nations, 2012), 9–10, http://www.un.org/esa/population/publications/expertpapers/Urdal_Expert %20Paper.pdf.

52. Mager, *Gender and the Making of a South African Bantustan*, 101–4.

53. Clegg, "*Ukubuyisa Isidumbu*—'Bringing Back the Body,'" 22.

54. John Iliffe, in his study of honor in African societies, makes the distinction between the honor of the young warrior and the honor of the mature householder in African societies. See *Honour in African History* (New York: Cambridge University Press, 2005), 6, 170–71, 284–86.

55. Anne Mager, "Youth Organisations and the Construction of Masculine Identities in the Ciskei and Transkei, 1945–60," *Journal of Southern African Studies* 24 (1998): 654.

56. South African National Archives, NTS 7687, File 309/332, Letter from the South African Police Divisional Headquarters, Umtata, to Commissioner for the South African Police, Pretoria, 27 August 1947.

57. South African National Archives, NTS 7687, File 309/332, Letter from the Office of the District Commandant, Umtata, to the Deputy Commissioner of the South African Police, Umtata, 17 April 1948; NTS 7687 File 309/332, Letter from the Office of the District Commandant, Umtata, to the Deputy Commissioner of the South African Police, Umtata, 8 June 1949; NTS 7687, File 309/332, Letter from the Office of District Commandant, Umtata, to the Deputy Commissioner of the South African Police, Umtata, 8 September 1949.

58. Cape Province Archives, 1/NQL 51, File 2/10/4, Letter from the Magistrate of Ngqeleni to the Chief Magistrate of the Transkei, 23 August 1949, with enclosed minutes of a meeting between the headman and the magistrate.

59. He was convicted of culpable homicide and sentenced to nine months in prison. Cape Province Archives, Cape Town, Records of the Magistrate of Libode (1/LBE) 1/1/12, Case 567/54, R. v. Xakiwe Zimbini, 8 October 1954.

60. Cape Province Archives, CMT 3/1477, File 42/3/8, Report from the South African Police, Elliotdale, to the District Commandant, Umtata, 20 February 1960.

61. Thornberry, *Colonizing Consent*, 280–83.

62. Cape Province Archives, Cape Town, Records of the Magistrate of Mqanduli (1/MQL) 6/1/60, File N1/9/2, Report from Constable Egling of the South African Police, Mqanduli, to the Magistrate of Mqanduli, June 1956.

63. Paul La Hausse, "'The Cows of Nongoloza': Youth, Crime and Amalaita Gangs in Durban, 1900–1936," *Journal of Southern African Studies* 16, no. 1 (1990): 79–111; M. C. O'Connell, "Xesibe Reds, Rascals and Gentlemen at Home and Work," in *Black Villagers in an Industrial Society*, ed. Philip Mayer (Cape Town: Oxford University Press, 1980), 255–303; Breckenridge, "Migrancy, Crime and Faction Fighting."

64. Breckenridge, "Migrancy, Crime and Faction Fighting," 71.

65. Although each of the group identities may have had at its core an ethic of violent masculinity. See Gary Kynoch, "From the Ninevites to the Hard Livings Gang: Township Gangsters and Urban Violence in Twentieth-Century South Africa," *African Studies* 58, no. 1 (1999): 60–62.

66. Mamdani, Citizen and Subject, 196; Ntsebeza, *Democracy Compromised*, 62–92.

67. William Beinart, "Conflict in Qumbu: Rural Consciousness, Ethnicity and Violence in the Colonial Transkei," in *Hidden Struggles in Rural South Africa*, ed. William Beinart and Colin Bundy (Berkeley: University of California Press, 1987), 106–8.

68. The district of Umzimkulu was part of East Griqualand. When East Griqualand was annexed by the Cape Province in 1878, it was incorporated into the Transkeian Territories, and then into the Transkei homeland until 1994. The provincial boundaries

have subsequently been changed and the district is part of KwaZulu-Natal. Nhlangwini and Bhaca people had both come from north of the Umzimkulu River in the early to mid-1800s. The Bhaca had migrated as a result of the military upheavals surrounding the creation of the Zulu kingdom; the Nhlangwini moved as white settlers (Boers) moved into what became Natal in the 1840s. See John Wright, "PMB Before the Voortrekkers," Natal Witness (n.d.), 1, http://www.pmbhistory.co.za/portal/witness history/custom_modules/TheWayWeWere/PMB%20before%20the%20Voortrekkers .pdf; and David Hammond-Tooke, *Bhaca Society* (Cape Town: Oxford University Press, 1962), 1–7.

69. Cape Province Archives, CMT 3/1483, File 42/25/8, Part 1, South African Police Progress Report on case R. v. Jobe Bukwana and 188 others on charges of affray, culpable homicide, and arson, 20 August 1930.

70. William Beinart, "The Anatomy of a Rural Scare: East Griqualand in the 1890s," in *Hidden Struggles in Rural South Africa*, ed. William Beinart and Colin Bundy (Berkeley: University of California Press, 1987), 46–78; Cape of Good Hope, *Report of a Commission Appointed to Inquire into the Causes of the Recent Outbreak in Griqualand East* (Cape Town: Solomon, 1879).

71. Cape Province Archives, Cape Town, Records of the Chief Magistrate of Griqualand East (CMK) 5/20, "Minutes of Enquiry Regarding the Causes of the Disturbances in Umzimkulu during January 1897, deposition of Field Cornet J. E. Hancock.

72. Cape Province Archives, CMK 5/20, "Minutes of Enquiry Regarding the Causes of the Disturbances in Umzimkulu during January 1897." See also Stanford's retrospective discussion of this episode in MacQuarrie, *Reminiscences of Walter Stanford*, 2:180–85.

73. Cape Province Archives, CMT 3/1483, File 42/25/8, Part 1, Letter from the Divisional Inspector of the South African Police, Transkei, to the Deputy Commissioner of the South African Police, 14 November 1923.

74. Cape Province Archives, CMT 3/1483, File 42/25/8, Part 1, Letter from the Magistrate of Umzimkulu, to the Chief Magistrate of the Transkei, 27 November 1923.

75. CMT 3/1483, File 42/25, "Report on Bantu Unrest: Expectation Trust Farm: Gowan Lea Police Area," 17 April 1962.

76. The anthropologist W. D. Hammond-Tooke, whose research among the Bhaca took place in the 1950s, also noted that fights were very common, and he adhered to the official analysis in his conclusion that the fights were "merely local quarrels" (Hammond-Tooke, *Bhaca Society*, 221).

77. Cape Province Archives, CMT 3/1483, File 42/25, "Report on Bantu Unrest: Expectation Trust Farm: Gowan Lea Police Area," 17 April 1962.

78. Cape Province Archives, CMT 3/1478, File 42/5/8, Police report, from the office of the South African Police, Flagstaff, to the District Commandant, Kokstad, 19 July 1959.

79. Cape Province Archives, CMT 3/1478, File 42/5/8, Police report, from the office of the South African Police, Flagstaff, to the District Commandant, Kokstad, 4 May 1960.

80. Cape Province Archives, 1/FSF 1/1/1/37, Case 221 of 1960, R. v. Mqelwa Sikonxo and 8 others, 28 July 1960.

81. Redding, *Sorcery and Sovereignty,* 175–200.

82. There were some emissaries from the African National Congress leadership and from the South African Communist Party who traveled to the region. But they mostly arrived after hostilities against state policies had begun and were most likely trying to get an idea of what was happening on the ground rather than instigating the revolt. See quotations from interviews with Harry Gwala and Thomas Nkobi in Philip Bonner et al., "The Road to Armed Struggle," in *The Road to Democracy in South Africa,* vol. 1, *1960–1970,* ed. South African Democracy Education Trust (Cape Town: Zebra Press, 2004), 58–61.

83. Cape Province Archives, 1/FSF 6/97, File C3/2, Typescript: "Unrest in Flagstaff District. 1960–1961," unsigned, undated, probably mid-1961.

84. Cape Province Archives, 1/FSF 6/97, File C3/2, Typescript: "Unrest in Flagstaff District. 1960–1961," unsigned, undated.

85. Cape Province Archives, CMT 3/1478, File 42/5, Pamphlet enclosed in a letter, marked "Confidential," from the Bantu Affairs Commissioner of Flagstaff to the Assistant Chief Bantu Affairs Commissioner, 27 October 1961.

86. Cape Province Archives, CMT 3/1478, File 42/5, Pamphlet enclosed in letter, 27 October 1961, emphasis in the original.

87. Bernard Magubane et al., "The Turn to Armed Struggle," in *The Road to Democracy in South Africa,* vol. 1, *1960–1970,* ed. South African Democracy Education Trust (Cape Town: Zebra Press, 2004), 58–61.

88. See Ntsebeza, *Democracy Compromised,* 175–89, 202.

89. Cape Province Archives, CMT 3/1451, File 38/A, "Report of the Chief Magistrate and Chief Native Commissioner of the Transkeian Territories for the Year Ending 31 December 1957," dated 8 September 1958.

90. Cape Province Archives, CMT 3/1481, File 42/15, Letter from the Bantu Affairs Commissioner of Mqanduli to the Chief Bantu Affairs Commissioner, 5 July 1961.

91. Cape Province Archives, CMT 3/1481, File 42/15, Letter from the Bantu Affairs Commissioner of Mqanduli to the Chief Bantu Affairs Commissioner.

92. Cape Province Archives, CMT 3/1477 File 42/3, Letter from the Bantu Affairs Commissioner, Elliotdale, to the Chief Bantu Affairs Commissioner, 21 June 1963.

Chapter 2. "The Girl Is Not Consulted"

1. Cape of Good Hope, *Commission on Native Laws and Customs,* 1:95.

2. Different sources use different spellings of the isiXhosa word. I have adopted the spelling that is most commonly used by scholarly authors and government sources since the mid-1990s, but I have retained the original spellings of the word in quoted materials.

3. Cape of Good Hope, *Commission on Native Laws and Customs,* 1:440.

4. Natasha Erlank, "Gendering Commonality: African Men and the 1883 Commission on Native Law and Custom," *Journal of Southern African Studies* 29, no. 4 (2003): 953.

5. James Ferguson, *Expectations of Modernity: Myths and Meanings of Urban Life on the Zambian Copperbelt* (Berkeley: University of California Press, 1999), 87–90.

6. Elizabeth Thornberry, "*Ukuthwala,* Forced Marriage, and the Idea of Custom in South Africa's Eastern Cape," in *Marriage by Force? Contestation Over Consent and Coercion in Africa,* ed. Annie Bunting, Benjamin Lawrance, and Richard Roberts (Athens: Ohio University Press, 2016), 147.

7. Nyasha Karimakwenda, "Rethinking Ukuthwala, the South African 'Bride Abduction' Custom," *The Conversation,* 12 September 2021, https://theconversation.com/rethinking-ukuthwala-the-south-african-bride-abduction-custom-165496.

8. Anonymous, "Lusikisiki Girl Abducted in Kwa Ncele," Treatment Action Campaign Newsletter, https://www.tac.org.za/news/lusikisiki-girl-abducted-in-kwa-ncele/.

9. Staff Reporter, "Forced Marriage in South Africa," *Sunday Times,* 10 December 2009.

10. Kate Rice has analyzed the literature on the practice of *ukuthwala.* "Ukuthwala in Rural South Africa," 382–83. See also the discussion of recent practices in Nyasha Karimakwenda, "Deconstructing Characterizations of Rape, Marriage, and Custom in South Africa: Revisiting the Multi-Sectoral Campaign against Ukuthwala," *African Studies Review* 63, no. 4 (2020): 763–81.

11. Glen S. Elder, *Hostels, Sexuality, and the Apartheid Legacy: Malevolent Geographies* (Athens: Ohio University Press, 2003), 44–63.

12. Magistrate J. C. Warner commented in 1856 that Africans' "wives are nevertheless mere slaves, and have all the drudgery and laborious work to perform" (quoted in John MacLean, *A Compendium of Kafir Laws and Customs* [Mt. Coke, 1858], 72).

13. Erlank, "Gendering Commonality."

14. Ferguson was drawing on the insights of Judith Butler in her discussion of gender as a performance in *Expectations of Modernity,* 99, citing Judith Butler, *Gender Trouble: Feminism and the Subversion of Identity* (New York: Routledge, 1990), 139.

15. Virginia Van der Vliet, "Traditional Husbands, Modern Wives? Constructing Marriages in a South African Township," in *Tradition and Transition in Southern Africa: Festschrift for Philip and Iona Mayer,* ed. Andrew Speigel and Patrick McAllister (New Brunswick, NJ: Transaction, 1991), 219–21.

16. Lynn M. Thomas, "The Modern Girl and Racial Respectability in 1930s South Africa," *Journal of African History* 47, no. 3 (2006): 461–90.

17. Vigh, "Motion Squared," 423.

18. Mats Utas, "West-African Warscapes: Victimcy, Girlfriending, Soldiering: Tactic Agency in a Young Woman's Social Navigation of the Liberian War Zone," *Anthropological Quarterly* 78, no. 2 (2005): 403–8.

19. Marjoke A. Oosterom, "Youth and Social Navigation in Zimbabwe's Informal Economy: 'Don't End Up on the Wrong Side,'" *African Affairs* 118, no. 472 (2019): 493.

20. See the testimony of Chief Dalindyebo of the Thembu in Union of South Africa, *Report from the Select Committee on Native Custom and Marriage Laws* (Cape Town: Solomon Printers, 1913), 84–85.

21. Elder, *Hostels, Sexuality and the Apartheid Legacy,* 103–9.

22. McAllister, *Xhosa Beer Drinking Rituals,* 123–57.

23. John Comaroff and Jean Comaroff, *Of Revelation and Revolution*, vol. 2, *The Dialectics of Modernity on a South African Frontier* (Chicago: University of Chicago Press, 1997), 258–59.

24. Shula Marks, "Patriotism, Patriarchy and Purity: Natal and the Politics of Zulu Ethnic Consciousness," in *The Creation of Tribalism in Southern Africa*, ed. Leroy Vail (Berkeley: University of California Press, 1991), 215–40; Hamilton Sipho Simelane, "The State, Chiefs and the Control of Female Migration in Colonial Swaziland, c. 1930s to 1950s," *Journal of African History* 45, no. 1 (2004): 103–24; Ferguson, *Expectations of Modernity*, 87–95; Moodie with Ndatshe, *Going for Gold*, 11–43.

25. Belinda Bozzoli, *Women of Phokeng* (Johannesburg: Ravan, 1992), 147–64.

26. Meghan Healy, "'To Control Their Destiny': The Politics of Home and the Feminisation of Schooling in Colonial Natal," *Journal of Southern African Studies* 37 (2011): 247–64; Sean Redding, "Women as Diviners and as Christian Converts in Rural South Africa, c. 1880–1963," *Journal of African History* 57, no. 3 (2016): 367–89.

27. South African National Archives, Pretoria, Records of the 1903–05 South African Native Affairs Commission (SANAC) C17, vol. 6, written replies by W. Holford, November 1903.

28. See the statements made by a deputation of chiefs and headmen to the magistrate of Pinetown in Natal in KwaZulu-Natal Province Archives, Pietermaritzburg, Records of the Secretary of Native Affairs (Natal) (SNA) 1/1/328, File 2678/1905, Letter from the Natal Undersecretary of Native Affairs, 2 November 1905.

29. Henri Junod, in his ethnography of the Thonga in northeastern South Africa, states that girls did have some say in choosing a marriage partner: "[A] father very seldom obliges his daughter to accept a husband whom she dislikes, except in the case of debt." *The Life of a South African Tribe*, 2 vols. (New Hyde Park, NY: University Books, 1962), 1:102.

30. Nafisa Essop Sheik, "Colonial Rites: Custom, Marriage Law and the Making of Difference in Natal, 1830s–c. 1910" (PhD diss., University of Michigan, Ann Arbor, 2012), 108–19.

31. See the testimony of the Reverend William Sigenu, "Fingo, Wesleyan Missionary," to the 1883 Native Laws Commission in Cape of Good Hope, *Commission on Native Laws and Customs*, 1:399–400; and the comments of Walter Stanford in MacQuarrie, *Reminiscences of Walter Stanford*, 1:100–102.

32. Cape of Good Hope, *Commission on Native Laws and Customs*, 1:517.

33. Cape of Good Hope, *Commission on Native Laws and Customs*, 1:517–18.

34. Cape of Good Hope, *Commission on Native Laws and Customs*, 1:304.

35. Cape of Good Hope, *Commission on Native Laws and Customs*, 1:439.

36. MacQuarrie, *Reminiscences of Walter Stanford*, 1:188–91.

37. Rev. E. J. Barrett, "Kaffir Marriages," *Wesleyan-Methodist Magazine*, June 1883, 426.

38. South African National Archives, Pretoria, SANAC C 17, vol. 3, Evidence of R. J. Dick, Special Magistrate, King William's Town, 2 November 1903.

39. Even in Natal, which had an official procedure of asking every girl who was marrying if she was marrying freely, Native commissioners noted that marriages

in which girls were forced to marry men against their wishes were common. See KwaZulu-Natal Province Archives, SNA 1/1/90, Letter from Assistant Native Commissioner of the Lower Tugela Division to the Secretary for Native Affairs, Natal, 16 April 1886.

40. Thomas V. McClendon, "Tradition and Domestic Struggle in the Courtroom: Customary Law and the Control of Women in Segregation-Era Natal," *International Journal of African Historical Studies* 28, no. 3 (1995): 532–33.

41. South African National Archives, SANAC C17, vol. 6, written replies by Peter Mti, "Native Clerk, East London," November 1903, 65. Mti identified himself as having grown up near Keiskamahoek, in Kingwilliamstown district in the eastern Cape.

42. Soga, *The Ama-Xosa*, 271.

43. There were differences in the laws pertaining to Africans throughout what is now South Africa until after the Act of Union in 1910. Even after 1910, though, some differences remained. In Natal and Zululand, technically, even a minor daughter's marriage without her consent was not permitted, but most magistrates acknowledged that it regularly occurred regardless.

44. An interesting instance of damages being paid by a man after his attempted abduction marriage was annulled (because the woman's father disapproved) is a 1931 case in the Cape Province Archives, Cape Town, Records of the Magistrate of Cofimvaba (1/COF) 1/1/2/4, Preparatory exam 13/1931, R. v. Mponqo Matumbu.

45. Cape Province Archives, 1/COF 1/1/1/36, R. v. Cetywayo Mayekiso, 20 December 1915.

46. Cape Province Archives, 1/COF 1/1/1/36, R. v. Cetywayo Mayekiso, 20 December 1915

47. Cape Province Archives, 1/NKE 1/1/1/39, Case 136 of 1916, R. v. Buti Swaartbooi and others, 5 June 1916.

48. Cape Province Archives, 1/NKE 1/1/1/39, Case 136 of 1916, R. v. Buti Swaartbooi and others, 5 June 1916.

49. Cape Province Archives, 1/NKE 1/1/1/39, Case 136 of 1916, R. v. Buti Swaartbooi and others, 5 June 1916.

50. Cape Province Archives, 1/NKE 1/1/1/39, Case 136 of 1916, R. v. Buti Swaartbooi and others, 5 June 1916.

51. See the testimony of the magistrates of Willowvale, Kentani, and Butterworth districts to the 1903–5 South African Native Affairs Commission in South African National Archives, SANAC C17, vol. 3, 996–1000.

52. Bozzoli, *Women of Phokeng*, 86–93; Philip Mayer, *Townsmen or Tribesman?*, 2nd ed. (Cape Town: Oxford University Press, 1961), 233–51.

53. Sean Redding, "Witchcraft, Women, and Taxes in the Transkei, South Africa, 1930–63," in *Stepping Forward: Black Women in Africa and the Americas*, ed. Catherine Higgs, Barbara Moss, and Earline Rae Ferguson (Athens: Ohio University Press, 2002), 87–99.

54. Union of South Africa, *Report from the Select Committee on Native Custom and Marriage Laws*, 53.

55. T. R. H. Davenport, "The Triumph of Colonel Stallard: The Transformation of the Natives (Urban) Areas Act Between 1923 and 1937," *South African Historical Journal* 2 (1970): 77–96.

56. One copy of the letter is in Cape Province Archives, 1/NKE 7/1/58, File N1/9/2, Letter, signed by J. D. Rheinallt Jones and H. Selby Msimang, to Native Chiefs, Transkei, April 1925. None of the chiefs' replies were in the file.

57. South African National Archives, NEC K26 16, Records of statements from the Orange Free State, Evidence presented by the Kroonstad Joint Council of Europeans and Natives dealing with Kroonstad Location, 17 February 1931.

58. Cape Province Archives, 3/UTA 18, File 48E, Letter from the Location Superintendent to the Town Clerk, 21 May 1931.

59. See also the testimony of a local African businessman in Umtata, Thomas Poswayo, to the Native Economic Commission: South African National Archives, NEC K26 15, File "Records of Statements from the Transkei," Evidence of Thomas Poswayo at Umtata, 1930; and Charlotte Maxeke's analysis in 1930 of the problems that women faced when they moved to cities to work, reprinted in Thomas Karis and Gwendolyn Carter, *From Protest to Challenge: A Documentary History of African Politics in South Africa, 1882–1990*, 5 vols. (Palo Alto: Hoover Institution, 1972–96), 1:344–46.

60. Mager, *Gender and the Making of a South African Bantustan*, 176–78.

61. D. H. Reader, *The Black Man's Portion* (Cape Town: Oxford University Press, 1961), 188.

62. It was of course not just daughters who sometimes balked at arranged marriages: Nelson Mandela famously escaped the rural Transkei and moved to Johannesburg to avoid a marriage arranged by his parents. See Mandela, *Long Walk to Freedom*, 10, 20.

63. Simelane, "The State, Chiefs and the Control of Female Migration," 109–11.

64. Union of South Africa, *Native Custom and Marriage Laws*, iii–iv.

65. South African National Archives, NTS 1772, File 64/276/6, Letter 11 August 1932, Native Commissioner, Nongoma, to the Secretary for Native Affairs.

66. Cape Province Archives, 1/COF 1/1/2/3, Preparatory Examination 11/1929, R. v. Motu Caso.

67. Cape Province Archives, 1/COF 1/1/2/3, Preparatory Examination 11/1929, R. v. Motu Caso.

68. Cape Province Archives, 1/COF 1/1/2/3, Preparatory Examination 11/1929, R. v. Motu Caso.

69. Elizabeth Thornberry discusses the legality of abduction marriages and the connection to rape law in the colonial eastern Cape in *Colonizing Consent*, 171–92.

70. Cape Province Archives, Cape Town, Records of the Magistrate of Kentani (1/KNT) 1/1/18, Case 6/39, R. v. Kuleni Gqugquta and Gade Gqugquta, 25 August 1939, appeal heard by Supreme Court of South Africa, Butterworth Circuit Local.

71. Cape Province Archives, 1/KNT 1/1/18, Case 6/39, R. v. Kuleni Gqugquta and Gade Gqugquta, 25 August 1939.

72. Cape Province Archives, 1/KNT 1/1/18, Case 6/39, R. v. Kuleni Gqugquta and Gade Gqugquta, 25 August 1939.

73. The law at the time was that a man could not rape his wife. Generally, magistrates did not routinely try abduction marriages, regardless of circumstances, as rapes, nor did they see numerous cases of rape in any circumstances. The acting magistrate in Engcobo stated in 1936 that "very few cases of rape come before this Court. It is considered that a large number are settled amongst the natives themselves." See Cape Province Archives, Cape Town, Records of the Magistrate of Engcobo (1/ECO) 6/1/28, File N1/18/2, letter from the Magistrate to Dr. B. J. F. Laubsher, Senior Physician, Mental Hospital, Queenstown, 12 June 1936.

74. Cape Province Archives, 1/KNT 1/1/18, Case 6/39, R. v. Kuleni Gqugquta and Gade Gqugquta, 25 August 1939. The case file does not state whether the marriage was annulled after the trial, or what became of the different people involved. Anne Mager recounts a similarly violent instance of a woman being forcibly married to a man she did not want, with ultimately fatal results for her husband. *Gender and the Making of a South African Bantustan*, 102–5.

75. For some other cases of *ukuthwala* abductions that came to trial, see Cape Province Archives, Cape Town, Records of the Magistrate of Tsolo (1/TSO) 1/1/22, Case 468 of 1949, R. v. Dickson Macutsha; 1/COF 1/1/1/38, Case 798/1941, R. v. Rulumente Mkontwana, 14 October 1941; 1/COF 2/1/1/59, Case 35/40, Lumkile Nkanti v. Nziponde Pilisani and Pendu Pilisani, 12 April 1940; Cape Province Archives, 1/MTF 2/1/1/20, Case 53/1939, Alfraim Zenzele Mbobo v. Ngcoyo Juqu, 18 October 1939; and Cape Province Archives, 1/NKE 1/1/1/40, Case 269 of 1931, R. v. Moyeni Tshemese and Bonakele Mapungu, 23 September 1931.

76. M. Wilson, *Reaction to Conquest*, 189.

77. Cape Province Archives, CMT 3/1033, File 6/D, Letter from the Bantu Affairs Commissioner of Libode, 15 November 1962

78. Anne Mager, "Sexuality, Fertility and Male Power," *Agenda: Empowering Women for Gender Equity* 28 (1996): 14.

79. Cape Province Archives, 1/LBE 1/1/12, Case 614/51, R. v. Manxelo Mneno and Elias Tshaka, 28 November 1951.

80. Cape Province Archives, 1/LBE 1/1/12, Case 614/51, R. v. Manxelo Mneno and Elias Tshaka, 28 November 1951.

81. Julia Wells, "Why Women Rebel: A Comparative Study of South African Women's Resistance in Bloemfontein (1913) and Johannesburg (1958)," *Journal of Southern African Studies* 10, no. 1 (1983): 39–55; Mayer, *Townsmen or Tribesman?*, 275–82.

82. M. Wilson, *Reaction to Conquest*, 187–88.

83. Joan Broster, *Red Blanket Valley* (Johannesburg: Hugh Keartland, 1967), 79.

84. Broster, *Red Blanket Valley*, 77–78.

85. Broster, *Red Blanket Valley*, 80.

86. Broster, *Red Blanket Valley*, 81.

87. Cape Province Archives, 1/COF 1/1/1/36, R. v. Cetywayo Mayekiso, 20 December 1915.

88. Adam Ashforth, *Witchcraft, Violence, and Democracy in South Africa* (Chicago: University of Chicago Press, 2005), 42.

89. Ashforth in *Witchcraft, Violence, and Democracy in South Africa*, 43, cites Alan Morris, *Change and Continuity: A Survey of Soweto in the Late 1990s* (Johannesburg: Sociology Department, University of the Witwatersrand, 1999).

90. Ashforth, *Witchcraft, Violence, and Democracy in South Africa*, 43.

91. Kate Wood, Helen Lambert, and Rachel Jewkes, "'Showing Roughness in a Beautiful Way': Talk about Love, Coercion, and Rape in South African Youth Sexual Culture," *Medical Anthropology Quarterly* 21 (2007): 277–300.

92. Wood, Lambert, and Jewkes, "Showing Roughness in a Beautiful Way," 295.

93. Deborah Posel, "The Scandal of Manhood: 'Baby Rape' and the Politicization of Sexual Violence in Post-Apartheid South Africa," *Culture, Health and Sexuality* 7, no. 3 (2005): 242.

94. Posel does not discuss abduction or forced marriages specifically in the article, however.

95. Memory Mphaphuli and Letitia Smuts, "'Give It to Him': Sexual Violence in the Intimate Relationships of Black Married Women in South Africa," *Signs: Journal of Women in Culture & Society* 46, no. 2 (2021): 445.

96. For a discussion of the many causes of coerced marriages across several African societies, see Annie Bunting, Benjamin Lawrance, and Richard L. Roberts, "Something Old, Something New: Conceptualizing Forced Marriage in Africa," in *Marriage by Force? Contestation Over Consent and Coercion in Africa*, ed. Annie Bunting, Benjamin Lawrance, and Richard L. Roberts (Athens: Ohio University Press, 2016), 1–40.

97. Ferguson, *Expectations of Modernity*, 99.

98. Vigh, "Motion Squared," 425.

99. Ferguson, *Expectations of Modernity*, 87–90.

100. The South African Department of Justice and Constitutional Development has an extensive discussion of *ukuthwala* and women's rights. See Republic of South Africa Department of Justice and Constitutional Development, *Ukuthwala: Let's Stop Stolen Childhoods*, pamphlet (Pretoria, 2010), https://www.justice.gov.za/brochure/ukuthwala/ukuthwala.html. See also Diana Mabasa, "Ukuthwala: Is It All Culturally Relative?," *DeRebus*, 23 July 2015, https://www.derebus.org.za/ukuthwala-culturally-relative/, for the legal analysis of a 2015 appeal case: "In a landmark judgment delivered by a full Bench of the Western Cape Division, the court held that ukuthwala is no defence to crimes of rape, human trafficking and assault with the intent to do grievous bodily harm."

101. Staff Reporter, "Forced Marriage in South Africa."

102. Pumza Fihlani, "Stolen Youth of SA's Child Brides," BBC News, 14 October 2009, 2, http://news.bbc.co.uk/2/hi/africa/8303212.stm.

103. Fihlani, "Stolen Youth of SA's Child Brides," 3.

104. Fihlani, "Stolen Youth of SA's Child Brides," 1.

Chapter 3. Deaths in the Family

1. Cape Province Archives, Cape Town, Records of the Magistrate of Butterworth (1/BUT) 1/1/26, Preparatory Examination, R. v. Nomagqwata Sitoti and Nompahla Sitoti, 14 January 1935.

2. Max Gluckman, "Moral Crises: Magical and Secular Solutions," *Hau* 4, no. 2 (2014): 377–82.

3. William Beinart, "The Family, Youth Organisation, Gangs and Politics in the Transkeian Area," conference presentation, Conference on the Family in Africa (School of Oriental and African Studies, London, 1981), 10–12; O'Connell, "Xesibe Reds, Rascals and Gentlemen at Home and Work," 258–60, 295–300.

4. Mager, "Youth Organisations and the Construction of Masculine Identities," 653–67; Mamphela Ramphele, *A Bed Called Home: Life in the Migrant Labour Hostels of Cape Town* (Athens: Ohio University Press, 1993), 70–83.

5. See the analysis of the martial content of Zulu male identity and the way that women frame their own participation in "Zuluness," in Jill Kelly, "'Women Were Not Supposed to Fight': The Gendered Uses of Martial and Moral Zuluness During UDlame, 1990–1994," in *Gendering Ethnicity in African Women's Lives*, ed. Jan Bender Shetler (Madison: University of Wisconsin Press, 2015), 178–205.

6. Robert Morrell, "Of Boys and Men: Masculinity and Gender in Southern African Studies," *Journal of Southern African Studies* 24 (1998): 609.

7. Clifton Crais, "Of Men, Magic, and the Law: Popular Justice and the Political Imagination in South Africa," *Journal of Social History* 32, no. 1 (1998): 53–59.

8. See Louise du Toit's analysis of different analytic frames for understanding men's violence toward women in the postapartheid era in "Shifting Meanings of Postconflict Sexual Violence in South Africa," *Signs: Journal of Women in Culture and Society* 40, no. 1 (2014): 101–23.

9. Tapiwa Zimudzi, "African Women, Violent Crime and the Criminal Law in Colonial Zimbabwe, 1900–1952," *Journal of Southern African Studies* 30, no. 3 (2004): 501–2.

10. Ashforth, *Witchcraft, Violence, and Democracy in South Africa*, 243–74; Selaelo Thias Kgatla, "Containment of Witchcraft Accusations in South Africa: A Search for a Transformational Approach to Curb the Problem," in *Imagining Evil: Witchcraft Beliefs and Accusations in Contemporary Africa*, ed. Gerrie ter Haar (Trenton, NJ: Africa World Press, 2007), 269–70.

11. Katherine Luongo, "Domestic Dramas and Occult Acts: Witchcraft and Violence in the Arena of the Intimate," in *Domestic Violence and the Law in Colonial and Postcolonial Africa*, ed. Emily S. Burrill, Richard L. Roberts, and Elizabeth Thornberry (Athens: Ohio University Press, 2010), 179–86.

12. Cape of Good Hope, *Commission on Native Laws and Customs*, 2:141. See also J. B. Peires, "The Central Beliefs of the Xhosa Cattle-Killing," *Journal of African History* 28 (1987): 43–63.

13. Cape of Good Hope, *Commission on Native Laws and Customs*, 2:416.

14. Members of the group who were answering the commissioners' questions included Ngangelizwe, chief of the Thembu, and several Thembu headmen. It is not clear which of these witnesses gave the answer quoted above. Cape of Good Hope, *Commission on Native Laws and Customs*, 2:436.

15. M. Wilson, *Reaction to Conquest*, 306–12; Peter Geschiere, *The Modernity of Witchcraft: Politics and the Occult in Postcolonial Africa* (Charlottesville: University of

Virginia Press, 1997), 1–25, 61–68; Ashforth, *Witchcraft, Violence, and Democracy in South Africa*, 111–21.

16. M. Wilson, *Reaction to Conquest*, 275.

17. M. Wilson, *Reaction to Conquest*, 303; Soga, *The Ama-Xosa*, 45.

18. T. O. Ranger, "Scotland Yard in the Bush: Medicine Murders, Child Witches and the Construction of the Occult," *Africa* 77, no. 2 (2007): 272–83.

19. Flint, *Healing Traditions*, 93–127; Geoffrey Cornelius, "Chicane: Double-Thinking and Divination among the Witch-Doctors," in *Divination: Perspectives for a New Millennium*, ed. Patrick Curry (Burlington, VT: Ashgate, 2010), 119–42.

20. Soga, *The Ama-Xosa*, 156.

21. M. Wilson, *Reaction to Conquest*, 318.

22. Sean Redding, "Witchcraft in Africa: Political Power and Spiritual Insecurity from the Precolonial Era to the Present," in *Oxford Research Encyclopedia of African History*, ed. Thomas Spear (Oxford University Press, 2019); W. D. Hammond-Tooke, "Urbanization and the Interpretation of Misfortune: A Quantitative Analysis," *Africa: Journal of the International African Institute* 40, no. 1 (1970): 27–28.

23. M. Wilson, *Reaction to Conquest*, 43; Soga, *The Ama-Xosa*, 317–20; Hammond-Tooke, "Urbanization and the Interpretation of Misfortune," 33–34.

24. Soga, *The Ama-Xosa*, 155–62.

25. Walter E. Stanford, "A Witch Doctor by Habit and Repute," *Cape Law Journal* (1893): 218–20.

26. Stanford, "A Witch Doctor by Habit and Repute," 218.

27. Cape Province Archives, 1/BUT 1/1/26, Preparatory Examination, R. v. Nomagqwata Sitoti and Nompahla Sitoti, 14 January 1935.

28. Cape Province Archives, 1/BUT 1/1/26, R. v. Nomagqwata Sitoti and Nompahla Sitoti.

29. Cape Province Archives, 1/BUT 1/1/26, R. v. Nomagqwata Sitoti and Nompahla Sitoti.

30. Cape Province Archives, 1/BUT 1/1/26, R. v. Nomagqwata Sitoti and Nompahla Sitoti.

31. Cape Province Archives, 1/BUT 1/1/26, R. v. Nomagqwata Sitoti and Nompahla Sitoti, Written statement on the charge sheet, signed with an *X* by Nomaqwata Sitoti.

32. Mayer, *Townsmen or Tribesman?*, 242; W. D. Hammond-Tooke, *The Tribes of King William's Town District*, Ethnological Publication #41 (Pretoria: Government Printer, 1958), 59.

33. Colin Murray and Peter Sanders, "Medicine Murder in Basutoland: Colonial Rule and Moral Crisis," *Africa* 70, no. 1 (2000): 49–52, 76–77.

34. Cape of Good Hope, *Commission on Native Laws and Customs*, 2:30–31.

35. M. Wilson, *Reaction to Conquest*, 289–90.

36. M. Wilson, *Reaction to Conquest*, 282–83.

37. M. Wilson, *Reaction to Conquest*, 232–33; Hammond-Tooke, *Tribes of King William's Town District*, 58; W. D. Hammond-Tooke, *The Tribes of Willowvale District*, Department of Native Affairs, Ethnological Publication #36 (Pretoria: Government

Printer, 1957), 60; Soga, *The Ama-Xosa*, 389–94; James Macdonald, "Manners, Customs, Superstitions, and Religions of South African Tribes, Part 1," *Journal of the Anthropological Institute of Great Britain and Ireland* 19 (1890): 266–67.

38. Cape Province Archives, Cape Town, Records of Government House (GH) 35/248, File 275, Minute from the Prime Minister's Office, Cape Town, signed L. S. Jameson, 30 June 1905.

39. Cape Province Archives, 1/UTA 1/1/1/43, Case 40, 14 January 1910, R. v. Joselina Ngese.

40. Cape Province Archives, 1/BUT 1/1/25, Case 5 of 1925, R. v. Nontwana Xeke, 5 March 1925.

41. Cape Province Archives, 1/ECO, Criminal Cases 1936–1946, Case 1133, R. v. Philicia Dalasile, 23 June 1939.

42. Cape Province Archives, 1/ECO, Criminal Cases 1936–1946, R. v. Notingolozi Mankomo, 22 March 1946. The chief magistrate, who heard the appeal, also suspended five months of the six-month sentence for three years, meaning that Mankomo would only serve one month in prison if she did not re-offend within three years.

43. Cape Province Archives, 1/TSO 1/1/22, Case 302, R. v. Madosini Maquina, 23 February 1959. The magistrate allowed some leniency in the sentencing by suspending three months of the sentence for three years, meaning that Maquina would leave prison after six months.

44. Mager, *Gender and the Making of a South African Bantustan*, 186–88.

45. Carolyn Westall and Pranee Liamputtong, *Motherhood and Postnatal Depression: Narratives of Women and Their Partners* (Dordrecht: Springer, 2011), 101–21.

46. Cape Province Archives, 1/UTA 1/1/1/77, Case 911 of 1951, R. v. Nohalala Mfana, 7 September 1951.

47. Cape Province Archives, 1/UTA 1/1/1/77, Case 911 of 1951, R. v. Nohalala Mfana.

48. Alan R. Booth, "'European Courts Protect Women and Witches': Colonial Law Courts as Redistributors of Power in Swaziland, 1920–50," *Journal of Southern African Studies* 18, no. 2 (1992): 253–75; Redding, *Sorcery and Sovereignty*.

49. Through the 1950s, chiefs continued to hear relatively petty criminal and civil cases, including, for example, the theft of small numbers of livestock, local disputes over land ("garden disputes"), or damage caused by livestock to another farmer's crops.

50. Cape Province Archives, 1/XAA 1/1/1/12, Case 237/1928, R. v. Mdunyelwa Kunana, 6 June 1928.

51. Patrick Harries, "Missionaries, Marxists and Magic: Power and the Politics of Literacy in South-East Africa," *Journal of Southern African Studies* 27, no. 3 (September 2001): 418.

52. Mayer, *Townsmen or Tribesman?*, 160–65.

53. M. Wilson, *Reaction to Conquest*, 540.

54. Randall Packard, "The 'Healthy Reserve' and the 'Dressed Native': Discourses on Black Health and the Language of Legitimation in South Africa," *American Ethnologist* 16, no. 4 (November 1989): 691–93.

55. Cape Province Archives, 1/XAA 1/1/1/12, Case 237/1928, R. v. Mdunyelwa Kunana, 6 June 1928.

56. Cape Province Archives, Cape Town, Records of the Magistrate of Idutywa (1/IDW) 1/1/1/25, Case 655/1931, R. v. Gxamtwana Tiwani, 20 January 1932.

57. Cape Province Archives, Cape Town, Records of the Magistrate of Lusikisiki (1/LSK) 1/1/13, Case 104/31, R. v. Mbizwa Mraji, 6 March 1931.

58. Cape Province Archives, 1/LSK 1/1/13, Case 104/31, R. v. Mbizwa Mraji, 6 March 1931.

59. Cape Province Archives, 1/LSK 1/1/13, Case 66/31, R. v. Konyelwayo Sigwaca, 13 February 1931.

60. M. Wilson, *Reaction to Conquest*, 316.

61. M. Wilson, *Reaction to Conquest*, 317.

62. Cape Province Archives, Cape Town, Records of the Magistrate of Umzimkulu (1/UKL) 1/1/27, Case 884/37, R. v. Lekenku Mjaja, 3 August 1937.

63. Niehaus, "Witchcraft and the South African Bantustans," 48–52.

64. Redding, *Sorcery and Sovereignty*, 147–73; Peter Geschiere and Cyprian Fisiy, "Domesticating Personal Violence: Witchcraft, Courts and Confessions in Cameroon," *Africa: Journal of the International African Institute*, no. 3 (1994): 326.

65. Cape Province Archives, 1/LSK 1/1/16, Case 285/62, R. v. M. Walaza and another, 15 June 1962.

66. Cape Province Archives, 1/LSK 1/1/16, Case 285/62, R. v. M. Walaza and another, 15 June 1962.

67. Flint, *Healing Traditions*, 113.

68. Francis Wilson, "Historical Roots of Inequality in South Africa," *Economic History of Developing Regions* 26, no. 1 (2011): 6–15.

69. Joan A. Broster, *Amagqirha: Religion, Magic and Medicine in Transkei* (Goodwood, South Africa: Via Afrika, 1981), 22–89; M. Wilson, *Reaction to Conquest*, 320–46.

70. For a fuller discussion of women acting as diviners in the rural areas, see Sean Redding, "Women as Diviners," 367–89.

71. Cape Province Archives, 1/COF 1/1/1/38, Case 34/1933, R. v. Nosengqi Silanga, 23 January 1933.

72. Cape Province Archives, 1/COF 1/1/1/38, Case 34/1933, R. v. Nosengqi Silanga.

73. Cape Province Archives, 1/NQL 1/1/1/14, Case 645, R. v. Matshezi alias Maxalanga Centani, 10 November 1952.

74. Flint, *Healing Traditions*, 117; Julie Parle, "Witchcraft or Madness? The Amandiki of Zululand, 1894–1914," *Journal of Southern African Studies* 29, no. 1 (March 2003): 123–24.

CHAPTER 4. SONS AND "HOOLIGANS,"
"WORLD-DESTROYERS" AND REBELS

1. Cape Province Archives, 1/LSK 1/1/16, Case 946/61, the State v. Mgoduzwa Tshezi, 25 October 1961. See also Cape Province Archives, CMT 3/1472, File 42/Q, "Report of the Departmental Committee of Enquiry into Unrest in Eastern Pondoland," 9 August 1960.

2. Cape Province Archives, 1/LSK 1/1/16, Case 946/61, the State v. Mgoduzwa Tshezi.

3. Cape Province Archives, 1/LSK 1/1/16, Case 946/61, the State v. Mgoduzwa Tshezi.

4. Sukude Matoti and Lungisile Ntsebeza, "Rural Resistance in Mpondoland and Thembuland, 1960–1963," in *The Road to Democracy in South Africa*, vol. 1, *1960–1970*, ed. South African Democracy Education Trust (Cape Town: Zebra Press, 2004), 177–208.

5. *Contact* Correspondent, "Pondoland Terror at Its Height," *Contact* 4, no. 1 (14 January 1961): 3.

6. Cape Province Archives, 1/LSK 1/1/16, Case 946/61, the State v. Mgoduzwa Tshezi. Half the sentence was suspended for three years, meaning that, if Tshezi did not commit another crime within three years, he would never have to serve the last half of the sentence.

7. Cape Province Archives, 1/XAA 5/1/168, File N1/9/2/1, "Address by Colonel J. A. C. Reay, Officer Commanding S.A. Police, Transkei Division, to the Transkeian Territorial Authority on 26th April, 1961," four mimeographed pages.

8. Cape Province Archives, 1/XAA 5/1/168, File N1/9/2/1, "Address by Colonel J. A. C. Reay."

9. *Contact* Correspondent, "Bloodshed: How Government 'Restores Peace,'" *Contact* 4, no. 1 (14 January 1961): 3.

10. Govan Mbeki, *South Africa: The Peasants' Revolt* (Harmondsworth: Penguin, 1963), 124.

11. Quoted in Staff Reporter, "Traders and Liberals Get Blame for Poqo Terror," *Rand Daily Mail*, 26 February 1963, 14.

12. Vigh, "Social Death and Violent Life Chances," 54.

13. Vigh, "Social Death and Violent Life Chances," 55.

14. Vigh, "Social Death and Violent Life Chances," 31.

15. J. B. Peires, "Ethnicity and Pseudo-Ethnicity in the Transkei," in *Segregation and Apartheid*, ed. William Beinart and Saul Dubow (New York: Routledge, 1995), 256–84; Sara Pugach, "Carl Meinhof and the German Influence on Nicholas Van Warmelo's Ethnological and Linguistic Writing, 1927–1935," *Journal of Southern African Studies* 30, no. 4 (2004): 825–28; Thembisa Waetjen, "The 'Home' in Homeland: Gender, National Space, and Inkatha's Politics of Ethnicity," *Ethnic & Racial Studies* 22, no. 4 (1999): 653–59.

16. Laura Evans, "South Africa's Bantustans and the Dynamics of 'Decolonisation': Reflections on Writing Histories of the Homelands," *South African Historical Journal* 64, no. 1 (2012): 117–28.

17. Jason Hickel, "Social Engineering and Revolutionary Consciousness: Domestic Transformations in Colonial South Africa," *History & Anthropology* 23, no. 3 (2012): 301–22.

18. Cape Province Archives, Cape Town, Records of the Magistrate of Bizana (1/BIZ) 6/47, File C9/6/C, Memorandum written by E.M. Warren, Bantu Affairs Commissioner of Bizana, 11 July 1960.

19. Anne Mager, "'The People Get Fenced': Gender, Rehabilitation and African Nationalism in the Ciskei and Border Region, 1945–55," *Journal of Southern African Studies* 18, no. 4 (December 1992): 761–82; Ntsebeza, *Democracy Compromised*, 140–51.

20. Cape Province Archives, 1/BIZ 6/47, File C9/6/C, Memorandum by E.M. Warren.

21. Niehaus, "Witchcraft and the South African Bantustans," *South African Historical Journal* 64, no. 1 (2012): 45–49; Redding, *Sorcery and Sovereignty*, 175–200.

22. Cape Province Archives, 1/BIZ 6/47, File C9/6/C, Memorandum by E.M. Warren.

23. Susan I. Blackbeard, "Worms, Frogs, Crabs, and the Eye of God: Mpondo and Hlubi Perceptions of White Malevolence and Surveillance," *South African Historical Journal* 63, no. 4 (December 2011): 514–36.

24. Sean Redding, "'Maybe Freedom Will Come from You': Christian Prophecies and Rumors in the Development of Rural Resistance in South Africa, 1948–1961," *Journal of Religion in Africa* 40, no. 2 (2010); Mxolisi R. Mchunu, "'We Have Finished Them': Ritual Killing and War-Doctoring in Kwazulu-Natal during the 1980s and 1990s," *African Historical Review* 47, no. 2 (2015): 58–84.

25. These were myths that white settlers in South Africa had in common with white settlers elsewhere. See Michael Taussig, "Culture of Terror—Space of Death. Roger Casement's Putumayo Report and the Explanation of Torture," *Comparative Studies in Society and History* 26, no. 3 (July 1984): 467–97.

26. C. Thomas, "Bloodier Than Black and White: Liberation History Seen through Detective Sergeant Donald Card's Narrative of His Investigations of Congo and Poqo Activities, 1960–1965," *New Contree*, no. 50 (2005): 39–58; Wessel Visser, "The Production of Literature on the 'Red Peril' and 'Total Onslaught' in Twentieth-Century South Africa," *Historia* 49, no. 2 (2004): 115–19.

27. Patrick Laurence, *The Transkei: South Africa's Politics of Partition* (Johannesburg: Ravan, 1976), 38.

28. Mbeki, *The Peasants' Revolt*, 120; Isak Niehaus, "Witch-Hunting and Political Legitimacy: Continuity and Change in Green Valley, Lebowa, 1930–91," *Africa* 63 (1993): 498–530; Redding, *Sorcery and Sovereignty*, 175–200.

29. Cape Province Archives, CMT 3/1471, File 42/C, pamphlet titled "Where there is neither back nor front there is no truth," enclosed in a letter from Chief K. D. Matanzima to the Chief Magistrate of the Transkei, 9 November 1957.

30. Cape Province Archives, CMT 3/1472, File 42/Q, "Report of the Departmental Committee of Enquiry into Unrest in Eastern Pondoland," 9 August 1960.

31. Cape Province Archives, 1/UKL 1/1/28, Case 368/63, the State v. Mboyi Sadry Mkulisi, 28 January 1964, testimony of Everett Ntanjana.

32. At the end of the trial, the Bantu Affairs commissioner convicted the defendant on all four arson counts and on one count of violating the Fencing Act, and he sentenced him to twelve months in prison. Cape Province Archives, 1/UKL 1/1/28, Case 368/63, the State v. Mboyi Sadry Mkulisi, 28 January 1964.

33. Cape Province Archives, Cape Town, Records of the Magistrate of Qumbu (1/QBU) 7/1/70, File N1/9/2, Letter from the Magistrate of Qumbu to the Chief Magistrate of the Transkei, 2 May 1957.

34. Cape Province Archives, CMT 3/1481, File 42/19, Letter from the Chief Bantu Affairs Commissioner of the Transkei to the Secretary for Native Affairs, Pretoria, 14 March 1957.

35. Cape Province Archives, CMT 3/1481, File 42/19, Letter from the Chief Bantu Affairs Commissioner of the Transkei to the Secretary for Native Affairs, 14 March 1957.

36. Saul Dubow, "Were There Political Alternatives in the Wake of the Sharpeville-Langa Violence in South Africa, 1960?," *Journal of African History* 56, no. 1 (2015): 119–42.

37. Tom Lodge, *Sharpeville: An Apartheid Massacre and Its Consequences* (Oxford: Oxford University Press, 2011), 102–42.

38. Stephen Ellis, "The Genesis of the ANC's Armed Struggle in South Africa, 1948–1961," *Journal of Southern African Studies* 37, no. 4 (2011): 657–76; Kwandiwe Kondlo, *In the Twilight of the Revolution: The Pan Africanist Congress of Azania (South Africa), 1959–1994*, 2nd ed. (Basel, Switzerland: Basler Afrika Bibliographien, 2010), 50–69.

39. Cape Province Archives, CMT 3/1471, File 42/1, marked "Confidential," Pamphlet in the original Xhosa with a translation into English enclosed in a letter from the Bantu Affairs Commissioner of Cofimvaba to the Chief Bantu Affairs Commissioner, February 22, 1961.

40. Thami ka Plaatjie, "The PAC's Underground Activities, 1960–1980," in *The Road to Democracy in South Africa*, vol. 2, *1970–1980*, ed. South African Democracy Education Trust (Pretoria: UNISA, 2007), 677–79.

41. Kondlo, *In the Twilight of the Revolution*, 68–69.

42. Lodge, "The Poqo Insurrection," 179–222; Staff Reporter, "Paarl: Ministers Not in Contempt," *Rand Daily Mail*, 9 January 1963, 4.

43. Bianca van Laun, "Of Bodies Captured: The Visual Representation of the Paarl March and Poqo in Apartheid South Africa," *Social Dynamics* 40, no. 1 (2014): 43–45; Madelaine Fullard, "State Repression in the 1960s," in *The Road to Democracy in South Africa*, vol. 1, *1960–1970*, ed. South African Democracy Education Trust (Cape Town: Zebra Press, 2004), 341–63.

44. Barry Streek and Richard Wicksteed, *Render unto Kaiser: A Transkei Dossier* (Johannesburg: Ravan, 1981), 115–24; Kaizer D. Matanzima, *Independence My Way* (Pretoria: Foreign Affairs Association, 1976), 29–45.

45. Cape Province Archives, CMT 3/1471, File 42/1 Confidential, Replies to Chief Bantu Affairs Commissioner's circular questionnaire, from the Bantu Affairs Commissioner of Engcobo, 18 February 1961. It is not clear whether the people who committed this murder were Poqo members. See Maaba, "The PAC's War Against the State," 273–85.

46. Cape Province Archives, CMT 3/1471, File 42/1, Confidential reply from the Bantu Affairs Commissioner of Umtata to a circular sent from the Chief Bantu Affairs Commissioner, 2 March 1961.

47. South African National Archives, Pretoria, Records of the Bantu Affairs Department (BAO) 5/514, File F109/1282, letter from the Bantu Affairs Commissioner of Qumbu to the Chief Bantu Affairs Commissioner, 4 March 1961. Emphasis in the original.

48. South African National Archives, BAO 5/514, File F109/1282, Letter from the Bantu Affairs Commissioner of Qumbu to the Chief Bantu Affairs Commissioner, 4 March 1961.

49. Cape Province Archives, CMT 3/1471, File 42/1, Confidential reply from the Bantu Affairs Commissioner of Cofimvaba to a circular sent from the Chief Bantu Affairs Commissioner, 22 February 1961.

50. South African National Archives, BAO 5/510, File F109/1128, Memo on J. Mpemba, marked "Geheim [Secret]," dated 1962. See additional information on hostility toward Matanzima in Transkei Archives, Mthatha, Chiefs and Headmen 197, File 3/24/3/1, part 2, letter from Headman M. Makaula to the Chief Bantu Affairs Commissioner, 3 April 1962.

51. Matoti and Ntsebeza, "Rural Resistance in Mpondoland and Thembuland, 1960–1963," 203–8.

52. Maaba, "The PAC's War Against the State, 1960–1963," 275–77.

53. Cape Province Archives, CMT 3/1481, File 42/20, Statement by James Funani, 17 December 1962, typescript, 2 pages.

54. Cape Province Archives, CMT 3/1481, File 42/20, Statement by James Funani, 17 December 1962.

55. Cape Province Archives, CMT 3/1481, File 42/20, Statement by James Funani, 17 December 1962.

56. Cape Province Archives, CMT 3/1481, File 42/20, Statement of Lawana Nto, 16 December 1962, typescript, 4 pages.

57. Cape Province Archives, CMT 3/1481, File 42/20, Statement by James Funani, 17 December 1962.

58. Cape Province Archives, CMT 3/1481, File 42/20, Statement by Maqadasa Magusha, 17 December 1962, 3 pages.

59. Staff Reporter, "Police Probe of the Poqo Riots Nears End," *Rand Daily Mail*, 18 January 1963, 9; Staff Reporter, "Poqo: Only Object Was to Kill Chief—Court Told," *Rand Daily Mail*, 5 March 1963, 3.

60. Cape Province Archives, CMT 3/1481, File 42/20, Letter, marked "Confidential," from the Bantu Affairs Commissioner of Cofimvaba to the Chief Bantu Affairs Commissioner, 13 December 1962.

61. Cape Province Archives, CMT 3/1481, File 42/20, Letter, marked "Confidential," from the Bantu Affairs Commissioner of Cofimvaba to the Chief Bantu Affairs Commissioner, 13 December 1962.

62. Staff Reporter, "Police Probe of the Poqo Riots Nears End."

63. *Contact* Correspondent, "The Battle Near Qamatapoort," *Contact* 5, no. 26 (27 December 1962): 6.

64. *Contact* Correspondent, "The Battle Near Qamatapoort."

65. Staff Reporter, "Police Hold 14 Poqo Suspects," *Rand Daily Mail*, 18 December 1962, 3.

66. Maaba, "The PAC's War Against the State, 1960–1963," 279–82.

67. Cape Province Archives, 1/XAA 5/1/168, File N1/9/2/4, titled "Bantu Administration and Development, Disturbances, Home Guard Weapons." The file contains an extensive list of headmen in the Xhalanga district and the weapons they owned or were issued by the state in 1963. As a result of rebels' threats, the state provided weapons to most chiefs and headmen who were considered state loyalists in the Transkei.

68. Karis and Carter, *From Protest to Challenge*, 3:671–72.

69. South African National Archives, BAO 5/510, File F109/1128, Letter from the Bantu Affairs Commissioner of Cofimvaba to the Chief Bantu Affairs Commissioner in Umtata, dated 8 April 1963. Other Bantu Affairs commissioners held similar meetings with a similar set of talking points. See, for example, Cape Province Archives, 1/BUT 7/1/88, File C25, Letter from the Bantu Affairs Commissioner of Butterworth to the Chief Bantu Affairs Commissioner, Umtata, dated 8 March 1963, enclosing a report of a recent meeting.

70. Cape Province Archives, 1/WVE 5/1/40, File C16, confidential memo titled "Propaganda Warfare," sent from the Chief Bantu Affairs Commissioner to all Bantu Affairs Commissioners in the Transkei, 25 March 1963.

71. Staff Reporter, "Manhunt in Transkei: The Scene at the Engcobo Caravan Slayings; Police Comb Area; Robbery Ruled Out as Motive," *Rand Daily Mail*, 6 February 1963, 1.

72. Staff Reporter, "Manhunt in Transkei." See also Maaba, "The PAC's War Against the State, 1960–1963," 282–83.

73. Staff Reporter, "Gen. Keevy (SAP) on Motives in Engcobo Killing," *Rand Daily Mail*, 8 February 1963, 2.

74. Staff Reporter, "Gen. Keevy (SAP) on Motives in Engcobo Killing."

75. Anonymous, "Transkei Tragedy," *News Check*, 15 February 1963. https://www.1820 settlers.com/genealogy/getperson.php?personID=I1364&tree=master.

76. Staff Reporter, "Shadow of Poqo over Transkei Killings—Keevy," *Rand Daily Mail*, 12 February 1963, 9.

77. Maaba, "The PAC's War Against the State, 1960–1963," 282–83; N. Nkosi, "Hanged Dad's Remains Dug Up after 52 Years," *Pretoria News*, 15 December 2016. https://www.iol.co.za/news/politics/hanged-dads-remains-dug-up-after-52-years-7186 033; Truth and Reconciliation Commission of South Africa, *Truth and Reconciliation Commission Final Report*, vol. 3 (Cape Town: Juta, 2003), 49–50.

78. Staff Reporter, "Transkei Chief Blames Liberals, Reds," *Rand Daily Mail*, 1 March 1963, 11.

79. Muriel Horrell, *A Survey of Race Relations in South Africa, 1963* (Johannesburg: South African Institute of Race Relations, 1964), 18–20.

80. Cape Province Archives, 1/BUT 7/1/88, File C25, Letter from the Bantu Affairs Commissioner of Butterworth to the Chief Bantu Affairs Commissioner, 8 March 1963.

81. Staff Reporter, "Talk Was of Killing Whites:—Poqo Witness," *Rand Daily Mail*, 16 January 1963, 2.

82. Staff Reporter, "Manhunt in Transkei."

83. Staff Reporter, "S.A. 'Like Kenya in 1951' Paarl Inquiry Told," *Rand Daily Mail*, 22 March 1963, 13.

84. Staff Reporter, "S.A. 'Like Kenya in 1951' Paarl Inquiry Told."

85. Gail Gerhart, *Black Power in South Africa* (Berkeley: University of California Press, 1979), 214–16.

86. *Contact* Correspondent, "Leballo vs. Vorster: Little Comfort from Shouts over the Veld," *Contact* 6, no. 7 (5 April 1963): 6; Matoti and Ntsebeza, "Rural Resistance in Mpondoland and Thembuland, 1960–1963," 285.

87. Staff Reporter, "'Pass Laws Cause of Paarl Riot,' Xhosa Pamphlet Blames Govt," *Rand Daily Mail*, 20 February 1963, 4.

88. Staff Reporter, "Poqo Report: 'No Alarm'—but Vorster Drafts Urgent Laws," *Rand Daily Mail*, 22 March 1963, 1–2. See also *Contact* Correspondent, "Police Brutality Worsens—Silence from Press and Bench?," *Contact* 6, no. 10 (17 May 1963): 1.

89. The commission on which Holloway served was tasked with suggesting appropriate accommodations for whites who resided in areas designated as African "homelands"; Staff Reporter, "If Transkei Fails So Will Apartheid—Commission," *Rand Daily Mail*, 22 November 1962, 3.

90. Anonymous, "Transkei: The Myth of Independence," *Sechaba* 10, no. 4 (Fourth Quarter 1976): 1–5; James Ferguson, *Global Shadows: Africa in the Neoliberal World Order* (Durham NC: Duke University Press, 2006), 58–62; Dubow, "Racial Irredentism, Ethnogenesis, and White Supremacy," *Kronos: Southern African Histories* 41, no. 1 (2015): 242–45.

91. Streek and Wicksteed, *Render unto Kaiser*, 110–32; Ntsebeza, *Democracy Compromised*, 175–94.

92. Mbeki, *The Peasants' Revolt*, 148.

93. Judge Snyman's comments were quoted in a news report: *Staff Reporter*, "Poqo's 'Plan for Revolt' in 1963; Banned P.A.C. Continues Underground, Says Shock Paarl Report; Judge Urges Drastic Government Action," *Rand Daily Mail*, 22 March 1963, 13.

94. Tom Lodge, "The Paarl Insurrection: A South African Uprising," *African Studies Review* 25, no. 4 (December 1982): 114.

95. Vigh, "Social Death and Violent Life Chances," 50–51.

Conclusion

1. Cape Province Archives, CMT 3/1478, File 42/4, Letter from the Bantu Affairs Commissioner of Engcobo to the Chief Bantu Affairs Commissioner, 8 January 1963.

2. South African National Archives, BAO 5/510, File F109/1128, Statement by Ngxatwana Kusele, dated 4 April 1963, taken in the office of the Bantu Affairs Commissioner of Cofimvaba, and BAO 5/510 File F109/1128, Letter from the Bantu Affairs Commissioner of Cofimvaba to the Chief Bantu Affairs Commissioner, 1 March 1963.

3. Cape Province Archives, CMT 3/1483, File 42/26, Letter from the Bantu Affairs Commissioner of Willowvale to the Chief Bantu Affairs Commissioner, 8 February 1963.

4. Henrik Vigh, *Navigating Terrains of War: Youth and Soldiering in Guinea-Bissau* (New York: Berghahn Books, 2006), 10.

5. Fullard, "State Repression in the 1960s," 381–90.

6. J. B. Peires, "The Implosion of Transkei and Ciskei," *African Affairs* 91, no. 364 (1992): 365–87; Timothy Gibbs, "Chris Hani's 'Country Bumpkins': Regional Networks in the African National Congress Underground, 1974–1994," *Journal of Southern African Studies* 37, no. 4 (2011): 677–91.

7. Sindiso Mnisi Weeks, "The Violence of the Harmony Model: Common Narratives between Women and Lower-Level Traditional Leaders" in *Traditional Leaders in a Democracy: Resources, Respect and Resistance*, ed. Mbongiseni Buthelezi, Dineo Skosana, and Beth Vale (Johannesburg: Mapungubwe Institute for Strategic Reflection [MISTRA], 2018), 182–223.

8. Fani Ncapayi, "Emerging Rural Struggles against Unelected Traditional Authorities and the Role of the Courts: Lessons from Rural Villages of the Eastern Cape," in *Traditional Leaders in a Democracy: Resources, Respect and Resistance*, ed. Mbongiseni Buthelezi, Dineo Skosana, and Beth Vale (Johannesburg: Mapungubwe Institute for Strategic Reflection [MISTRA], 2018), 262–96.

9. Caroline Elkins discusses the way in which white settler administrations in colonial Africa generally constructed their own versions of tyranny, through "forced evictions, vagrancy laws, communal labor ordinances, taxation, corvée, and the like," all of which catered to settlers' self-interests. "Race, Citizenship and Governance: Settler Tyranny and the End of Empire," in *Settler Colonialism in the Twentieth Century: Projects, Practices, Legacies*, ed. C. Elkins and S. Pedersen (New York: Routledge, 2005), 207.

10. Alberti, *Account of the Tribal Life and Customs of the Xhosa in 1807*, 41.

11. Cape Province Archives, 1/FSF 1/1/1/30, Case 119 of 1944, R. v. Mkosana Dlepu and others, 6 March 1944.

12. Thornberry, *Colonizing Consent*, 36–74.

13. Staff reporters, "8 Dead in Panga Riot: Berserk Mob Surge Off Train," *Rand Daily Mail*, 14 December 1962, 1.

14. Donham, "Staring at Suffering," 28.

15. See, for example, Cape Province Archives, CMT 3/90, Blue Book Report for 1899, From the Magistrate of Engcobo, 20 January 1899.

16. Cape Province Archives, CMT 3/1483, File 42/26/8, Police Report from the South African Police of Willowvale to the District Commandant, Umtata, 5 February 1960.

17. Nancy Scheper-Hughes, *Death without Weeping: The Violence of Everyday Life in Brazil* (Berkeley: University of California Press, 1993), 219–20.

18. Scheper-Hughes, *Death without Weeping*, 267.

19. Elder, *Hostels, Sexuality, and the Apartheid Legacy*, 41–51. See also the comments of Mark Hunter in *Love in the Time of AIDS*, 3–6.

20. Vigh, *Navigating Terrains of War*, 10.

21. Vigh, *Navigating Terrains of War*, 235.

22. Henrik Vigh, "Bandits Fall from Grace: Liberation Heroes and Alter-Politics in Bissau," *Terrain* 74 (March 2021): 1–14.

23. Kondlo, *In the Twilight of the Revolution*, 250–51, 272–79.

BIBLIOGRAPHY

Archival Sources

South African National Archives, Pretoria:
  Records of the Native Affairs Department/Bantu Administration and Development
    Department (BAO)
  Records of the 1903–1905 South African Native Affairs Commission (SANAC)
  Records of the 1930–1932 Native Economic Commission (NEC)
  Records of the Ministry of Justice (JUS)
  Records of the Secretary of Native Affairs (NTS)
Cape Province Archives (now the Western Cape Province Archives), Cape Town:
  Records of the Chief Magistrate of Griqualand East (CMK)
  Records of the Chief Magistrate of the Transkei (1/CMT and CMT 3)
  Records of Government House (GH)
  Records of the Municipality of Umtata (3/UTA)
  Records of the Magistrate of Bizana district (1/BIZ)
  Records of the Magistrate of Butterworth district (1/BUT)
  Records of the Magistrate of Cofimvaba district (1/COF)
  Records of the Magistrate of Elliotdale district (1/EDL)
  Records of the Magistrate of Engcobo district (1/ECO)
  Records of the Magistrate of Flagstaff district (1/FSF)
  Records of the Magistrate of Idutywa district (1/IDW)
  Records of the Magistrate of Kentani district (1/KNT)
  Records of the Magistrate of Libode district (1/LBE)
  Records of the Magistrate of Lusikisiki district (1/LSK)
  Records of the Magistrate of Mount Frere district (1/MFE)
  Records of the Magistrate of Mqanduli district (1/MQL)
  Records of the Magistrate of Ngqeleni district (1/NQL)
  Records of the Magistrate of Nqamakwe district (1/NKE)
  Records of the Magistrate of Qumbu district (1/QBU)
  Records of the Magistrate of Tsolo district (1/TSO)

Records of the Magistrate of Umtata district (1/UTA)
Records of the Magistrate of Umzimkulu district (1/UKL)
Records of the Magistrate of Willowvale district (1/WVE)
Records of the Magistrate of Xhalanga district (1/XAA)
KwaZulu-Natal Province Archives, Pietermaritzburg:
Records of the Secretary for Native Affairs, Natal (SNA)
Transkei Archives, Mthatha:
Chiefs and Headmen Files

Newspapers, Newsletters, and Periodicals

Alice Times
BBC News online
Contact
Guardian
Natal Witness
Pretoria News
Rand Daily Mail
Sechaba
Sunday Times (South Africa)
Wesleyan-Methodist Magazine
Treatment Action Campaign Newsletter

Published Sources

Alberti, Ludwig. *Account of the Tribal Life and Customs of the Xhosa in 1807.* Cape Town: Balkema, 1968.

Anonymous. "Lusikisiki Girl Abducted in Kwa Ncele." In *Treatment Action Campaign Newsletter.* https://www.tac.org.za/news/lusikisiki-girl-abducted-in-kwa-ncele/.

———. "Transkei: The Myth of Independence." *Sechaba* 10, no. 4 (Fourth Quarter 1976): 1–5.

———. "Transkei Tragedy." *News Check*, 15 February 1963. https://www.1820settlers.com/genealogy/getperson.php?personID=11364&tree=master.

Archambault, Julie Soleil. "Cruising Through Uncertainty: Cell Phones and the Politics of Display and Disguise in Inhambane, Mozambique." *American Ethnologist* 40, no. 1 (2013): 88–101.

Ashforth, Adam. *Witchcraft, Violence, and Democracy in South Africa.* Chicago: University of Chicago Press, 2005.

Barchiesi, Franco. "The Violence of Work: Revisiting South Africa's 'Labour Question' through Precarity and Anti-Blackness." *Journal of Southern African Studies* 42, no. 5 (2016): 875–91.

Barrett, Rev. E. J. "Kaffir Marriages." *Wesleyan-Methodist Magazine*, June 1883, 424–37.

BBC. "South Africa's Ancient Art of Stick Fighting." BBC News, 3 March 2011. http://www.bbc.com/news/world-africa-12632447.

Beall, Jo. "Cultural Weapons: Traditions, Inventions and the Transition to Democratic Governance in Metropolitan Durban." *Urban Studies* 43, no. 2 (2006): 457–73.

Becker, Heike. "History: Colonialism, Christianity, and Tradition." In *Unravelling Taboos: Gender and Sexuality in Namibia*, edited by Suzanne LaFont and Dianne Hubbard, 22–38. Windhoek, Namibia: Legal Assistance Center, 2007.

Beinart, William. "The Anatomy of a Rural Scare: East Griqualand in the 1890s." In *Hidden Struggles in Rural South Africa*, edited by William Beinart and Colin Bundy, 46–78. Berkeley: University of California Press, 1987.

———. "Beyond Homelands: Some Ideas about the History of African Rural Areas in South Africa." *South African Historical Journal* 64, no. 1 (2012): 5–21.

———. "Conflict in Qumbu: Rural Consciousness, Ethnicity and Violence in the Colonial Transkei." In *Hidden Struggles in Rural South Africa*, edited by William Beinart and Colin Bundy, 106–37. Berkeley: University of California Press, 1987.

———. "The Family, Youth Organisation, Gangs and Politics in the Transkeian Area." Conference presentation. Conference on the Family in Africa. School of Oriental and African Studies, London, 1981.

———. "Political and Collective Violence in Southern African Historiography." *Journal of Southern African Studies* 18, no. 3 (September 1992): 455–86.

Beningfield, Jennifer. *The Frightened Land: Land, Landscape and Politics in South Africa in the Twentieth Century*. New York: Routledge, 2006.

Blackbeard, Susan I. "Worms, Frogs, Crabs, and the Eye of God: Mpondo and Hlubi Perceptions of White Malevolence and Surveillance." *South African Historical Journal* 63, no. 4 (December 2011): 514–36.

Bonner, Philip, Bernard Magubane, Peter Delius, Jabulani Sithole, Janet Cherry, Pat Gibbs, and Thozana April. "The Road to Armed Struggle." In *The Road to Democracy in South Africa*, vol. 1, *1960–1970*, edited by the South African Democracy Education Trust, 53–145. Cape Town: Zebra Press, 2004.

Booth, Alan R. "'European Courts Protect Women and Witches': Colonial Law Courts as Redistributors of Power in Swaziland, 1920–50." *Journal of Southern African Studies* 18, no. 2 (1992): 253–75.

Bozzoli, Belinda. "Marxism, Feminism and Southern African Studies." *Journal of Southern African Studies* 9 (1983): 139–71.

———. *Women of Phokeng*. Johannesburg: Ravan, 1992.

Bradford, Helen. "Women, Gender and Colonialism: Rethinking the History of the British Cape Colony and Its Frontier Zones, c. 1806–70." *Journal of African History*, no. 3 (1996): 351–70.

Breckenridge, Keith. "The Allure of Violence: Men, Race and Masculinity on the South African Goldmines, 1900–1950." *Journal of Southern African Studies* 24, no. 4, Special Issue on Masculinities in Southern Africa (December 1998): 669–93.

———. "Migrancy, Crime and Faction Fighting: The Role of the Isitshozi in the Development of Ethnic Organisations in the Compounds." *Journal of Southern African Studies* 16, no. 1 (March 1990): 55–78.

Broster, Joan A. *Amagqirha: Religion, Magic and Medicine in Transkei*. Goodwood, South Africa: Via Afrika, 1981.

Broster, Joan. *Red Blanket Valley*. Johannesburg: Hugh Keartland, 1967.

Brownlee, Charles. *Reminiscences of Kaffir Life and History, and Other Papers.* 2nd ed. Fort Hare: Lovedale Press, 1916.

Bunting, Annie, Benjamin Lawrance, and Richard L. Roberts. "Something Old, Something New: Conceptualizing Forced Marriage in Africa." In *Marriage by Force? Contestation Over Consent and Coercion in Africa,* edited by Annie Bunting, Benjamin Lawrance, and Richard L. Roberts, 1–40. Athens: Ohio University Press, 2016.

Buthelezi, Mbongiseni, and Beth Vale. "Collisions, Collusions and Coalescences: New Takes on Traditional Leadership in Democratic South Africa: An Introduction." In *Traditional Leaders in a Democracy: Resources, Respect and Resistance,* edited by Mbongiseni Buthelezi, Dineo Skosana, and Beth Vale. 1–20. Johannesburg: Mapungubwe Institute for Strategic Reflection (MISTRA), 2018.

Butler, Judith. *Gender Trouble: Feminism and the Subversion of Identity.* New York: Routledge, 1990.

Cape of Good Hope. *Report of a Commission Appointed to Inquire into the Causes of the Recent Outbreak in Griqualand East.* Cape Town: Solomon Printers, 1879.

———. *Report of the Government Commission on Native Laws and Customs, 1883.* 2 vols. Facsimile Reprint. Cape Town: Struik, 1968.

Carton, Benedict. "Locusts Fall from the Sky: Manhood and Migrancy in KwaZulu." In *Changing Men in Southern Africa,* edited by Robert Morrell, 129–40. London: Zed Books, 2001.

Carton, Benedict, and Robert Morrell. "Zulu Masculinities, Warrior Culture and Stick Fighting: Reassessing Male Violence and Virtue in South Africa." *Journal of Southern African Studies* 38, no. 1 (2012): 31–53.

Chidester, David. *Wild Religion: Tracking the Sacred in South Africa.* Berkeley: University of California Press, 2012.

Christopher, A. J. "The Union of South Africa Censuses, 1911–1960: An Incomplete Record." *Historia* 56, no. 2 (2011): 1–18.

Clegg, Jonathan. "*Ukubuyisa Isidumbu*—'Bringing Back the Body': An Examination into the Ideology of Vengeance in the Msinga and Mpofana Rural Locations, 1882–1944." In *Working Papers in Southern African Studies,* vol. 2, edited by P. Bonner, 164–98. Johannesburg: Ravan, 1979.

Comaroff, Jean, and John L. Comaroff. *The Truth about Crime: Sovereignty, Knowledge, Social Order.* Chicago: University of Chicago Press, 2016.

Comaroff, John, and Jean Comaroff. *Of Revelation and Revolution.* Vol. 2, *The Dialectics of Modernity on a South African Frontier.* Chicago: University of Chicago Press, 1997.

Contact Correspondent. "The Battle Near Qamatapoort." *Contact* 5, no. 26 (27 December 1962): 6.

———. "Bloodshed: How Government 'Restores Peace.'" *Contact* 4, no. 1 (14 January 1961): 3.

———. "Leballo vs. Vorster: Little Comfort from Shouts over Veld." *Contact* 6, no. 7 (5 April 1963): 6.

———. "Police Brutality Worsens—Silence from the Press and Bench?" *Contact* 6, no. 10 (17 May 1963): 1.

———. "Pondoland Terror at Its Height." *Contact* 4, no. 1 (14 January 1961): 3.

Cornelius, Geoffrey. "Chicane: Double-Thinking and Divination among the Witch-Doctors." In *Divination: Perspectives for a New Millennium*, edited by Patrick Curry, 119–42. Burlington, VT: Ashgate, 2010.

Crais, Clifton. "Of Men, Magic, and the Law: Popular Justice and the Political Imagination in South Africa." *Journal of Social History* 32, no. 1 (1998): 49–72.

Crais, Clifton C. *Poverty, War, and Violence in South Africa*. New York: Cambridge University Press, 2011.

Davenport, T. R. H. "The Triumph of Colonel Stallard: The Transformation of the Natives (Urban) Areas Act Between 1923 and 1937." *South African Historical Journal* 2 (1970): 77–96.

Department of Justice and Constitutional Development, Republic of South Africa. *Ukuthwala: Let's Stop Stolen Childhoods*. Pamphlet. Pretoria, 2010. https://www.justice.gov.za/brochure/ukuthwala/ukuthwala.html.

Dodson, Belinda. "Locating Xenophobia: Debate, Discourse, and Everyday Experience in Cape Town, South Africa." *Africa Today* 56, no. 3 (2010): 2–22.

Donham, Donald L. "Staring at Suffering: Violence as a Subject." In *States of Violence: Politics, Youth, and Memory in Contemporary Africa*, edited by Edna G. Bay and Donald L. Donham, 16–33. Charlottesville: University of Virginia Press, 2006.

du Toit, Louise. "Shifting Meanings of Postconflict Sexual Violence in South Africa." *Signs: Journal of Women in Culture and Society* 40, no. 1 (2014): 101–23.

Dubow, Saul. "Holding 'a Just Balance between Black and White': The Native Affairs Department in South Africa c. 1920–33." *Journal of Southern African Studies* 12, no. 2 (1986): 217–39.

———. "Racial Irredentism, Ethnogenesis, and White Supremacy in High-Apartheid South Africa." *Kronos: Southern African Histories* 41, no. 1 (2015): 236–64.

———. "Were There Political Alternatives in the Wake of the Sharpeville-Langa Violence in South Africa, 1960?" *Journal of African History* 56, no. 1 (2015): 119–42.

Durrheim, K., X. Mtose, and L. Brown. *Race Trouble: Race, Identity and Inequality in Post-Apartheid South Africa*. Lanham, MD: Lexington Books, 2011.

Elder, Glen S. *Hostels, Sexuality, and the Apartheid Legacy: Malevolent Geographies*. Athens: Ohio University Press, 2003.

———. "Malevolent Traditions: Hostel Violence and the Procreational Geography of Apartheid." *Journal of Southern African Studies* 29, no. 4 (December 2003): 921–35.

Eldredge, Elizabeth. "Sources of Conflict in Southern Africa c. 1800–1830: The 'Mfecane' Reconsidered." In *The Mfecane Aftermath: Reconstructive Debates in Southern African History*, edited by Carolyn Hamilton, 123–61. Johannesburg: Witwatersrand University Press, 1995.

Elkins, Caroline. "Race, Citizenship and Governance: Settler Tyranny and the End of Empire." In *Settler Colonialism in the Twentieth Century: Projects, Practices, Legacies*, edited by C. Elkins and S. Pedersen, 203–21. New York: Routledge, 2005.

Ellis, Stephen. "The Genesis of the ANC's Armed Struggle in South Africa 1948–1961." *Journal of Southern African Studies* 37, no. 4 (2011): 657–76.

Erlank, Natasha. "Gendering Commonality: African Men and the 1883 Commission on Native Law and Custom." *Journal of Southern African Studies* 29, no. 4 (2003): 937–53.

Etherington, Norman. "Putting the Mfecane Controversy into Historiographical Context." In *Mfecane Aftermath: Reconstructive Debates in Southern African History*, edited by Carolyn Hamilton, 13–20. Johannesburg: Witwatersrand University Press, 1995.

Evans, Ivan. *Bureaucracy and Race: Native Administration in South Africa*. Berkeley: University of California Press, 1997.

Evans, Laura. "South Africa's Bantustans and the Dynamics of 'Decolonisation': Reflections on Writing Histories of the Homelands." *South African Historical Journal* 64, no. 1 (2012): 117–37.

Ferguson, James. *Expectations of Modernity: Myths and Meanings of Urban Life on the Zambian Copperbelt*. Berkeley: University of California Press, 1999.

———. *Global Shadows: Africa in the Neoliberal World Order*. Durham, NC: Duke University Press, 2006.

Fihlani, Pumza. "Stolen Youth of SA's Child Brides." BBC News, 14 October 2009. http://news.bbc.co.uk/2/hi/africa/8303212.stm.

Flint, Karen. *Healing Traditions: African Medicine, Cultural Exchange, and Competition in South Africa, 1820–1948*. Athens: Ohio University Press, 2008.

Fry, Poppy. "Re-Reading the 1835 'Fingo Emancipation': Women and Ethnicity in the Colonial Archive." In *Gendering Ethnicity in African Women's Lives*, edited by Jan B. Shetler, 87–99. Madison: University of Wisconsin Press, 2015.

Fullard, Madelaine. "State Repression in the 1960s." In *The Road to Democracy in South Africa*, vol. 1, *1960–1970*, edited by the South African Democracy Education Trust, 341–90. Cape Town: Zebra Press, 2004.

Gerhart, Gail. *Black Power in South Africa*. Berkeley: University of California Press, 1979.

Geschiere, Peter. *The Modernity of Witchcraft: Politics and the Occult in Postcolonial Africa*. Charlottesville: University of Virginia Press, 1997.

———. *The Perils of Belonging: Autochthony, Citizenship, and Exclusion in Africa and Europe*. Chicago: University of Chicago Press, 2009.

Geschiere, Peter, and Cyprian Fisiy. "Domesticating Personal Violence: Witchcraft, Courts and Confessions in Cameroon." *Africa: Journal of the International African Institute*, no. 3 (1994): 323–41.

Gibbs, Timothy. "Chris Hani's 'Country Bumpkins': Regional Networks in the African National Congress Underground, 1974–1994." *Journal of Southern African Studies* 37, no. 4 (2011): 677–91.

Gluckman, Max. "Moral Crises: Magical and Secular Solutions." *Hau* 4, no. 2 (2014): 369–405.

Gqola, Pumla Dineo. "How the 'Cult of Femininity' and Violent Masculinities Support Endemic Gender Based Violence in Contemporary South Africa." *African Identities* 5, no. 1 (2007): 111–24.

Hammond-Tooke, David. *Bhaca Society*. Cape Town: Oxford University Press, 1962.

Hammond-Tooke, W. D. *The Tribes of King William's Town District*. Ethnological Publication #41. Pretoria: Government Printer, 1958.

———. *The Tribes of Willowvale District*. Department of Native Affairs, Ethnological Publication #36. Pretoria: Government Printer, 1957.

———. "Urbanization and the Interpretation of Misfortune: A Quantitative Analysis." *Africa: Journal of the International African Institute* 40, no. 1 (1970): 25–39.

Harries, Patrick. "Missionaries, Marxists and Magic: Power and the Politics of Literacy in South-East Africa." *Journal of Southern African Studies* 27, no. 3 (September 2001): 405–27.

Hassim, Shireen, Tawana Kupe, and Eric Worby. *Go Home or Die Here: Violence, Xenophobia and the Reinvention of Difference in South Africa*. Johannesburg: Witwatersrand University Press, 2008.

Healy, Meghan. "'To Control Their Destiny': The Politics of Home and the Feminisation of Schooling in Colonial Natal." *Journal of Southern African Studies* 37 (2011): 247–64.

Hedlund, Anna. "Simple Soldiers?: Blurring the Distinction between Compulsion and Commitment among Rwandan Rebels in Eastern Congo." *Africa: The Journal of the International African Institute* 87, no. 4 (2017): 720–37.

Hickel, Jason. "Social Engineering and Revolutionary Consciousness: Domestic Transformations in Colonial South Africa." *History & Anthropology* 23, no. 3 (2012): 301–22.

———. "'Xenophobia' in South Africa: Order, Chaos, and the Moral Economy of Witchcraft." *Cultural Anthropology* 29, no. 1 (2014): 103–27.

Horrell, Muriel. *A Survey of Race Relations in South Africa, 1963*. Johannesburg: South African Institute of Race Relations, 1964.

Hunter, Mark. *Love in the Time of AIDS: Inequality, Gender, and Rights in South Africa*. Bloomington: Indiana University Press, 2010.

Iliffe, John. *Honour in African History*. New York: Cambridge University Press, 2005.

Junod, Henri A. *The Life of a South African Tribe*. 2 vols. New Hyde Park, NY: University Books Inc., 1962.

ka Plaatjie, Thami. "The PAC's Underground Activities, 1960–1980." In *The Road to Democracy in South Africa*, vol. 2, *1970–1980*, edited by the South African Democracy Education Trust, 669–701. Pretoria: UNISA, 2007.

Karimakwenda, Nyasha. "Deconstructing Characterizations of Rape, Marriage, and Custom in South Africa: Revisiting the Multi-Sectoral Campaign Against Ukuthwala." *African Studies Review* 63, no. 4 (2020): 763–81.

———. "Rethinking Ukuthwala, the South African 'Bride Abduction' Custom." *The Conversation*, September 12, 2021. https://theconversation.com/rethinking-ukuthwala-the-south-african-bride-abduction-custom-165496.

Karis, Thomas, and Gwendolyn Carter. *From Protest to Challenge: A Documentary History of African Politics in South Africa, 1882–1990*. 5 vols. Palo Alto, CA: Hoover Institution, 1972–96.

Kelly, Jill. *To Swim with Crocodiles: Land, Violence, and Belonging in South Africa, 1800–1996*. East Lansing: Michigan State University Press, 2017.

———. "'Women Were Not Supposed to Fight': The Gendered Uses of Martial and Moral Zuluness during UDlame, 1990–1994." In *Gendering Ethnicity in African Women's Lives*, edited by Jan Bender Shetler, 178–205. Madison: University of Wisconsin Press, 2015.

Kgatla, Selaelo Thias. "Containment of Witchcraft Accusations in South Africa: A Search for a Transformational Approach to Curb the Problem." In *Imagining Evil: Witchcraft Beliefs and Accusations in Contemporary Africa*, edited by Gerrie ter Haar, 269–92. Trenton, NJ: Africa World Press, 2007.

King, Brian H., and Brent McCusker. "Environment and Development in the Former South African Bantustans." *Geographical Journal*, no. 1 (2007): 6–13.

Kondlo, Kwandiwe. *In the Twilight of the Revolution: The Pan Africanist Congress of Azania (South Africa), 1959–1994*. 2nd ed. Basel, Switzerland: Basler Afrika Bibliographien, 2010.

Kuschminder, Katie. "Before Disembarkation: Eritrean and Nigerian Migrants Journeys within Africa." *Journal of Ethnic & Migration Studies* (2020): 1–16.

Kynoch, Gary. "From the Ninevites to the Hard Livings Gang: Township Gangsters and Urban Violence in Twentieth-Century South Africa." *African Studies* 58, no. 1 (1999): 55–86.

———. "Reassessing Transition Violence: Voices from South Africa's Township Wars, 1990–94." *African Affairs* 112 (2013): 283–303.

———. "Urban Violence in Colonial Africa: A Case for South African Exceptionalism." *Journal of Southern African Studies* 34, no. 3 (2008): 629–45.

La Hausse, Paul. "'The Cows of Nongoloza': Youth, Crime and Amalaita Gangs in Durban, 1900–1936." *Journal of Southern African Studies* 16, no. 1 (1990): 79–111.

Laurence, Patrick. *The Transkei: South Africa's Politics of Partition*. Johannesburg: Ravan, 1976.

Leibbrandt, Murray, Ingrid Woolard, and Christopher Woolard. "Poverty and Inequality Dynamics in South Africa: Post-Apartheid Developments in the Light of the Long-Run Legacy." *South African Economic Policy under Democracy* 10 (2009): 270–300.

Lodge, Tom. "The Paarl Insurrection: A South African Uprising." *African Studies Review* 25, no. 4 (December 1982): 95–116.

———. "The Poqo Insurrection, 1961–1968." In *Resistance and Ideology in Settler Societies*, edited by John Lonsdale, 179–222. Johannesburg: Ravan, 1986.

———. *Sharpeville: An Apartheid Massacre and Its Consequences*. Oxford: Oxford University Press, 2011.

Luongo, Katherine. "Domestic Dramas and Occult Acts: Witchcraft and Violence in the Arena of the Intimate." In *Domestic Violence and the Law in Colonial and Postcolonial Africa*, edited by Emily S. Burrill, Richard L. Roberts, and Elizabeth Thornberry, 179–200. Athens: Ohio University Press, 2010.

Maaba, Brown Bavusile. "The PAC's War Against the State, 1960–1963." In *The Road to Democracy in South Africa*, vol. 1, *1960–1970*, edited by the South African Democracy Education Trust, 257–98. Cape Town: Zebra Press, 2004.

Mabasa, Diana. "Ukuthwala: Is It All Culturally Relative?" *DeRebus*, July 23, 2015. https://www.derebus.org.za/ukuthwala-culturally-relative/.

Macdonald, James. "Manners, Customs, Superstitions, and Religions of South African Tribes, Part 1." *Journal of the Anthropological Institute of Great Britain and Ireland* 19 (1890): 264–96.

MacLean, John. *A Compendium of Kafir Laws and Customs*. Mt. Coke, 1858.

MacQuarrie, J. W., ed. *The Reminiscences of Walter Stanford*. 2 vols. Cape Town: Struik, 1958.

Magaziner, Daniel R. "Pieces of a (Wo)Man: Feminism, Gender and Adulthood in Black Consciousness, 1968–1977." *Journal of Southern African Studies* 37, no. 1 (2011): 45–63.

Mager, Anne. "'The People Get Fenced': Gender, Rehabilitation and African Nationalism in the Ciskei and Border Region, 1945–55." *Journal of Southern African Studies* 18, no. 4 (December 1992): 761–82.

———. *Gender and the Making of a South African Bantustan: A Social History of the Ciskei, 1945–59*. Portsmouth, NH: Heinemann, 1999.

———. "Sexuality, Fertility and Male Power." *Agenda: Empowering Women for Gender Equity* 28 (1996): 12–24.

———. "Youth Organisations and the Construction of Masculine Identities in the Ciskei and Transkei, 1945–60." *Journal of Southern African Studies* 24 (1998): 653–68.

Magubane, Bernard, Philip Bonner, Jabulani Sithole, Peter Delius, Janet Cherry, Pat Gibbs, and Thozama April. "The Turn to Armed Struggle." In *The Road to Democracy in South Africa*, vol. 1, *1960–1970*, edited by the South African Democracy Education Trust, 53–145. Cape Town: Zebra Press, 2004.

Mahoney, Michael R. *The Other Zulus: The Spread of Zulu Ethnicity in Colonial South Africa*. Durham, NC: Duke University Press, 2012.

Mamdani, Mahmood. *Citizen and Subject*. Princeton, NJ: Princeton University Press, 1994.

Mandela, Nelson. *Long Walk to Freedom: The Autobiography of Nelson Mandela*. New York: Little, Brown, 1994.

Mann, Kristin, and Richard Roberts, eds. *Law in Colonial Africa*. Portsmouth, NH: Heinemann Educational Books, 1991.

Marks, Shula. "Patriotism, Patriarchy and Purity: Natal and the Politics of Zulu Ethnic Consciousness." In *The Creation of Tribalism in Southern Africa*, edited by Leroy Vail, 215–40. Berkeley: University of California Press, 1991.

Matanzima, Kaizer D. *Independence My Way*. Pretoria: Foreign Affairs Association, 1976.

Matoti, Sukude, and Lungisile Ntsebeza. "Rural Resistance in Mpondoland and Thembuland, 1960–1963." In *The Road to Democracy in South Africa*, vol. 1, *1960–1970*, edited by the South African Democracy Education Trust, 177–208. Cape Town: Zebra Press, 2004.

Mattes, Robert. "The 'Born Frees': The Prospects for Generational Change in Post-Apartheid South Africa." *Australian Journal of Political Science* 47, no. 1 (2012): 133–53.

Mayer, Philip. *Townsmen or Tribesman?* 2nd ed. Cape Town: Oxford University Press, 1961.

Mbeki, Govan. *South Africa: The Peasants' Revolt.* Harmondsworth, UK: Penguin, 1963.

McAllister, Patrick. *Xhosa Beer Drinking Rituals: Power, Practice and Performance in the South African Rural Periphery.* Durham, NC: Carolina Academic Press, 2006.

McClendon, Thomas V. "Tradition and Domestic Struggle in the Courtroom: Customary Law and the Control of Women in Segregation-Era Natal." *International Journal of African Historical Studies* 28, no. 3 (1995): 527–61.

———. *White Chief, Black Lords: Shepstone and the Colonial State in Natal, South Africa, 1845–1878.* Rochester, NY: University of Rochester Press, 2010.

McClintock, Anne. "'No Longer in a Future Heaven': Gender, Race and Nationalism." In *Dangerous Liaisons: Gender, Nation, and Postcolonial Perspectives*, edited by Anne McClintock, Mufti Aamir, and Ella Shohat, 89–112. Minneapolis: University of Minnesota Press, 1997.

Mchunu, Mxolisi R. "'We Have Finished Them': Ritual Killing and War-Doctoring in Kwazulu-Natal during the 1980s and 1990s." *African Historical Review* 47, no. 2 (2015): 58–84.

Moffat, Helen. "'These Women, They Force Us to Rape Them': Rape as Narrative of Social Control in Post-Apartheid South Africa." *Journal of Southern African Studies* 32, no. 1 (March 2006): 129–44.

Moodie, T. Dunbar, with Vivienne Ndatshe. *Going for Gold: Men, Mines, and Migration.* Berkeley: University of California Press, 1994.

Morrell, Robert. "Of Boys and Men: Masculinity and Gender in Southern African Studies." *Journal of Southern African Studies* 24 (1998): 605–30.

Morrell, Robert, Rachel Jewkes, Graham Lindegger, and Vijay Hamlall. "Hegemonic Masculinity: Reviewing the Gendered Analysis of Men's Power in South Africa." *South African Review of Sociology* 44, no. 1 (2013): 4–21.

Morris, Alan. *Change and Continuity: A Survey of Soweto in the Late 1990s.* Johannesburg: Sociology Department, University of the Witwatersrand, 1999.

Mphaphuli, Memory, and Letitia Smuts. "'Give It to Him': Sexual Violence in the Intimate Relationships of Black Married Women in South Africa." *Signs: Journal of Women in Culture & Society* 46, no. 2 (2021): 443–64.

Murray, Colin, and Peter Sanders. "Medicine Murder in Basutoland: Colonial Rule and Moral Crisis." *Africa* 70, no. 1 (2000): 49–78.

Naidu, Sam. "Three Tales of Theal: Biography, History and Ethnography on the Eastern Frontier." *English in Africa* 39, no. 2 (2012): 51–68.

Ncapayi, Fani. "Emerging Rural Struggles against Unelected Traditional Authorities and the Role of the Courts: Lessons from Rural Villages of the Eastern Cape." In *Traditional Leaders in a Democracy: Resources, Respect and Resistance*, edited by Mbongiseni Buthelezi, Dineo Skosana, and Beth Vale, 262–96. Johannesburg: Mapungubwe Institute for Strategic Reflection (MISTRA), 2018.

Niehaus, Isak. "Witchcraft and the South African Bantustans: Evidence from Bushbuckridge." *South African Historical Journal* 64, no. 1 (2012): 41–58.

———. "Witch-Hunting and Political Legitimacy: Continuity and Change in Green Valley, Lebowa, 1930–91." *Africa* 63 (1993): 498–530.

Nkosi, N. "Hanged Dad's Remains Dug Up after 52 Years." *Pretoria News*, 15 December 2016. https://www.iol.co.za/news/politics/hanged-dads-remains-dug-up-after-52-years-7186033.

Ntsebeza, Lungisile. *Democracy Compromised: Chiefs and the Politics of Land in South Africa*. Cape Town: HRSC Press/Brill, 2005/6.

O'Connell, M. C. "Xesibe Reds, Rascals and Gentlemen at Home and Work." In *Black Villagers in an Industrial Society*, edited by Philip Mayer, 255–303. Cape Town: Oxford University Press, 1980.

Oosterom, Marjoke A. "Youth and Social Navigation in Zimbabwe's Informal Economy: 'Don't End Up on the Wrong Side.'" *African Affairs* 118, no. 472 (2019): 485–508.

Packard, Randall. "The 'Healthy Reserve' and the 'Dressed Native': Discourses on Black Health and the Language of Legitimation in South Africa." *American Ethnologist* 16, no. 4 (November 1989): 686–703.

Parle, Julie. "Witchcraft or Madness? The Amandiki of Zululand, 1894–1914." *Journal of Southern African Studies* 29, no. 1 (March 2003): 105–32.

Peires, J. B. "The Central Beliefs of the Xhosa Cattle-Killing." *Journal of African History* 28 (1987): 43–63.

———. "Ethnicity and Pseudo-Ethnicity in the Transkei." In *Segregation and Apartheid*, edited by William Beinart and Saul Dubow, 256–84. New York: Routledge, 1995.

———. "The Implosion of Transkei and Ciskei." *African Affairs* 91, no. 364 (1992): 365–87.

Pinker, Steven. *The Better Angels of Our Nature: Why Violence Has Declined*. New York: Viking, 2011.

Posel, Deborah. "The Scandal of Manhood: 'Baby Rape' and the Politicization of Sexual Violence in Post-Apartheid South Africa." *Culture, Health and Sexuality* 7, no. 3 (2005).

Pugach, Sara. "Carl Meinhof and the German Influence on Nicholas Van Warmelo's Ethnological and Linguistic Writing, 1927–1935." *Journal of Southern African Studies* 30, no. 4 (2004): 825–45.

Ramphele, Mamphela. *A Bed Called Home: Life in the Migrant Labour Hostels of Cape Town*. Athens: Ohio University Press, 1993.

Ranger, T. O. "The Invention of Tradition in Colonial Africa." In *The Invention of Tradition*, edited by T. O. Ranger and E. Hobsbawm, 211–62. Cambridge: Cambridge University Press, 1983.

———. "Scotland Yard in the Bush: Medicine Murders, Child Witches and the Construction of the Occult." *Africa* 77, no. 2 (2007): 272–83.

Reader, D. H. *The Black Man's Portion*. Cape Town: Oxford University Press, 1961.

Redding, Sean. "'Maybe Freedom Will Come from You': Christian Prophecies and Rumors in the Development of Rural Resistance in South Africa, 1948–1961." *Journal of Religion in Africa* 40, no. 2 (2010): 163–91.

———. *Sorcery and Sovereignty: Taxation, Power and Rebellion in South Africa, 1880–1963*. Athens: Ohio University Press, 2006.

———. "Witchcraft in Africa: Political Power and Spiritual Insecurity from the Precolonial Era to the Present." In *Oxford Research Encyclopedia of African History*, edited by Thomas Spear, 1–22. Oxford University Press, 2019.

———. "Witchcraft, Women and Taxes in the Transkei, South Africa, 1930–63." In *Stepping Forward: Black Women in Africa and the Americas*, edited by Catherine Higgs, Barbara Moss, and Earline Rae Ferguson, 87–99. Athens: Ohio University Press, 2002.

———. "Women as Diviners and as Christian Converts in Rural South Africa, c. 1880–1963." *Journal of African History* 57, no. 3 (2016): 367–89.

Rice, Kate. "Ukuthwala in Rural South Africa: Abduction Marriage as a Site of Negotiation about Gender, Rights and Generational Authority among the Xhosa." *Journal of Southern African Studies* 40, no. 2 (2014): 381–99.

Scheper-Hughes, Nancy. *Death without Weeping: The Violence of Everyday Life in Brazil*. Berkeley: University of California Press, 1993.

Schneider, Geoffrey E. "The Post-Apartheid Development Debacle in South Africa: How Mainstream Economics and the Vested Interests Preserved Apartheid Economic Structures." *Journal of Economic Issues* 52, no. 2 (2018): 306–22.

Seekings, Jeremy. "The Social and Political Implications of Demographic Change in Post-Apartheid South Africa." *The Annals of the American Academy of Political and Social Science* 652, no. 1 (2014): 70–86.

Sheik, Nafisa Essop. "Colonial Rites: Custom, Marriage Law and the Making of Difference in Natal, 1830s–c. 1910." PhD diss., University of Michigan, Ann Arbor, 2012.

Simelane, Hamilton Sipho. "The State, Chiefs and the Control of Female Migration in Colonial Swaziland, c. 1930s to 1950s." *Journal of African History* 45, no. 1 (2004): 103–24.

Sithole, Jabulani. "Land Disputes, Social Identities and the State in the *Izimpi Zemibango* in the Umzinto District, 1930–1935." *Journal of Natal and Zulu History* 27 (2009): 60–82.

Skosana, Dineo. "Traditional Leadership and the African National Congress in South Africa: Reflections on a Symbiotic Relationship." In *Traditional Leaders in a Democracy: Resources, Respect and Resistance*, edited by Mbongiseni Buthelezi, Dineo Skosana, and Beth Vale, 50–74. Johannesburg: Mapungubwe Institute for Strategic Reflection (MISTRA), 2018.

Smith, Alex Duval. "South African Townships Take Stick-Fighting Tradition into New Future." *Guardian*, 30 January 2011.

Soga, J. H. *The Ama-Xosa: Life and Customs*. Lovedale, South Africa: Lovedale, 1931.

Spivak, Gayatri Chakravorty. "Preface to Concerning Violence." *Film Quarterly* 68, no. 1 (2014): 61–62.

Staff Reporter. "8 Dead in Panga Riot: Berserk Mob Surge Off Train." *Rand Daily Mail*, 14 December 1962, 1.

———. "Forced Marriage in South Africa." *Sunday Times*, 10 December 2009.

————. "Gen. Keevy (SAP) on Motives in Engcobo Killing." *Rand Daily Mail*, 8 February 1963, 2.

————. "If Transkei Fails So Will Apartheid—Commission." *Rand Daily Mail*, 22 November 1962, 3.

————. "Manhunt in Transkei: The Scene at the Engcobo Caravan Slayings; Police Comb Area; Robbery Ruled Out as Motive." *Rand Daily Mail*, 6 February 1963, 1.

————. "Paarl: Ministers Not in Contempt." *Rand Daily Mail*, 9 January 1963, 1, 4.

————. "'Pass Laws Cause of Paarl Riot,' Xhosa Pamphlet Blames Govt." *Rand Daily Mail*, 20 February 1963, 4.

————. "Police Hold 14 Poqo Suspects." *Rand Daily Mail*, 18 December 1962, 3.

————. "Police Probe of the Poqo Riots Nears End." *Rand Daily Mail*, 18 January 1963, 9.

————. "Poqo: Only Object Was to Kill Chief—Court Told." *Rand Daily Mail*, 5 March 1963, 3.

————. "Poqo Report: 'No Alarm'—but Vorster Drafts Urgent Laws." *Rand Daily Mail*, 22 March 1963, 1–2.

————. "Poqo's 'Plan for Revolt' in 1963; Banned P.A.C. Continues Underground, Says Shock Paarl Report; Judge Urges Drastic Government Action." *Rand Daily Mail*, 22 March 1963, 13.

————. "S.A. 'Like Kenya in 1951' Paarl Inquiry Told." *Rand Daily Mail*, 22 March 1963, 13.

————. "Shadow of Poqo over Transkei Killings—Keevy." *Rand Daily Mail*, 12 February 1963, 9.

————. "Talk Was of Killing Whites—Poqo Witness." *Rand Daily Mail*, 16 January 1963, 2.

————. "Traders and Liberals Get Blame for Poqo Terror." *Rand Daily Mail*, 26 February 1963, 14.

————. "Transkei Chief Blames Liberals, Reds." *Rand Daily Mail*, 1 March 1963, 11.

Stanford, Walter E. "A Witch Doctor by Habit and Repute." *Cape Law Journal* (1893): 218–20.

Stapleton, Timothy J. *Faku: Rulership and Colonialism in the Mpondo Kingdom (c. 1780–1867)*. Waterloo, ON: Wilfrid Laurier University Press, 2001.

————. "'Him Who Destroys All': Reassessing the Early Career of Faku, King of the Mpondo, c. 1818–1829." *South African Historical Journal*, no. 38 (1998): 55–78.

Steinberg, Jonny. "Xenophobia and Collective Violence in South Africa: A Note of Skepticism about the Scapegoat." *African Studies Review* 61, no. 3 (2018): 119–34.

Stoler, Ann Laura. *Along the Archival Grain: Epistemic Anxieties and Colonial Common Sense*. Princeton, NJ: Princeton University Press, 2009.

Streek, Barry, and Richard Wicksteed. *Render unto Kaiser: A Transkei Dossier*. Johannesburg: Ravan Press, 1981.

Taussig, Michael. "Culture of Terror—Space of Death. Roger Casement's Putumayo Report and the Explanation of Torture." *Comparative Studies in Society and History* 26, no. 3 (July 1984): 467–97.

Thomas, C. "Bloodier Than Black and White: Liberation History Seen through Detective Sergeant Donald Card's Narrative of His Investigations of Congo and Poqo Activities, 1960–1965." *New Contree*, no. 50 (2005): 39–58.

Thomas, Kylie. *Homophobia, Injustice and "Corrective Rape" in Post-Apartheid South Africa*. Center for the Study of Violence and Reconciliation Report. CVSR, 2013.

Thomas, Lynn M. "The Modern Girl and Racial Respectability in 1930s South Africa." *The Journal of African History* 47, no. 3 (2006): 461–90.

Thornberry, Elizabeth. *Colonizing Consent: Rape and Governance in South Africa's Eastern Cape*. African Studies Series. Cambridge: Cambridge University Press, 2019.

———. "*Ukuthwala*, Forced Marriage, and the Idea of Custom in South Africa's Eastern Cape." In *Marriage by Force? Contestation Over Consent and Coercion in Africa*, edited by Annie Bunting, Benjamin Lawrance, and Richard Roberts, 137–58. Athens: Ohio University Press, 2016.

Tropp, Jacob A. *Natures of Colonial Change: Environmental Relations in the Making of the Transkei*. Athens: Ohio University Press, 2006.

Truth and Reconciliation Commission of South Africa. *Truth and Reconciliation Commission Final Report*. Vol. 3. Cape Town: Juta, 2003.

Union of South Africa. *Report from the Select Committee on Native Custom and Marriage Laws*. Cape Town: Solomon Printers, 1913.

Urdal, Henrik. *A Clash of Generations? Youth Bulges and Political Violence*. Expert Paper Series No. 2012/1. New York: United Nations, 2012. Http://www.un.org/esa/popu lation/publications/expertpapers/Urdal_Expert%20Paper.pdf.

Utas, Mats. "West-African Warscapes: Victimcy, Girlfriending, Soldiering: Tactic Agency in a Young Woman's Social Navigation of the Liberian War Zone." *Anthropological Quarterly* 78, no. 2 (2005): 403–30.

Vail, Leroy. "Introduction: Ethnicity in Southern African History." In *The Invention of Tribalism in Africa*, edited by Leroy Vail, 1–20. Berkeley: University of California Press, 1991.

Van der Vliet, Virginia. "Traditional Husbands, Modern Wives? Constructing Marriages in a South African Township." In *Tradition and Transition in Southern Africa: Festschrift for Philip and Iona Mayer*, edited by Andrew Speigel and Patrick McAllister, 219–42. New Brunswick, NJ: Transaction, 1991.

van Laun, Bianca. "Of Bodies Captured: The Visual Representation of the Paarl March and Poqo in Apartheid South Africa." *Social Dynamics* 40, no. 1 (2014): 43–65.

van Warmelo, N. J., ed. *History of Matiwane and the AmaNgwane Tribe, as Told by Msebenzi to His Kinsman Albert Hlongwane*. Ethnological Publication #7. Pretoria: Government Printer, 1938.

Vigh, Henrik. "Bandits Fall from Grace: Liberation Heroes and Alter-Politics in Bissau." *Terrain* 74 (March 2021): 1–14.

———. "Motion Squared: A Second Look at the Concept of Social Navigation." *Anthropological Theory* 9, no. 4 (2009): 419–38.

———. *Navigating Terrains of War: Youth and Soldiering in Guinea-Bissau*. New York: Berghahn Books, 2006.

———. "Social Death and Violent Life Chances." In *Navigating Youth, Generating Adulthood: Social Becoming in an African Context*, edited by Catrine Christiansen, Mats Utas, and Henrik Vigh, 31–60. Uppsala, Sweden: Nordic Africa Institute, 2006.

Visser, Wessel. "The Production of Literature on the 'Red Peril' and 'Total Onslaught' in Twentieth-Century South Africa." *Historia* 49, no. 2 (2004): 105–28.

Waetjen, Thembisa. "The 'Home' in Homeland: Gender, National Space, and Inkatha's Politics of Ethnicity." *Ethnic & Racial Studies* 22, no. 4 (1999): 653–78.

Weeks, Sindiso Mnisi. *Access to Justice and Human Security: Cultural Contradictions in Rural South Africa*. London: Routledge, 2018.

———. "The Violence of the Harmony Model: Common Narratives between Women and Lower-Level Traditional Leaders." In *Traditional Leaders in a Democracy: Resources, Respect and Resistance*, edited by Mbongiseni Buthelezi, Dineo Skosana, and Beth Vale, 182–223. Johannesburg: Mapungubwe Institute for Strategic Reflection (MISTRA), 2018.

Wells, Julia. "Why Women Rebel: A Comparative Study of South African Women's Resistance in Bloemfontein (1913) and Johannesburg (1958)." *Journal of Southern African Studies* 10, no. 1 (1983): 39–55.

Westall, Carolyn, and Pranee Liamputtong. *Motherhood and Postnatal Depression: Narratives of Women and Their Partners*. Dordrecht: Springer, 2011.

Whitehead, Neil. "On the Poetics of Violence." In *Violence*, edited by Neil Whitehead, 55–78. Santa Fe, NM: School of American Research Press, 2004.

Wilson, Francis. "Historical Roots of Inequality in South Africa." *Economic History of Developing Regions* 26, no. 1 (2011): 1–15.

Wilson, Monica. *Reaction to Conquest: Effects of Contact with Europeans on the Pondo of South Africa*. London: International Institute of African Languages and Cultures, 1936.

Wood, Kate, Helen Lambert, and Rachel Jewkes. "'Showing Roughness in a Beautiful Way': Talk about Love, Coercion and Rape in South African Youth Sexual Culture." *Medical Anthropology Quarterly* 21 (2007): 277–300.

Wright, John. "PMB Before the Voortrekkers." *Natal Witness* (n.d.). http://www.pmbhistory.co.za/portal/witnesshistory/custom_modules/TheWayWeWere/PMB%20before%20the%20Voortrekkers.pdf.

Zimudzi, Tapiwa. "African Women, Violent Crime and the Criminal Law in Colonial Zimbabwe, 1900–1952." *Journal of Southern African Studies* 30, no. 3 (2004): 499–517.